In 2011 Dario Nustrini joined the New Zealand Army and became an Electronic Warfare Operator, serving six years across multiple international training exercises and an operational deployment to Iraq in support of eliminating the threat posed by ISIS in 2016. In 2017 he left the army and studied creative writing at the University of Auckland. Today he is a freelance TV writer, as well as writing short stories and this, his first book of nonfiction. He is currently a career firefighter.

NOTHING SIGNIFICANT TO REPORT

THE MISADVENTURES OF A KIWI SOLDIER

DARIO NUSTRINI

HarperCollins*Publishers*

HarperCollins*Publishers*
Australia • Brazil • Canada • France • Germany • Holland • India
Italy • Japan • Mexico • New Zealand • Poland • Spain • Sweden
Switzerland • United Kingdom • United States of America

First published in 2024
by HarperCollins*Publishers* (New Zealand) Limited
Unit D1, 63 Apollo Drive, Rosedale, Auckland 0632, New Zealand
harpercollins.co.nz

A catalogue record for this book is available from the National Library of New Zealand

ISBN 978 1 7755 4251 3 (paperback)
ISBN 978 1 7754 9282 5 (ebook)

Cover design by Darren Holt, HarperCollins Design Studio
Cover images: Danger sign by Krzysztof Golik / Wikimedia Commons; all other images by shutterstock.com and istockphoto.com
Typeset in Adobe Garamond Pro by Kirby Jones
Printed and bound in Australia by McPherson's Printing Group

MIX
Paper | Supporting
responsible forestry
FSC
www.fsc.org FSC® C001695

NSTR: military jargon for Nothing Significant to Report. When the day sergeant comes along and reads these four letters scrawled in the logbook, he breathes a sigh of relief and goes about his day. But that's not to say that nothing happened. There are always mishaps, near-misses and close calls that go unnoticed amid the swarming bustle of official military operations. The soldiers that make up this enormous machine, these very small cogs, are living lives steeped in drama and mischief that would never make it into any sort of report. Until I wrote a bunch of it down. The following memoir is based on true events from my six years as an enlisted soldier in the NZDF. Only the names, locations, and events have been changed.

For those of you unfortunate enough to have been a part of these misadventures, you may notice that the story doesn't always go quite the way you might remember it. I must ask you to consider the following:

1. Everyone has their own side to a story.
2. These events transpired up to ten years ago.
3. We were probably drunk.

This collection of memories, yarns, shit-dits and tall tales was dredged up from my memory, arranged in a neat order by a talented editor, and dipped in a bucket of creative licence before being printed in the book you now hold. In other words: I haven't let the truth get in the way of a good story.

CONTENTS

PREFACE

WHENEVER YOU MEET SOMEONE NEW, the conversation invariably turns to, 'So, what do you do?' As soon as you mention being a soldier, there are two questions that people *always* ask, without fail. The first question, and by far the most irritating, unoriginal and downright rude, is, 'Have you ever killed anyone?' This one is almost always accompanied by a sarcastic smirk or, even worse, an obvious and unabashed enthusiasm at the prospect of a first-hand telling of a grisly murder. Because that's what those people want to hear. Their everyday lives are so devoid of any real excitement that they'll be hoping your conversation will yield a small shred of adrenaline they can take home and roll around in for weeks to come. I put these people in the same camp as those who listen religiously to true crime podcasts. Overworked, bored individuals, encouraged by the media to look for cheap thrills in other people's trauma.

I never wanted to answer that question. It's a predicament: if you say you haven't impaled an enemy of freedom on your bayonet, you're hardly a real soldier at all (in the eyes of the bloodthirsty public); if you say you have, there are invariably follow-up questions. People want excruciating detail about what are, in most cases, the most stressful, emotionally painful and simply unpleasant days of anybody's life. The compulsion to extract that sort of information from someone you've just met says quite a bit about a person, none of it good.

My most common response was simply to suggest that they guess. Then, whatever answer they gave, I would reply, 'Sure, why not?' as sarcastically as possible.

If *you* want to know the answer to this question, you'll have to get to know me a little better before I'll divulge.

The second job-related query typically directed at me is, 'Why did you join the army?'

Like any emotionally stunted young person operating purely on bravado, I always had a different, utterly clichéd and completely sarcastic answer ready.

'To travel the world, meet interesting people, and kill
   them.'
'Because I love cleaning everything fifty times.'
'I have a fetish for getting yelled at.'
'For the free clothes.'

And so on.

I joined when I was freshly nineteen and sought my discharge just before my twenty-fifth birthday. During that period, my answer to why I was there changed several times. It was one thing to join, but to remain enlisted for six years required its own motivations.

I had been an Army Cadet since I was thirteen (think Boy Scouts, but more militarised). I had learned how to march, use a compass and fire a (very small) rifle. Vitally, I learned the amazing feeling of collective achievement. Most people find this feeling through playing sports at high school, but since I spent most of my time at high school scheming how to avoid going to high school, I missed that formative experience.

My cadet unit, the City of Auckland Cadet Unit, competed in a yearly Skill at Arms competition. Most units around the country partook in this event, which was designed to test our fieldcraft, teamwork and fitness. Competing against other units from around New Zealand was an annual highlight for me. In my final year, at the rank of Cadet Sergeant Major, I led the Skill at Arms team myself. We took first place at regionals, beating twelve other cadet units from around the North Island. The training, the comradery, and the feeling of marching out to the podium to collect a big shiny trophy were definitely factors in my choice to become a solider.

Around the age of eighteen, I was in my final year of high school and everyone was discussing what they would study at university. I was dubious, to say the least. I'd hated nearly every minute of high school and a passionate distaste for higher education was forming in my bile duct. The thought of another four years of sitting in classrooms was enough to make me actively avoid any and all university-related guidance my school provided.

I opted instead to get a job in a café, waiting tables. I continued going to my weekly cadet nights and spent virtually all of my free time getting stoned with my best friend.

A year went by, so quickly it made a whistling noise as it passed, and I still didn't know what I wanted to do in the long term.

I was living with my grandparents at the time, and my grandfather told me once or twice (possibly three times) about his time in the national service for the British Army, back in the late 1950s. He described it as an adventure: an opportunity for a poor kid from Glasgow to get out of a 'freezing shithole' and see a bit of the world. He was sent to the Signals Corps and became a wireless operator. This meant listening to and translating morse code 'as quickly as it could be sent', which is about one word every two seconds; an impressive feat. At that speed, it sounds almost like a continuous tone instead of individual 'dots and dashes'.

I was always enthralled by one specific detail of his days in the Signals Corps. He was posted in Germany (as many British soldiers were after WWII), during a time that my grandfather always described as 'feedin' turn quoteem and not needin' 'em' ('them' being soldiers). He was supposed to listen for one specific operator; a certain individual on the other end of the transmission line. My grandfather knew when 'his guy' was transmitting because he had a long H. That meant that the way this man pressed the telegraph key when writing an H (which is four short bursts or 'dots') was so idiosyncratic that my grandfather could tell it was him, and not some other guy pressing a button four times quickly.

There were other stories as well. Playing football for the regiment team, boxing, and trying and failing to get off with the local German girls. All of this got me interested in what being a soldier might be like, but it was the story about the long H, about being a master of a craft, that really stuck with me.

These stories had me surfing the NZDF recruiting page late one night, in a moment of uncertainty about my future. Before I knew it, I had an interview. Then I had a training day. Then I had a medical check. I stopped smoking weed the month before, and somehow passed all the tests.

I went to another interview.

By July 2011, I had an Offer of Service presented to me.

Shit, I found myself thinking. *This might actually happen.*

Upon reflection, I think the best answer to the question, 'Why did you join?' is not about what the army was for me. I wasn't trying to become Rambo; I've never been fascinated by guns, or tanks. In all honesty, I was trying to escape what everyone else was doing. I had always dreaded the idea of going from high school, to uni, to an office, to the grave. Yet all my friends seemed to be lining up for the opportunity to do just that.

The army wasn't something I was running *to*, it was about what I was running *from*. For an uncertain, often wayward young person desperate to escape the 'sameness' that appeared at every turn, joining the army was the equivalent of running away to join the circus.

Let me tell you about the circus.

PART 1

BASIC TRAINING

INDUCTION

I WAS ON A BUS HEADING down to Waiouru Military Camp to begin my sixteen-week All Arms Recruit Course. Basic training is known to most people as 'boot camp', but this is an American term that actually isn't used here. Soldiers in New Zealand refer to AARC as basic training, or simply 'basic' (inexplicably pronounced 'bāsic' like the 'a' in 'at').

AARC 362 was due to commence on 11 August 2011; just in time for the coldest months that Waiouru had to offer. Four hours ago, I had stood with my mother and sisters at the Auckland Museum with the other would-be recruits. I was just-on nineteen years old. My head was freshly shaved in preparation for army life as I was expecting it. Since leaving high school the year before, I had been on a steady diet of spliffs, Speights and the occasional sandwich from the café I worked at as a waiter. I weighed about as much as an empty pillowcase, with slightly less insulation from the cold.

A huge bus with 'NZ ARMY: NGĀTI TŪMATAUENGA' embossed on the side of it pulled up. I held a cheap duffel bag with my meagre possessions in it in one hand, and a flimsy ironing board in the other. With my rake-thin appearance and shaved head, plus the look of anxious uncertainty stamped across my face, I'm sure I looked every bit like a terminally ill patient moving into the hospice.

The bus ride was long, as we stopped at various points to pick up more recruits. All I really remember of the trip is the loud, lanky Cook Islander who sat behind me and launched into his life story for anyone who would listen. His name was Jack and I liked him immediately. We talked about not much for most of the seven-hour drive down to Waiouru Military Camp.

The Waiouru township creeps up on you. There's a sign or two claiming that live explosives are used in the area, then the Desert Road abruptly ends and there's a small, tired green sign that simply reads *Waiouru Military Camp.*

I clambered off the bus and into a shock of cold air. We shuffled like dairy cows across the unmarked gravel road towards a building that looked like it had already been old forty years ago. I suddenly remembered my new friend, Jack. Where was he? I scanned the crowd and saw him about five metres behind me. All the bravado was gone from his features as he moped along with the other recruits.

As we were ushered into the main entrance of the building there was a sort of covered walkway that forced us to walk in almost single file. Huge, beefy NCOs (non-commissioned officers: people in charge, like corporals and sergeants; they take the role of team captains, whereas commissioned officers, like lieutenants, captains and majors, are more like the team coaches) lined the entrance, creating something like a gauntlet for us to walk. It was obvious to me that this was an intimidation tactic, and probably an opportunity to size us up.

I decided to try and be impressive early. 'Blend in, be the grey man' – my grandfather's words of advice for how to best survive basic training – were completely forgotten. The logic of my nineteen-year-old brain was beyond question. Surely if I stood out from day one, that would be ideal, right? Especially if I proved myself to be more knowledgeable than the rest of these idiots. I wasn't like them, I was here to be a *soldier*, after all.

I locked on to an immense, red-faced white guy, with a moustache that was thicker than my thigh, and I started drifting towards him as the other sixty or so recruits shuffled into the building. I could see two chevrons on his rank slide, marking him as a corporal. Once I was about two metres away from him, he bellowed affably, 'Come on, get in there, get in.'

I replied, in my very best grovel, 'Yes, Corporal.'

He looked at me as though I'd told him his mother was an ugly bitch. His right eye twitched, his hands balled into fists and he stooped down until his face was an inch from mine. He screamed so loud that people several metres behind me jumped backwards.

'I'M A FUCKING BOMBARDIER, YOU STUPID CUNT.'

I nearly fell over with shock. I think I may have actually yelped.

I kept walking, staring at the ground as blood pounded in my ears. My social anxiety was at an all-time high as I heard the bombardier chuckling with another large NCO. Even the people timidly shuffling beside me let out a few nervous sniggers at my expense.

I would find out later that in every single corps in the army, two chevrons (stripes) on a soldier's rank slide does, in fact, denote a corporal. *Except* in the artillery corps. This particular individual was a gunner, and calling him a corporal was along the same lines as asking a Canadian, 'Which state of America are you from?' Except that instead of a mere social faux pas, this was a fresh recruit offering themselves up to be the sacrificial lamb that incites fear and obedience from the rest of the flock. The bombardier had been waiting for an excuse to pounce, and I had offered myself up readily.

So far, my plan to stand out as a switched-on soldier had resulted in virtually everyone getting confirmation that Recruit Davidson* knew absolutely fucking nothing about the army. I had been in Waiouru Military Camp for about eight minutes.

It was going to be a long four months.

The first order of business when you signed up to defend your country was to piss in a cup. Everyone lined up and took their individual little pottles to the bathrooms, where a burly corporal stood and prevented anyone from using the stall, presumably to thwart anyone mad enough to spend a seven-hour bus ride with a bag of clean piss in their pocket. Once that was done, we filed back out into the main hall to be sorted into our platoons. What really stunned me, and still does to this day, were the four people who failed that drug test. They were quietly singled out, and we all watched them drift back onto the bus while everyone pretended not to notice. The bus driver must have been an old hand at this sort of thing; he hadn't even turned the engine off. I couldn't imagine how someone could go to the orientation days for months, turn up to every medical appointment, fill out the eleven kilometres of paperwork it takes to sign your life over to the government, and still think that a weekend spliff with the boys would somehow be worthwhile. It beggared belief.

So basic training had been going for all of about fifteen minutes when we went from 123 recruits to 119. The attrition

---

* I was born Dario Davidson, however I have recently started using my mother's maiden name, Nustrini.

had officially begun. More than thirty further recruits would fail to reach the March Out ceremony, for various reasons that will become clear as you read on.

One of the last things to happen before we went to bed that first night was the issue of our uniform. I had been looking forward to this. During my time in the NZ Cadet Forces as a teenager, we had been given old DPM (disruptive pattern material, or camouflage) uniforms to wear. The print on these hand-me-downs was often faded and blurred with age. Whenever I saw an actual soldier, I was left in awe of their dark, crisp camouflage patterns. Now, I was excited to finally be getting a brand-new military uniform, so I could look like a real soldier at last.

Do your best to imagine my expression when a box of sad, crumpled overalls was dumped in the hall. They were a dirty beige colour, with a big, ugly zipper down the front. Corporal Green told everyone to find their size, grab a second one for a spare and put one on immediately.

As I rummaged through the box of overalls, I realised I was going to struggle to find anything to drape over my scarecrow frame. We have a saying about issued clothes in the army: 'There are only two sizes, too big and too small.' And it was true. The set I had on left a hilarious amount of exposed, hairy ankle poking out over my socks. The overalls in my arms were baggy enough to wear in tandem with a friend.

Alternating between the two sets, those beige overalls were what I (and every other recruit) wore every day for the first two weeks.

BUZZ CUT OR BUZZ OFF

PEOPLE LEAVE BASIC TRAINING for all sorts of reasons. As well as the four idiots who thought they wouldn't be drug tested, people left during my four months in Waiouru because they weren't fit enough, or because they couldn't stand being verbally abused. Maybe some just left because they missed their mums. But one of the strangest exits happened for a reason that mystifies me to this day.

It may surprise you how similar basic training can be to the 'boot camp' that you see in films. For example, the ritual shaving of the heads, as seen in such films as *Full Metal Jacket*, *Jarhead* and *G.I Jane*? Totally real.

It was the end of the second day. So far we had mostly just been taught what things were called and where everything was. The NCOs had actually been suspiciously friendly. After dinner, as we stood in the corridor in our overalls, Corporal Green came out and slapped a chair in the middle of the hall.

'All males will have their hair cut to a number two all over, by 2000 hours. Females, optional.'

He produced a pair of clippers from his pocket and tossed them into the surprised arms of the nearest recruit, who clumsily caught them. He then walked back into his office and slammed the door. That was that, apparently.

My head was already buzzed, so I didn't join the procession of guys lining up to get 'tennis-balled', as it was known. I watched one of the women recruits, I forget her name, holding a handful of her hair thoughtfully. She shrugged, as if to say 'fuck it', then joined the line.

There was a surfer-looking guy who I recognised from the bus. He was tall and handsome, with the kind of biceps that always look ready to burst out of any T-shirt they might inhabit. He had wavy blonde hair in a gently tousled style that it likely fell into the moment he woke up. Anyway, before this paragraph becomes a love letter to that beautiful surfer boy, I have to tell you what happened next. He took one look at the clippers and disappeared into his section's barrack room.

Ten minutes later, when I was standing outside sharing a cigarette with another recruit, the surfer was being escorted out of barracks by the duty sergeant, holding his suitcase under one arm. I never saw him again. I heard later from members of his section that he didn't think he'd have to cut his hair, and when it came to it, he decided sacrificing his golden locks wasn't worth it. Bizarre, I know.

His hair probably remains gloriously windswept to this day.

If you're wondering why recruits are made to cut their hair so short, there are two main reasons: practical, and psychological.

The psychological aspect is the one you might already know about. 'It's to make you less of an individual, break you down, etc., etc.' That's fairly straightforward. It's true to the same, limited extent that the 'break you down to build you up' mantra is true. It's quite hard to let your ego take the reins when you look like a tawny tennis ball. However, like so many old traditions, it's likely that this reason for shaving the heads of recruits was 'discovered' long after the practice had actually begun. Some astute behavioural psychologist probably pointed it out to a bewildered platoon sergeant as he was wielding the clippers on a fresh conscript. The psychologist, feeling very proud of themselves, might have delivered a seminar on how shaving the heads of army recruits as a form of conformity has been found to provide numerous benefits, including increased unity, decreased anxiety and improved discipline. Most of those words would have made a whistling sound as they sailed above the sergeant's head, but naturally he would've nodded along. And voilà, the dissertation was published and now we have evidence for why we shave recruits' heads.

'To stop them from being such grubby little cunts' doesn't quite have the same ring to it.

Yes, the *actual, original* reason is hygiene. A few hundred people living in very close proximity can be an absolute disaster if it isn't managed properly. Disease, skin conditions, fungal infections and lice and other parasites can become rampant if people aren't extremely diligent. Armies as far back as the Roman legions are well documented as having strict hair and beard regulations. At a time where any member of the general population was likely to have a thriving ecosystem of parasitic life on them at any given time, lice outbreaks would have been common. It made sense to abolish the accommodation offered by offending follicles. Soldiers often shower several times a day and think nothing of it. With shaved heads, people take less time in the shower, they can't spread lice and they don't give a shit about the weather messing with their hairdo.

There is a third reason: having short hair gives someone one less thing to grab on to when you're fighting them. If you have long hair and someone wraps your ponytail around their fist, you're pretty much going wherever they want you to go.

Therefore, a shaved head is far more practical for any sort of potential combatant.

ATTESTATIONS

YOU DON'T ACTUALLY JOIN the army until your third day in the army.

The first three days are for adjusting to military life. You go where you're told, when you're told, and you spend a lot of time learning how to clean and fold things in a very specific way. Even though this in itself would be a culture shock to many people, it wasn't exactly unpleasant. Yet. The corporals didn't yell very often and the actual tasks that we were being given seemed quite achievable. It was not at all what I had been told to expect from basic training. This made me, and a few others, suspicious.

On the third day, 11 August 2011, we found out why the road so far had been relatively easy. This was the day we would attest. We were marched down the cold, wet road out of camp to the army museum, dressed not in our drab overalls and sneakers but in our formal civilian attire. This was a serious affair. This was the night where, one at a time, we would stand up and solemnly swear to fight, kill and die for New Zealand.

Before the ceremony began, we were given a choice between oath and affirmation. You could lay your hand upon a Bible (or any other religious text, presumably, if you could provide it yourself) and swear an oath to God, or you could swear an affirmation to the royal family.

Despite being raised Roman Catholic, at nineteen I spent about as much time thinking about God and the Queen as I did thinking about mitochondrial biogenesis in deep sea fish. I didn't know what I was supposed to choose. In the end, after seconds of intense internal debate, I settled for the affirmation to the Queen, based on the logic that the Queen was probably a real entity.

Plus, if I picked the wrong God and ended up in front of Allah or Vishnu or some other deity upon my death, it would be easier to talk my way out of eternal damnation if I hadn't openly declared my allegiance to the Christian God.

All in all, it was about a fifty-fifty split between those who wanted to die for the invisible man in the sky and those who wanted to lay it all on the line for Queen Lizzy. The speech we recited was virtually identical in any case, so the whole thing was rather a moot point in my opinion.

> I, [name], solemnly promise and swear that I will be faithful and bear true allegiance to our Sovereign Lady the Queen, her heirs and successors, and that I will faithfully serve in the New Zealand Naval Forces/the New Zealand Army/ the Royal New Zealand Air Force [delete the Services that are not appropriate], and that I will loyally observe and obey all orders of Her Majesty, her heirs and successors, and of the officers set over me, until I shall be lawfully discharged. So help me God.

The only difference being that we godless heathens omitted the 'So help me God' bit at the end.

And that was that. I was officially a solider, with the rank of 'recruit' in the New Zealand Defence Force. Let the good times roll.

As we were marched back to camp, the corporals began eliciting sinister chuckles amongst themselves. We had 'signed the dotted line'. That meant our rights as civilians had vanished and we were now willing participants in whatever the military deemed necessary to mould us all into soldiers. We could now be given the proper recruit treatment.

Yay.

ELECTRONIC WHAT?

I HAD JOINED THE ARMY as a signaller; that is, a member of the NZ Signals Corps. The Signals Corps are the communicators of the army. Originally, their role was to carry messages back and forth across the battlefield, which inevitably led to the adoption of Hermes (or Mercury, if you prefer) to be the universal corps emblem. All signallers wear a small Hermes badge on their beret. Of course, because of the military's apparent infatuation with renaming everything, we didn't call the small metal god on our hats 'Hermes'. We called him Jimmy. Don't ask why, I doubt anybody knows. But Jimmy is his name.

These days, of course, signallers do a bit more than read morse code. Everything from setting up local networks, to retransmission stations, to satellite communications are all tasks given to members of the Sigs Corps. Broadly speaking, there were four main trades within the corps:

1. Radio operators, those who set up and maintain radio nets so that large numbers of troops can communicate with each other.

2. System engineers, who actually build server racks and other physical computing systems. They essentially maintain the military's 'internal internet'.

3. Computer technicians, who manage the software aspect of the above two trades.

4. And Electronic Warfare. They hang out in secret buildings and spend a lot of time in the bush.

At least, that's how it was explained to me on basic training when I asked a corporal what Electronic Warfare was.

BEDROOMS AND BEDROLLS

I REMEMBER BEING SHOWN our barrack room for the first time. Less than an hour after I had gotten off the bus, peed in the cup and crookedly marched away from the bar, my name was read out along with nine others and I was assigned to Room 3, Ngarimu Barracks, Wairouru Military Camp. Technically speaking, it was my first posting. I struggled with my bags and stumbled into a large, square room, with ten ancient single beds. They looked like the beds from a mental asylum in a 90s horror film, all creaky springs and metal frames. The blankets were a murky grey that had likely inherited most of their pigment from decades of accumulated dust, and they had a dark red line running down one of the long sides, to orientate you when you were folding them. Two feet from each bed was a large wooden cupboard, known as a tallboy, where you would hang your clothes. Adjacent to the tallboy was a waist-high set of rickety drawers, creatively called a lowboy. There were ten of these setups in each barrack room; you shared a room with nine other men.

Your personal space, the area that is undisputedly yours, is about the size of a queen-sized mattress. You are responsible for that forlorn little patch of carpet and its furniture-shaped relics.

One of the first things we were shown during those initial few days was how to make a bedroll. If you ever want an example of a futile military task, look no further than the NZ Army bedroll. Contrary to popular belief, you do not have to perfectly make your bed each and every morning during basic training. The idea that you have to get up and pull up your blanket, fold your sheet over to a precise length, fluff your pillow, smooth out any creases and finish the job with a 45-degree hospital corner is incorrect; that would be far too simple.

Instead, recruits at Waiouru have to make a bedroll from their sheets and blankets. It is essentially an alternating series of sheets and grey blankets folded to the same size, with the creases facing in a uniform direction, bound as tightly as possible by yet another grey blanket that wraps around the outside. When it's finished, it closely resembles an ugly, grey hamburger. This should be sat at the foot of your bed, with the creases all facing the same way as everyone else's. Every blanket and sheet must be folded to the same thickness, width and length. It's deceptively time consuming; if you're really onto it, a genuine bedroll savant, you might be able to smash one out in five minutes. With several refolds, minor adjustments and a good amount of swearing, it would take me closer to ten minutes each time. You had to be precise, because the corporals were passionately pedantic about examining them each morning. They would check the width of each fold with a fingertip, the angle of the creases with the edge of a piece of paper, and so on.

How can the corporals tell if it's wrapped tightly enough, you may ask? If they were in a good mood (and this was rare), they would jam their fingers into a gap and quicky withdraw them. If the gap had been widened by their fingers, it was deemed 'looser than your whore mother' and you'd be told to remedy it immediately, while the corporal stood over you, telling you how you should've been a blowjob instead of being born. If they weren't in a good mood, they would pick up your bedroll and launch it into the hallway, or at the wall beside your head. When it inevitably fell to pieces, they'd look at you with pure disappointment in their eyes, shake their head and say, 'See what I mean? You call *that* folded?' Then they'd turn on their heel and – maybe stopping to give your crumpled sheets another kick – they'd stride out of the room, leaving you to scrape your bedding up off the floor like some kind of sad interpretive dance performance.

TEAMWORK

THE MORNING ROUTINE ON basic training goes a little something like this. Each night, before you get into your skinny little bed, pull the ancient scratchy blankets up to your chin and fall unconscious ('sleep' is too gentle a word to describe the nose dive that your brain makes after a day of basic training), you have to make sure that your tiny island of solitude is as neat and tidy as it possibly can be. It's essential to find and remedy any scrap of leaf, or drawer that isn't closed the whole way. Taking those extra three seconds can save you *hours* of misery in the morning.

At 0545 *every* morning, seven days a week, for sixteen weeks, a corporal will wrench open the door to your room, flick on the light switch and bark something loud, crass and painfully unfunny about masturbation. Some that stuck with me:

'Hands off cocks, into your socks!'

'Wakey wakey, hands off snakey!'

'Drop your dicks and grab your shit!'

There were dozens more, but you get the gist. There was something undeniably wholesome about being woken up with a poem, each and every morning.

The room would then explode into activity. Everyone would be up and running towards the showers, their jandals flopping furiously on the linoleum floors and their towels streaking out behind them like the flag on a ship. We were expected to be showered, shaved, in our uniforms and standing in formation on the parade square by 0615 each morning. With our beds made into a perfect bedroll, of course.

There were sixty people in our barracks, with thirty in each platoon. Fifty-two of those people were male. There was a shared bathroom in the middle: six showers and six sinks. If you didn't make it to the front of either line, the preferred tactic was to stand, naked, in the line, and start soaping yourself up. As soon as a shower was free, you would dash in, rinse all the soap off and weave your way towards the sinks to run a razor around your cheeks.

When we started basic training, it was late August in Waiouru. Mornings would occasionally get above two degrees Celsius, but not often. Although our rooms each had a small, overworked bar heater in them, the corridors and bathrooms in these barracks did not. The bathrooms were always a haze of steam mixed with visible breath from everyone shuffling into the showers.

We also had to make sure our uniforms were immaculate. This meant boots polished, ironed creases, symmetrically rolled sleeves, and not a single loose thread on our clothes. Army corporals have a vendetta against loose threads that can only be described as passionate. The speed and precision at which they will sight and hone in on a loose thread on a recruit's unform suggests it must be, at some level, personal.

In the beginning our platoon never managed to be outside by 0615, and we were regularly punished for being late by being tasked with push-ups in the hall, picking leaves out of the small garden, and things of that nature. Within the first two weeks, I was getting really sick of these punishments. I decided I *would* make the 0615 timing, no matter what.

One night, I made my bedroll *before* I went to sleep and I stashed it under my bed. When I went to the bathroom to brush my teeth, I shaved as closely and carefully as I dared. I had my soap and shaving kit on the ground beside my bed, wrapped in my army-issue green towel. I found a single, spare blanket and slept wrapped in that, wearing warm clothes instead of getting under the covers of my made bed.

When the corporal stomped his way into our room the next morning, I was ready for him. I launched myself out of bed and, to his surprise, actually had to squeeze past him to get out of the room. I sprinted towards the showers, flip-flopping like a drunk cricket fan. I was in and out of the shower by the time the lines started forming. I didn't bother shaving; I was nineteen and my fuzz hadn't returned since the previous night. I stormed back into our room to see that three guys hadn't even gotten their jandals on yet. *Suckers*, I thought to myself. I was in my clothes and straightening my jungle hat before the first of them returned from the showers.

I made one small adjustment to the covers I had slept on top of, and then I was out towards the parade ground. I checked my watch: it was 0609. I was going to be a full five minutes *early*.

I sighted the spot on the parade square where Ngarimu Platoon always formed up, jogged over and took the position of the marker (this position is essentially the reference person for the rest of the platoon to form up on). I then stomped into the 'at ease' stance: feet shoulder-width apart, arms behind the back, right hand inside the left, gaze slightly above eye-level. The morning was cold, and still as dark as night, but the residual heat from my brief shower combined with the anticipation of victory kept me toasty.

I saw two corporals off to the side of the parade ground. They stopped talking to one another and stared at me.

I continued to look straight ahead, pretending I hadn't noticed. After what seemed like an age, I heard Corporal Arapeta's boots booming towards me. His stride was longer than I was tall, so it was easy to recognise without turning my head.

He stopped about five feet from me, off to my left. 'Who's that?' he snapped.

I tried to not be offended, despite the fact that the name DAVIDSON was scrawled across the front of my hat in giant, black lettering. 'Davidson, Corporal.'

In the silence that followed, I guess he vaguely remembered that he was responsible for me. 'Well, what the fuck are you doing?'

This was a curveball, I must admit. Nevertheless, I was not without purpose. I straightened up and tried to remove any trace of smugness from my voice (I undoubtedly failed).

'Ready for parade, Corporal!'

He laughed. A short, sharp bark that was entirely devoid of mirth.

'Oh *are you*? Ready for parade, eh?' He took a step closer, now standing directly in front of me. This was not going according to plan.

'Um, yes?' I managed.

'Like fuck you are. It's just you. Where is your platoon? Where's your section, Davidson?'

'They're, um, getting ready, Corporal.'

'And you're standing out here.'

I didn't know how to answer this, so instead I settled for trying to see if I could learn to turn invisible in the next few seconds. I failed.

'You aren't in there, helping your platoon? You just took care of yourself and here you are. Do you want a gold star? Or maybe a handjob for being such a good boy?'

'No, Corporal,' I mumbled.

I became vaguely aware that other members of the platoon had started to arrive. They gave the corporal and me the respectful distance that other animals might give a wolf when they see it has a struggling rabbit in its jaws.

'What the fuck am I meant to do with just you? I wanted a platoon out here. Not Recruit Ballbag standing on his own. I can't get anything done with just you. Can't take a hill, can't move supplies, can't dig an entrenchment. YOU are useless. On your own, YOU aren't worth shit. What possible use could I have for just you. I need your *team*.'

I could feel dozens of eyes on me. The bright lights of the parade ground seemed to be a spotlight just on me. I was sweating.

'Davidson, get back in the barracks and get every *single* person from Ngarimu Platoon out here. You don't come back until they're all out here, got it?'

Oh my God, thank you Jesus, he was going to let me go.

'Yes, Corporal!' I made to sprint away to the barracks, but before I made it two steps, he stopped me.

'Oi!'

I froze.

'I didn't say you could run.'

My heart sank.

'Get on your fucking guts. Crawl there.'

So I did. I got on my stomach and leopard-crawled the hundred metres of cold, wet concrete. It took a long time. People ran past me; I couldn't tell who. The others in my platoon knew better than to ask me what I was doing. The smartest thing to do was to go around and then promptly forget they had seen me. By the time I made it into the barracks, my front was soaked, I had gravel and dirt all over me, and my elbows were raw. I shakily stood up and lurched between the barrack rooms. Of course, they were all empty.

I shuffled back to the platoon. They were all standing there, ready to march to breakfast. Corporal Arapeta spotted me.

'Hurry up, Davidson. Don't make us wait for you.'

Humiliated, I avoided eye contact with everyone and took my spot in the platoon. That was my very own, personalised lesson in the value of teamwork.

FORWARD, MARCH!

WHAT IS THE DEAL with soldiers and marching? What's the point of walking in lines, with your footsteps all syncing up? You may have asked this question at some point.

Like many things, both in and out of the military, the reason it began and the reason it continues are very different from one another. Marching in formation, or 'drill', was invented back when soldiers used to form up in ranks and hack at each other until one side was left standing. Yet again, we owe the tradition of this discipline to the Romans. Walking in formation meant that the distances between you and the guy next to you, and the next two thousand guys next to him, were all consistent. This is important if you're trying to stop a cavalry charge or envelop a phalanx of enemy troops. In pre-modern warfare, it made practical sense as a commander to want your soldiers to know how to move around a battlefield without completely destroying their own formations. The big shields and spears at the front needed to stay at the front, and the guys holding bows needed to remain at the back.

But what about now? Why do we still teach soldiers how to march? There is a succinct mantra that every soldier is forced to recite, that captures the essence of this question. We would chant this in the morning before being marched off to breakfast.

> The aim of drill is to produce a soldier who is proud, alert
> and obedient, and forms the basis of ALL teamwork.

It really is that simple.

Proud. The army was the first place where I actually cared about my appearance beyond the question of whose pants it could get me into. Drill emphasises keeping your uniform immaculate, your hair cut neat and short and your boots polished. It also requires you to stand up straight, something I had never managed in my nineteen years of slouching. When I first got back from basic training, virtually everyone I knew would have sworn I'd gotten taller. I hadn't; they had just never seen me with decent posture before.

Alert. Drill keeps you alert, because you are constantly listening for the next command. Thirty sets of ears have to listen and thirty sets of feet must come together to make one sound. If you aren't alert, you'll be the odd one out that makes the whole thing look and sound like shit, like a member of a dance troupe who is half a beat behind everyone else.

Obedient. Well, obviously. You just stand there, doing what you're told.

The basis of all teamwork. Hard to say if it's *all* teamwork, but it's certainly a start. Drill is about having everyone aimed at the same goal, becoming one entity and working for the same outcome. Taking a group of civilians from all walks of life and teaching them to move in perfect unison is actually an ideal way to get them all to develop a sense of trust and comradery, especially if you make them do push-ups every time someone falls out of step. Before you ever touch a rifle or throw a grenade, you will learn to stand to attention and stomp your foot at the exact same time as everyone else.

We had been in barracks for almost a week when Corporal Green took Ngarimu Platoon to the drill square near the back of camp for the first time. It wasn't impressive, as drill squares go; just a large expanse of old cement the size of four tennis courts. It looked vast and bleak.

Behind us, the rest of Waiouru camp went about its daily business. Trucks roared, sergeants barked orders and other platoons of freshly shaved recruits shuffled around like stunned cattle. Out in front of us, behind Corporal Green, lay the edge of the Waiouru training area. It started out as a flat paddock of grass, but quickly developed into a series of rolling hills that seemed to stretch on endlessly. I began picturing myself wandering through it on any number of adventures. I later learned that the entire training area is 900 square kilometres.

I snapped out of my reverie when a fresh gust whipped through my overalls and cut straight through the thermals I wore underneath. My cheap sneakers provided no insulation. I immediately began to shake. It wasn't freezing, but I had lived my entire life in Auckland. We were 800 metres above sea level and I had the same body fat content as a peeled carrot. It was perhaps just below ten degrees this morning, but I was already starting to suffer. Evidently, so were others, because Corporal Green now delivered a speech that has stayed with me ever since.

'Discomfort is the constant companion of the field soldier!' His harsh voice rasped across the parade square from where he stood. I tried to ignore the cold momentarily and strained to take in every word, despite the tremoring in my bony knees. 'Right now, you are not cold,' he said, staring right at me. I didn't move, or even blink, but my eyes earnestly disagreed with him. 'You have a stomach full of hot food. You have been moving for at least fifteen minutes. Your clothes are dry, and you had eight hours of sleep last night. You have been standing in the wind for four minutes. You are not cold.'

My fingers began to ache.

'What you are experiencing now is discomfort. Learn it well. Acknowledge what it feels like. When you are outside, doing your job, this is how you will feel. This will always be manageable, if you are disciplined and you have everything in order.'

He began to pace. My numb toes burned with jealousy.

'Do not mistake discomfort for cold. Being cold means you need to do something about it. Currently, you are just uncomfortable. Feel it. Embrace this sensation.'

We stood there, most of us silently shaking. To my left, though, was a recruit named Daniel Smith, who was barely moving. He was from somewhere in the deep South Island. This was probably barbeque weather to him.

My nose burned and my cheeks felt numb. I began tensing my quads and calves to try and squeeze some hot blood around my lower body. It probably did nothing, but I felt better for trying.

After what seemed like an age, Corporal Green barked again.

'Platoooooon. Platoon, attenSHUHn!' (Translation: I am talking to you, I am about to give a command to you, stand at attention.)

In ramshackle unison, thirty-five people each picked up their left foot and stomped it in beside their right. It sounded like hail on a tin roof. Having been a drill instructor in Cadet Forces, it was hard for me not to visibly wince at the sound. More importantly, the prospect of moving had me genuinely happy.

From there we began to learn the most basic drill moves. I mentally checked out of the lesson, having learned these manoeuvres years ago. Left turn at the halt, right turn at the halt, about turn, left wheels and right wheels. This took all morning, but eventually the entire platoon had a semblance of cadence happening on about 75% of all given instructions. It was a start.

It felt good to be making progress as a platoon. It was the first real day that I didn't feel like a civilian with a shaved head, too far from home.

AHH WAYNE, YOU'VE DONE IT AGAIN

IN EVERY BOX OF AMMUNITION, there is a dud; in every bunch of grapes, one is sour; and in every platoon in every army since the main battle tactic was CHAAAAARGE, there is one soldier who is utterly, completely hopeless.

Ours was a thin, rat-faced creature named Wayne. If Gomer Pyle from *Full Metal Jacket* and Peter Pettigrew from *Harry Potter* had a love child, and viciously beat them any time they displayed an ounce of common sense, that creature would still have been a better recruit than Sig Wayne.

It wasn't just that he was slow, or sloppy. It wasn't the fact that he couldn't lift his rifle over his head without breaking into a sweat. It wasn't just that his uniform always looked like it was made entirely of wrinkles. It wasn't even that he would intentionally skip showering to 'save time' and his odour would follow him from room to room like a stray dog. It was that no matter how many times he screwed something up, or how often the corporals thrashed him, he would continue to make the same, simple errors, over and over and *over* again.

He wasn't in my section, so fortunately I only suffered indirect repercussions of Wayne's shortcomings. The rest of his section, however, were almost continuously spending their time making up for Wayne's latest fuckup.

The army has long stood by the philosophy of 'win together, lose together'. When an individual makes a careless error, it is more often than not their comrades who are punished. This tactic *usually* motivates people to get their act together, to reduce the suffering of their friends.

This principle didn't seem to permeate Wayne's oddly shaped skull in the slightest. It became commonplace to see Wayne's section outside, picking up leaves in the rain, or recleaning their rifles for the umpteenth time. Eventually our platoon adopted a little catchphrase for him.

We were sitting in the corridor, cleaning our weapons. We'd had dinner, not much was happening for the night and most of us were just enjoying the opportunity to sit down and chat. Cleaning a rifle isn't especially difficult, but it is time consuming. You have to work your brush and rag into a lot of different crevices, again and again, alternating between using oil and a dry rag to clean off the black carbon that sticks to the metal. After less than ten minutes, Wayne stood up and started walking towards Corporal Jones. Most of us looked confused, astonished even. Everyone in Wayne's section looked murderous.

Jones looked Wayne up and down, without getting out of his chair. 'Done already?'

'Yes, Corporal.'

Everyone was diligently staring at their weapons, but thirty sets of ears were listening intently to the exchange.

'You must have a bloody good technique. Are you sure you don't need to check any of the parts again?'

Incredible, I thought; Jones was actually giving him an out.

Wayne shook his head. I saw several members of his section die a little inside.

Jones smirked and took the rifle. He didn't even open the breach or pull off the barrel. Instead, he whipped off the gas plug, a small, piston-shaped attachment on the side of the barrel. Its job is to regulate the gas released while the rifle is firing. Understandably, it gets *filled* with carbon.

Wayne's looked like it hadn't been cleaned since Vietnam.

Jones smirked and tossed it back to him.

'Break down your rifle. Give a piece to everyone in your section. *They* can clean it for you, and they can show you what you're meant to be doing as you go. You are not to touch your rifle again until it is sparkling and reassembled. If it's not the cleanest rifle I've ever seen in my entire fucking *life*, your section will be marching down to the armoury and cleaning every machine gun we have. Got it?'

Wayne mumbled a 'yes, Corporal' and scurried over to his section.

It took me almost an hour to clean my rifle properly, after which I enjoyed a cigarette, chatted some shit and took a shower. I don't know what time they finished, but when I went to bed, Wayne's section were still there, cleaning his rifle while he sat on the floor and picked his nose.

Sean Newark and I were walking past to give Callahan our sympathies when Newark gave birth to our platoon catchphrase. He looked at Wayne and shook his head, evoking the melody of the old 'McCain' TV advertisement of the late 90s. 'Ah Wayne, you've done it again.'

Another fun Wayne incident involved a barrack inspection, a towel and a lighter. Almost every morning on basic training, the entire platoon was subjected to a barrack inspection. After breakfast, we would usually spend close to an hour cleaning the entire barracks, top to bottom, polishing all that could be polished and sweeping everything that wasn't bolted to the ground. By 0800 everyone would be standing rigidly to attention at the foot of their beds, staring directly ahead. The duty corporal would saunter through the rooms, checking for dust, or a slight crease in the bedsheets, or some other nebulous detail that would justify them dolling out a cruel and unusual punishment.

Because there are four rooms for each platoon, and the corporal inspects all of them, you can't see or hear what's happening when the corporal is inspecting the other room.

Usually there's just a muffled murmur as the corporal struts around, thinking out loud.

'Dusty light.' 'Shirt's untucked.' 'That's shit.' And so on.

So, imagine our surprise when, during one such inspection, we all heard Corporal Arapeta's booming voice resonate through the walls, crystal clear.

'JESUS FUCK, put it OUT you clown!'

There followed a dozen hurried footsteps and a good deal more swearing.

What happened, as Callahan told me over a cigarette later that morning, was this:

Wayne's section was cleaning their room, as they did every morning. Wayne was doing his usual routine of moving around and talking a lot but not actually helping in any significant way. There was less than a minute to go before Corporal Arapeta was due to come in and inspect the place. Someone passed by Wayne's bed and noticed it ponged of B.O., quite badly.

'Eugh, what's that stink?'

'Nothing, I don't smell anything,' was Wayne's response.

'Well, I do and so will Arapeta. Fix it.'

Wayne searched around frantically. He was given a can of Lynx to obscure the offensive odour, which he sprayed around his bed. A good amount settled on the towel laid out neatly on top of his lowboy. We all had a towel just like that one, in a faded green colour.

The boys were stood in front of their beds just in time, as Corporal Arapeta's size thirteen boots stomped down the hall. As he was approaching, Wayne noticed that there was a loose thread hanging off his towel. Knowing how corporals felt about loose threads, and not wanting to get fragged for such a heinous infringement, he whipped his lighter out of his pocket and tried to incinerate the offending fibre. Of course, it burned, and so did the heavy dousing of Lynx on the towel. The entire thing burst into flames exactly as Arapeta entered the room.

That's when the shouting began. Once it had been established that the room and, by extension, the barracks were not in any immediate danger, Corporal Arapeta dished out the section's collective punishment. While the rest of us smoked, did laundry and studied our workbooks for the week's lessons, they were busy indeed.

They began by measuring the distance between every article in their room. The distance between the beds, the distance from the door to each tallboy, and so on. Once that was done, they began moving everything out the door. Everything. Every bed, closet and drawer was hauled out and carried across to the parade ground. They began setting up their room, exactly as it was, but outside. And I do mean *exactly* as it was: to the millimetre. It took them over an hour. And once they were done, sweating and exhausted, Corporal Arapeta didn't even give their setup a glance. He just nodded and said, 'Fine, bring it back in. Hurry up.'

After Callahan had finally finished hauling ten beds, ten closets and ten drawers the few hundred metres across camp, he related the story to me. I was in near hysterics by the end.

Callahan just shook his head. 'I wonder what it'll be next time. Probably burn the fucking barracks down.'

'Ah Wayne, you've done it again,' I agreed.

LATE AUGUST 2011

ON ONE OF OUR FIRST nights in Waiouru, we were standing in the corridor, all lined up as usual. Corporal Green rasped a command.

'Smokers, prove.'

'Prove' was a term that I had quickly learned meant 'Stick your arm out, or otherwise identify yourself.'

I had been smoking since I was fifteen (when I could afford it) so I stuck my arm out without thinking. It occurred to me a split-second after I had done this that he had probably found a cigarette butt on the ground and was going to make anybody who smoked go around licking the windows clean or something. There were only three others who stuck their arms out.

Corporal Green continued. 'For the duration of this recruit course, these are the *only* four people from this platoon I want to see smoking. Understand?'

'Yes, Corporal!' we barked in response. His sentiment came from a good place. The army has a disproportionally high volume of people who smoke (because they're not allowed to do any decent drugs). And a lot of people start smoking on basic training. The stress and lack of anything better to do, along with the social aspect, are all contributing factors to this statistic. So, as far as Ngarimu Platoon was concerned, there were only four smokers to worry about.

We were an eclectic bunch of characters and we got along almost immediately. Malohi was an American-born Tongan, who spoke slow, thoughtful English when he was happy and loud, expletive-riddled Tongan when he wasn't. Sean Newark had already been singled out as one of the corporals' favourite punching bags. It was almost entirely self-inflicted: he was one of those people who was born to touch the 'wet paint' signs and run along any verge that read 'keep off the grass'. Getting into trouble was simply in his bones, but he made up for it by being hysterically funny. Callahan was just like me: a nondescript, white teenager who wasn't entirely sure what he was doing there.

On basic training, you have to ask permission to go out for a cigarette. We didn't know this going in, but we four smokers of Ngarimu Platoon gathered fairly quickly that if we didn't ask, the opportunity was never offered. We were therefore constantly bickering over who would be the next one to timidly raise their hand after receiving the night's instructions and meekly chirp, 'Permission to have a cigarette, Corporal.'

Sometimes you'd get a reluctant yes, other times you'd get a flat no. And just as often, you'd just found a way to volunteer for some awful task that the duty corporal hadn't assigned to anyone yet.

Alas, even if one of us did muster up the courage to ask for a precious gasp of nicotine, most smoking breaks went the same way. No sooner would the four of us shuffle into our smoking corner to huddle away from the vicious winds, like a tiny flock of green-garbed penguins, than we would hear the dreaded 'FORM UP' being hollered from the corporals' office. We would swear in frustration, drag furiously for another few seconds, then sigh and tuck our partially spent cigarettes back into their packets and jog over to the parade ground to join the rest of the platoon.

EX COMPASS ROSE

IT TAKES ALMOST TWO weeks of basic training before you get issued your uniform, pack, sleeping bag and every other little bit of equipment deemed necessary for a modern solider trying to survive New Zealand's winter desert. It's actually a pretty good day when it happens. You aren't running around carrying out menial tasks; you get to sit and wait for everyone to file through the clerks. Most crucially, the prospect of finally being out of those heinous overalls is downright titillating. Once we had our DPMs, everyone was absolutely rapt.

We were told in excruciating detail about how to adhere to the uniform standards. Black, immaculately polished boots, pants ironed flat (no creases) and tucked into your socks with a paratrooper's billow over the top that should cover the tops of the boots. Shirts also ironed flat and sleeves rolled up to your biceps, with the fold measuring exactly four fingers' width. Our collars had to be ironed flat. There couldn't be a single lose thread *anywhere* on the entire ensemble. Lastly, we would slap our wide-brimmed, DPM jungle hats (J-hats) on our heads, with a large piece of duct tape across the front. The duct tape had our surnames in capital letters.

Real soldiers wore berets in camp, and J-hats in the field. Recruits wear wide-brimmed J-hats all day, every day. Once you left basic, one of the first orders of business was to seek out a short-brimmed J-hat, resulting in a look that has become the trademark of the NZ field soldier. As for berets, as much as I loved them, and each of us desperately wanted to wear one, we wouldn't even get to touch a beret until our final week of basic training.

Each and every morning, as we stood either on the parade ground or in the corridor, the duty corporal would go over every recruit and look for faults. Each infraction would become a 'minute' that we as a platoon owed the corporal. We had to pay these minutes back in increasingly painful ways. In the first few weeks, at least half of the platoon would have at least one thing wrong with their uniform, so we would regularly end up owing more than twenty minutes a day.

One of the most common punishments was to 'mark time'. This is essentially walking in place, but you have to raise your knee until your thigh is parallel with the ground and, most importantly, you all have to do it in time, at a rate of 120 beats per minute. This is the difficult part. Maintaining a cadence with thirty other people, for minutes at a time, without letting fatigue speed you up or slow you down requires inhuman discipline. Each time we fell out of time, the corporals would stop the clock until we got back in sync. Quite often the twenty-odd minutes we owed in the morning would turn into over half an hour spent marking time that evening.

After I'd left basic training, and had started instructing fresh soldiers myself, the reasons for this exhausting and frustrating punishment became quite obvious.

1. It's practise for drill. Like everything else on basic, it all comes back to teamwork. Learning to aim for a group goal and prioritise being in time above everything else gives you a feeling of unity.

2. It's physically hard. Walking on the spot might not
    sound fatiguing, but doing it at that speed for ten
    minutes or more will set a fire in your quads that you
    wouldn't believe.

Because of the increasingly hard tasks set for us on basic – and almost everyone who shows up is either chubby, or cartoonishly thin, like I was – the first few weeks of punishment are as much about raising your fitness level as they are about discipline. I have no doubt that the hours spent marking time, raising the heaviest footwear I'd ever worn in my life, contributed massively to the gains I made in leg strength during basic training.

About three days after we had been issued our gear and were getting used to our nice, shiny new uniforms, it was time to go into the field for the very first time and get them completely filthy.

We had been in classrooms, learning about maps and compasses, among other things. It wasn't too much of a learning curve for me: one thing that the NZ Cadet Forces are really, *really* big on is using a map and compass. Orienteering is practically half of what they do when they go out for the weekend. However, when the instructing corporal first came around and gave everyone a map and a compass to start familiarising themselves with, I was downright startled to see that around the housing of my compass, the numbers were all wrong.

It probably isn't news to you that a compass contains as many degrees as a circle. Due east sits at 90 degrees, south is at 180, west 270, and north is at 0/360. These numbers were burned into my brain from years of running around Whatipu and Whangaparoa trying to locate little numbered tags nailed to trees. So, imagine my surprise when I looked at east on this compass and saw the numbers 1600 etched there.

The concept of dividing a circle into 6400 units instead of 360 has been around for a long time, however it was during the Second World War, when artillery and longer-range weapons were being used regularly (a naval warship could fire projectiles at distances of twenty *kilometres*), that something more precise than degrees was needed.

Although it was difficult for me to unlearn what had become instinctive measurements, I had to admit that mils were the superior means of navigation.

A week later, we were standing out on the road, in our shiny new DPM uniforms and our army ALICE packs bulging with sleeping bags, hoochie shelters, warm clothes and the ugly, brown packets of sludge they called 'ration packs'.

I don't remember much about that first night. We walked maybe two kilometres from camp, stumbling on rocks and crashing into one another as the afternoon sun faded, and took an outrageous amount of time to set up our hoochies. Looking back, I'm amazed the corporals instructing us didn't simply spend the whole time laughing. It was farcical.

My most vivid memory of that night was the cold. It wasn't wet, and the snow hadn't made it into the pine forest we were staying in, but the wind was bitter. It cut through my thermals and my smock and struck my chest relentlessly. My ears, my nose, my fingers, even my nipples *throbbed* with cold. I had just finished an hour of shivering on guard duty, and was trying to get excited about getting into my sleeping bag ... except I couldn't get my fingers to work. I couldn't unlace my boots, or unzip my jacket. My hands literally wouldn't grip anything. I started to get worked up. I was so frustrated, and so cold. I just wanted to get into my sleeping bag. I must've been making some desperate, exasperated sighs, because I was wrenched out of my personal misery by Corporal Prim, a short, severe woman covered in freckles.

She shook my hoochie, which is essentially a single sheet of nylon that can be tied between trees and pegs to form a roof over your head: imagine a tent with no walls or floor. They're covered in a green and black camouflage print, naturally.

'Davidson, is that you?' she demanded in a whisper.

I was terrified. I suddenly realised that if she started yelling at me right now, in front of everyone, there was a very real possibility that I would cry. 'Yes, Corporal,' I managed to squeak.

There was a long pause.

'You alright?' she asked.

'Yes, Corporal. Just cold.'

She grunted. 'Here, eat this.' An army-issue chocolate bar appeared before me. I took it, using both hands as a sort of crude pincer.

'Thank you, Corporal,' I mumbled.

'Now, get in your bag and go the fuck to sleep.' She stalked off without another word.

I was grateful, and excited to eat the waxy, cheap chocolate. But of course I couldn't get the chocolate bar open. I finally chewed through the wrapper, eating more than a little of the foil covering. As for removing my clothes, I ended up having to place my zipper between my frozen fingers, and then bend over so that I could clamp my hand shut using my teeth. It took almost twenty minutes, by my reckoning, but eventually I was safely wrapped inside my winter-proof sleeping bag. My first night in the field was blissfully over.

THIS IS MY RIFLE

WE HAD BEEN ON basic training for almost a month before we got to touch a rifle. Honestly.

It makes sense. Despite all the vetting and screenings and interviews you go through to qualify for basic, there's still a decent amount of weirdos who make it through the first few weeks before they get sent to the bus.

We were lined up, standing outside the armoury. We knew where we were. Corporal Green could sense our giddy anticipation. He gave us all our first, and only, warning.

'You are about to be issued your rifles that you'll carry for the remainder of basic. I will tell you this now. The first person to point their rifle at someone, *anyone*, or any other dicking around with their weapon, and I'll wrap it around your head.'

Firearm safety 101, with Corporal Green.

I took this lesson to heart immediately. Over the six years that followed, I spent the majority of the time holding or wearing a weapon of some kind. As far as that rule goes, I have to say I agree completely.

There are seven official firearm safety rules (T.A.L.I.S.C.A) that comprehensively cover all the dos and don'ts of how to handle an extremely dangerous piece of metal.

1. Treat all firearms as loaded.
2. Always point your weapon in a safe direction (down is good).
3. Load only when ready to fire.
4. Identify your target beyond all doubt.
5. Store weapons and ammunition separately.
6. Check your firing zone.
7. Avoid drugs and alcohol when shooting.

But the most fundamental rule, the one that sits above all others in my opinion, is this:

> *Do not point a firearm at ANYTHING you aren't willing to destroy.*

It really is that simple. The use of the verb 'destroy', not kill, is deliberate. Destroy fits better, because when people are shot, they don't neatly fall down dead like in films. Bits of them go across the floor, the walls, and so on. Guns are made solely to destroy things, and they do so spectacularly well.

This rule should be applied whether or not the weapon is loaded, whether it has a magazine or not – hell, even if the barrel is off. A bullet travelling at half speed out of a partially disassembled weapon will still kill you stone dead.

Just don't point it at anything or anyone you don't want to dig a grave for.

Sadly, this is a rule that is often forgotten, leading to tragic, unnecessary deaths. Anyone who skims the news will eventually hear about an accidental firearm death, and 99% of the time, it's because this one simple rule wasn't followed.

I had handled the odd rifle during my time in the cadets, but they had either been the ancient, museum display-worthy Lee-Enfield (literally a Second World War weapon) or the cheap and cheerful, Canadian-made Norinco rifle. Both were bolt-action, .22 calibre. Pea shooters, really. In 2011, the NZDF official weapon was the IW Steyr. If you've played *Call of Duty* or *Counter-Strike*, you've probably seen this weapon, except it's called a bullpup or an AUG. It's a futuristic-looking assault rifle made largely of dark green, ballistic plastic. It takes 5.56 calibre rounds and can fire on semi or fully automatic. Compared to what I was used to, this was an entire arsenal as far as I was concerned.

We spent the afternoon in the barracks, learning how to strip and assemble the rifles. When Corporal Green pulled one apart for the first time and laid out all the tiny, bizarrely shaped pieces of metal on the carpet, I was completely overwhelmed. There was a random little spring, a piece that looked like a cog, a long, thin rod that had to be jiggled in and out of place and about ten other tiny little pieces.

Another part of basic that is surprisingly like the movies: I must've pulled that rifle apart and put it back together over a hundred times that first day.

We did relays, we did races, we even made blindfolds and pulled the firearms apart by touch alone. It took less than a week for me to go from being utterly baffled by the sight of those little twisted pieces of metal to being able to completely strip and reassemble my rifle in a little over forty seconds.

The point of learning to do it so quickly is not so you can quickly pull apart and clean your weapon during a firefight. It's so you can clean your weapon after you've been marching all day, or when there's barely enough light to see by, or when it's raining sideways. Each and every day, you need to put some time into your weapon, no matter how you're feeling.

I'm not into firearms. They don't excite me in any way. But I did come to respect them as a useful tool. And any tradesman will tell you, you always take care of your tools before you take care of yourself. We had an expression for this in the army: 'Gears before beers.' It's an ethos I've carried with me ever since.

FIRST TOUCH OF SNOW, AND LANDMINES

I HAD LIVED IN Auckland my entire life. While I'd visited Italy a few times to meet various chain-smoking, moustached aunties, it had always been during the summer. What I'm getting at is that I had never felt snow until it started falling on me on my second day in Waiouru. For anyone reading who has fond memories of spending weekends absconding to Ruapehu, skiing by day and drinking hot cocoa by night, while Father drank cognac and the maid polished the silverware, snow in Waiouru was quite different. At first, it was magical and beautiful and gloriously new to me. I loved the way it crunched underfoot and seemed to eat up all the sound that touched it, giving the world a sort of muffled feel. But I can precisely remember when snow stopped being fun.

After two weeks of physical training (PT), classroom lessons and quite a lot of drill, snow was firmly and decisively ruined for me.

For the first week or so of basic training, you spend a lot of time indoors. You're still adjusting to military life, and the skinny (or chubby) new recruits can barely make it through the morning routine without gasping for air. Army PT is only thrown at you four or five days a week. They use the time between physical training sessions to educate you on all sorts of theory. Ranks, NZ Army history, the army ethos, and so much more. You file into little classrooms and you actually have to *learn* things. My ADHD brain seriously struggled with this component. It was only my background in cadets, which meant I already knew a lot of this stuff, that saved me from falling seriously behind.

One of the weapon systems that the NZDF still teaches every soldier to use is the Claymore anti-personnel mine. For the uninitiated, it's a small, nondescript hunk of metal about the size of a small takeaway container. You stick its little retractable legs into the ground, run a wire from it to a handheld detonator (called a 'clacker') that has a switch attached. You cover the Claymore in bits of grass and twigs, point it at where you think someone unfriendly might approach, and when you hear them coming you duck (most definitely you should duck first), hit the clacker and send 900 ball bearings towards your enemy at 4,000 feet per second (yes, you read that right) in a cone of destruction that can extend as far back as 200 metres.

Anyone caught in this cone quickly stops being unfriendly.

Of course, before you can trust someone to carry one of these in their pack all day and set it up somewhere without blowing their own face off, they need to practise. On basic training, they have boxes of 'training Claymores', which are exact replicas that weigh the same and have the same basic design as a live Claymore. They are also bright blue.

To maximise safety – and because the army loves rote learning – there is a specific manner in which Claymores should be set and laid out. We would spend evenings reading the by-numbers instructions for placing the mines, quizzing each other before our TOETS (Test of Elementary Training Skills). On a blustery, snowy Friday morning, we marched out to the back of camp where the training sheds (basically an open shelter with a corrugated iron roof) were, to learn how to place a Claymore. We took turns at walking out the detonator wire, then had to lie down on our stomachs and go through the TOETS *exactly* as they were written. Any deviation at all resulted in an instant fail. The corporal looming above you would give an exaggerated sigh, whisper 'ballbag' at you, just loud enough to hear, and then send you to the back of the line to wait your turn to try again.

You had to do all of these things by memory, perfectly, whilst lying on your stomach in the snow and frozen mud.

1. Given an M18A1 Claymore mine in a bandoleer, an M57 firing device, an M40 test set, and a firing wire with blasting cap, all packed in an M7 bandoleer; a sandbag; and two wooden stakes.
2. Conduct a circuit test of the firing device, with the blasting cap secured under a sandbag.
3. Install the M18A1 Claymore mine so that:
   a. the front of the mine centres on a kill zone
   b. the firing device is 16 metres to the rear or side

of the emplaced mine and is fired from a covered
position

c. the mine, firing wire and firing device are
camouflaged

d. he installation is confirmed by conducting a final
circuit test.

4. Circuit test of the M57 firing device and M40 test set:

a. Remove the electrical wire and accessories while
leaving the mine in the bandoleer

b. Remove the dust cover from the connector of the
M57 firing device and from the female connector of
the M40 test set

c. Plug the test set into the firing device

d. Position the firing device bail to the FIRE position

e. Activate the handle of the firing device with a firm,
quick squeeze, observing the flash of light through
the window of the test set

f. Remove the shorting plug cover from the connector
of the firing wire and from the end of the test set

g. Plug the connector of the firing wire into the test set.

h. Place the blasting cap under a sandbag, behind a
tree, or in a hole in the ground to protect the person
performing the circuit check should the blasting cap
detonate

i. Place the M57 firing device bail in the FIRE position
and actuate the firing handle

j. Place the firing device on SAFE; remove the firing
device and the M40 test set

k. Place the shorting plug cover on the firing wire.

Once you get through all of those, the corporal will say something like 'enemy approaching front' and you squeeze the detonator. The corporal says 'mine detonated', you repeat this back to them (because for some reason, they need confirmation that you would have heard 650 grams of plastic explosive going off and turning several people into wet confetti).

I don't remember exactly how many attempts it took me that day, but it was more than three. I do remember my hands being so cold that I had to pry my fingers off the cord with my teeth. My clothes were sodden and I was shaking. I so desperately wanted to be done with this stupid thing, but I needed to pass. The corporals warned that anyone who didn't pass that day would be back out there first thing the next morning while everyone else got the relatively enjoyable task of ironing their clothes. I did muddle my way through it, eventually. But it was another stark reminder that I was just a new recruit who didn't know much of anything. I wasn't the naturally gifted soldier that I assumed I was going to be, not by a long shot.

RADIOS IN THE DARK

IT'S INTERESTING HOW desperately people organise themselves into groups, isn't it? How even when you've spent months with the same people, being a part of a team, you'll all still do your best to sort one another into categories that separate you somehow. One of the first things you learn about your roommates on basic training is what trade and corps they are heading into. Everyone in the army receives what they call 'Basic Infantry Training' on basic training. This is based on the ethos that every soldier is an infantry soldier first and foremost, and a skilled tradesperson second. Then, once you 'march out' (complete basic training), you get shipped off to your various corps and units, where you are reminded regularly that everyone else in the army is a wanker or an idiot or a useless sack of shit, and it's only thanks to you and your unit that the New Zealand Military even manages to carry on each day.

By far the most common assignment is Infantry. Many people think that the army is made up of only foot soldiers who sit in trenches or run around collecting Nazi scalps for Brad Pitt. Unsurprisingly, so do many people who sign up. They want to spend as much time as possible doing the good soldiery stuff they've seen in movies, and so being an infantry solider seems like the best way to fulfil this fantasy. A word of warning for any prospective grunts out there looking to join New Zealand's Infantry Battalions: I hope you love digging holes.

That's what they don't show you in the movies: infantry soldiers spend nearly as much time holding a shovel as a rifle. To their credit, an infantry section (ten men) can smash out a platoon entrenchment – enough shelter and holes to conceal thirty people – in a matter of hours. A section from every other corps in the army (with the notable exception of the mole-people we call the Engineering Corps) will take almost an entire day to complete this horrid task.

Virtually everyone else in my section was heading to what they call 'Teeth Arms' corps. Infantry, Artillery, Engineers, etc. Those real 'war-dog' corps. The only exceptions were Louis, the medic, and me, the signaller.

For the most part, this was a big advantage. My section was full of big, physical guys who knew they were heading into a trade that would only throw them more challenges, so they embraced the bullshit that basic training threw at us with an almost masochistic relish.

But there was a downside too. Despite the fact that all eleven of us had received *exactly* the same level of training and were by all accounts identically skilled soldiers, when it came time to go out into the field for the first time as a section, guess who got the radio, without any discussion at all. Of course, it was the smallest guy there, yours truly.

I was already dreading carrying my food, water, ammunition, sleeping bag, cooking equipment, warm clothes and all the other little trinkets they like to load recruits up with. The first time I put that pack on I remember thinking that it was as heavy as it could possibly be; surely there was nothing more you could load onto a man's back? I would guess that my pack came to a laughable twenty kilos, probably twenty-two at the most. By now, two months into basic training, I had put on several kilos of muscle, but I was still skinnier than a hungry greyhound.

As soon as it was determined that we were indeed ready to carry a section radio as a part of our equipment, it was obvious to everyone in the section that I should be the one to carry it. 'Because you're a sig,' was the oft-repeated justification.

I tried to point out that I wasn't a sig just yet, and that when they all got to the Infantry Battalion they would still need to know how to operate a radio, but this fell on deaf ears. Especially once the lads had seen the radio. It was the length of two laptops taped together and weighed slightly less than seven kilos. It also used two huge batteries at a time, that each lasted about eight hours. I made sure that others in my section carried all my spare and dead batteries at all times, and I received very little pushback on this concession at least.

So there I was, the so-called section signaller, conducting radio checks, keeping us in contact with the other sections, learning by trial and error where the best place to put up my antenna was, as we got deeper and deeper into the bush. When you patrol in the military, you do it in total silence, trying to listen for people who are looking for you. You communicate through hand signals. The only person who talks at all during patrols is the poor bastard dragging the radio along.

The 117F radio comes with two main antennas. One is three feet long, and the other is ten feet long and segmented like a tent pole. The three-foot antenna is good for shorter distances and, more importantly, doesn't get caught on every stray twig as you're walking through the bush. It does have one tough lesson that comes with it though. It is attached by screwing it into place, and the antenna itself, made entirely of metal (known as a blade, because of its thin, sharp shape), is attached to the base by a very thick coiled spring. This means it can wobble about and poke out of your pack at a weird angle without getting damaged. Brilliant. What I didn't realise is that springs are quite ... springy. I was walking, huffing and puffing, thinking about how the single kilometre we had walked through the bush was surely the most heroic distance ever covered by a man under such encumbrance as mine, when the blade brushed up against a tree and was pulled back. It then snapped into the side of my head like a steel ruler.

It fucking hurt. A lot. I whimpered and went down on one knee. Amazingly, my fear of getting bollocked must have surpassed my sense of self-preservation, because I didn't tell anyone what had happened. I just felt the side of my head for blood and stood up, swaying slightly. Dan, who was behind me, must not have seen what happened, because he caught up to me and merely gestured for me to go faster. I felt like shooting a blank right into his face at that moment. But instead, I nodded and waited for the white-hot pain behind my eyes to subside.

When we finally got into our LUP (lay-up point) for the night, I had an angry red grape of blood under the skin beside my temple. I was irate and my headache had only gotten worse over the course of the day.

When you get into a platoon position, you place your 'section assets' at your sentry position. This means the machine gun and the radio get sent up to the spot and anybody who is on stag (sentry) has the ability to A: call for help on the radio, and B: fire many, many bullets into anybody they don't like the look of.

It had been a cold, wet walk on a cold, wet day. The night was colder and wetter still. I did the first sentry after dinner and was elated to get into my sleeping bag and lie unconscious for as long as humanly possible. By my estimate I had at least six hours before anybody should be bothering me. Fucking marvellous.

At 2300, while the wind whipped the roof of my hoochie, and rain ran in tiny rivers all around me, somebody prodded my leg with their boot.

It is hard to describe how unpleasant it is to be woken up under such circumstances, but I would compare it to being told you have to complete some vital chore, moments after sitting down to eat a meal you've been looking forward to all day.

'Dario.'

It was Spike. He spoke in that appalling whisper that large, baritone men have, which is somehow louder than their normal speaking voice.

'Dario.'

I heard him the first time, as I'm sure I would have even if I'd been six feet underground. But I didn't move. Playing possum was a perfectly valid strategy as I saw it.

Spike wasn't deterred. 'Dario, oi.' He punctuated this greeting with another boot prod.

'What?' I replied with a scowl.

'It's the radio, you need to come fix it.'

I was very tired, my head hurt and I was not on shift. I wanted to articulate how this was very much not my issue to deal with at the present time.

'Fuck off.'

'I'm serious,' he pleaded. 'We can't hear anything and there was supposed to be a radio check at 2200.'

I wracked my brains. Hopefully I could troubleshoot this without getting out of my nice, warm bag.

'Is it on the right freq? Have you got the ten-foot whip on it? Have you tried unplugging the handset and cleaning the contacts?'

'Yes, yes and yeah, obviously.' A little bit of panic and urgency was creeping into his booming whisper. 'Can you *please* come and take a look.'

I sat up. Please? This was some serious shit.

I grumbled and swore as I put on my cold, wet boots, zipped up my jacket and stuffed a beanie over my still-throbbing head.

'Alright,' I huffed. 'Lead the fuck on.'

Spike breathed a sigh of relief and shuffled along the path towards the gun pit. I stumbled along behind him, in almost total darkness, cursing the piece-of-shit defective radio that my decent, hardworking section had been plagued with.

I got to the gun pit and saw Dan and Watson hunched over the radio, neither of them looking into the woods.

Great, I thought. Any second now a corporal is going to come screaming out of the bushes and tell us we're all dead for not keeping a proper watch. That'll be fun.

I squatted down and poked Dan. 'What's up?'

He knew it was me without turning around.

'Radio's fucked. Can't hear a thing.'

Now that I was awake, I realised how odd this was.

'No static? No squelch?'

'Nothing,' he confirmed. He handed me the handset to verify.

I held the receiver to my ear and, indeed, could hear no background static. I pressed the transmit button, expecting to hear the transmission elevate above the 'noise floor' in a universally recognised noise officially known as 'squelch' but better described as the 'kcchhhh' sound that a radio makes.

I heard nothing. That was weird.

I wriggled into the gun pit between Dan and Watson. I was small, but Dan was regular-sized and Watson was roughly the size of an expensive fridge, so we were comically crushed together. I managed to get my hand onto the radio knob.

'Did you guys fuck with this? I loaded up the night frequency before I went to sleep.'

They both insisted they hadn't touched it, and neither had anyone else. I immediately identified this as a piping hot lie. Because the radio was off.

I turned the knob to the appropriate setting. It lit up. Before they could say anything, I depressed the transmit button and rattled off a radio check.

'All call signs, this is Charlie-Three, radio check, over.'

I stared at Watson and Dan with utter exasperation as the responses came back immediately.

'Charlie-Three, this is Charlie-Two, loud and clear. Where have you been, over?'

I didn't reply. Instead I thrust the handset into Dan's hands and scrambled out of the hole.

Spike started to giggle. So did Watson. Dan tried to smooth things out a bit.

'Cheers bro, you're going to be an awesome sig.'

'And you three are already perfect grunts,' I replied. I stomped off back to bed, doing my utmost to conceal a grin at the ridiculousness of the scenario.

NGĀTI TŪMATAUENGA

THERE ARE SOME DAYS on basic training that could be described as enjoyable, depending on who is doing the describing. But if there is one occasion that every recruit unanimously enjoys, it's the visit and subsequent stay at the Army Marae.

Not many people know this, I certainly didn't prior to enlisting, but every single member of the NZDF are members of the iwi Ngāti Tūmatauenga. (For those of you hazy on the Māori pantheon, Tūmatauenga is the war god.)

As a member of an iwi, you need a home marae. The one in Waiouru military camp is very large, very old and extremely hallowed. Even my naïve and arrogant teenage brain could sense the reverence with which all the soldiers treated the building as soon as we arrived. The walls of the entrance were adorned with photos of high-status visitors. Pacific Island kings and queens, members of the British monarchy, even a US president or two had walked onto this lawn, and been received by a fierce welcoming haka as a part of the pōwhiri.

It was our turn to learn the Army Haka.

Being a Pākehā child with immigrant parents, I hadn't had much exposure to the haka or any other kapa haka practices, besides seeing other people do them at school, or watching the All Blacks. Actually being in one, being encouraged to search inside of myself for the energy and the commitment to deliver an unflinching scream, was an experience I'll never forget.

I had always been a typical teenager in that I never took anything seriously. Never fully committed to anything. My time at basic had started to change that. If you don't fully commit to climbing a wall, you might fall off it. If you don't fully commit to cleaning your uniform, you'll find yourself going for a long crawl around the parade ground.

If you don't fully, 100% commit to delivering a haka with every shred of energy that your body can deliver, you end up looking like a fucking fool. It is something that cannot, must not *ever* be conducted at less than full power. When it is delivered with proper commitment, and you are one out of 120 other people also giving it 100%, it's the most exhilarating feeling you can experience. It immediately made perfect sense why warriors would do this before battle, or when receiving guests from neighbouring iwi, and why the All Blacks have made it a part of their indisputable success.

Being in a haka makes you feel ten feet tall and bulletproof.

The Army Haka is performed during deployments and other large-scale occasions. Every corps (and some individual units) in the NZ Army also has their own haka. During my enlistment, I actually performed the Signals Haka more often than the Army Haka.

As well as learning the Army Haka, the stay at the marae is a time to relax. Even the corporals, who so far had spent most of the time yelling and screaming at us, spoke in hushed tones around the marae.

We sat in the main room, listening to stories about soldiers that had come before us. We spent the morning digging a hāngī pit, and we ate kūmara and lamb for dinner.

It was truly special.

HURRY THE RUCK UP

FOR FELLOW WORSHIPPERS OF the egg-shaped ball, you may remember that 2011 was a special year: the Rugby World Cup was being hosted on our own soil. While most people have fond memories of watching the games either in person, or in pubs with friends and family, I spent most of it cleaning something, or being yelled at for not cleaning something enough. On the night of the final, between New Zealand and France, we were rushed through our cleaning duties so we could be ushered into the camp bar. We thought it was a special gift to us, the recruits, but the truth was, the corporals were dammed if they were going to miss the final just because of some stinking recruits. We couldn't drink of course, but we were allowed to crowd around the projector screen to watch Steven Donaldson be immortalised by the deeds of his late penalty kick. So, in case you had any doubt, when the All Blacks play, everybody stops, even the Army. Little did I know, I would have a much better view of New Zealand's next World Cup performance.

EXERCISE WARRIOR

OF ALL THE FIELD exercises that you do on basic training, Exercise Warrior is the one you hear about (and therefore dread) the most. It starts at an indeterminate time, on a random day, in the final month of training. The main objective of Exercise Warrior is to be as unpleasant, difficult and miserable as possible. It's the NCO's final opportunity to see which recruits will give up, spit the dummy or rage-quit their way out of the army and back to civilian life. All I knew about it was rumours and whispers from people who were on their second attempt at basic training, and none of them had anything positive to say.

As I've mentioned, reveille is at 0545 every morning, without exception. Exercise Warrior is the exception. At the eye-watering time of 0400 one Monday morning, Corporal

Green came thundering into our room and hoarsely bellowed at us to get out of bed, 'Like, RIGHT FUCKING NOW,' as he so charmingly put it.

We were immediately up and moving. At this stage in training, we were a well-oiled machine. The morning routine was a breeze. There was one slight deviation from the norm, however. We were instructed to get into our field dress (sleeves rolled down) and carry our full FSMO (pronounced 'fizmoe') with us. FSMO stands for Field Service Marching Order, and it means carrying everything you would need to go out on exercise. Your pack, with water, sleeping bag, bivvie bag, warm gear, spare uniform, cooking gear, entrenching tool (E-tool), pruning saw and so on. Plus your webbing, with more water, (empty) magazines, and all the numerous small pieces of equipment that somehow end up adding six kilograms.

We were all standing on the parade ground. Aside from the fact that we had packs on our backs and webbing on, it was business as usual, except it still felt like the middle of the night. I'd overheard someone theorising in the showers that this must be the dreaded Exercise Warrior. And since nobody had a better guess, that's what we all started thinking.

We were arranged into formation and Corporal Green started double-timing us towards the mess hall.

'At least we'll get some breakfast first,' murmured Jack, who was next to me.

As if in response to this, right at that very moment Corporal Green wheeled us away from the mess hall and towards the end of camp where the gym was located.

'Shit.' Jack was not happy.

I echoed the sentiment. But we passed the gym and kept going down the road. We had jogged well over a kilometre at this point. Not a huge distance, but it feels like a long way with a pack (even a half-filled one) at 0430.

We reached the complex at the end of the road. It was made mostly of ugly, painted stone. A familiar smell wafted out from the double doors, transporting each and every one of us straight back to primary school. Chlorine.

We were at the Waiouru Olympic swimming pool.

Yay.

We filed into the building and were instructed to line our packs up along the pool's edge. We took off our boots and stood in rows at the short edge of the rectangular pool. Nobody wasted much breath on small talk. Everybody was acutely aware that whatever followed was going to require as much oxygen as our lungs could hold.

The water was heated, just. I remember being surprised when I first jumped in, but that surprise was quickly replaced by despair once the platoon sergeant started rattling off the list of tasks we had to do before breakfast.

First task, swim to the far end of the pool and back again in your uniform (without boots, blessedly). If you've ever tried to swim in long pants and a thick shirt, you'll know how deceptively difficult it is. Your legs have about half the range you're used to, so you have to move them twice as fast to stay afloat. Your arms become far heavier. Raising them out of the water quickly becomes exhausting, so you resort to a breaststroke, or in some cases a doggie paddle. But this doesn't help much. With each stroke there is so much water flowing in and out of your sleeves and collar that you don't move forward much at all. Every movement creates small currents that push you backwards as you're trying to go forward.

The huge complex was filled with echoes of people gasping, spluttering and splashing their way up the pool. I was third in the line. Like always, I took off at an unsustainably rapid pace. The first twenty metres disappeared, but then my arms started burning. I mistimed a stroke and swallowed water. I have never been an exceptional swimmer, but I wasn't terrible. What I lacked was any real technique. This was apparent as I flailed my way up the pool. At the other end I clung to the edge for a full minute, gasping for air.

People were catching up to me. I had to make my way back to where I had entered. I groaned, took a deep breath and tried to kick off the wall, hoping to get a good start. My waterlogged uniform ballooned with my kick and I feebly floated about a metre and a half off the wall. Back to my pitiful breaststroke. By the time I clambered out the other end, I was absolutely shattered.

That was the very first task of what would turn out to be forty hours of continuous labour.

The next step was to line up along the long edge of the pool, 'dragging' a partner in what was known as a survival stroke. As usual, I looked around for someone my size, and was rewarded with Matt Armstrong. All six foot three inches and ninety-something kilos of him. Fuck.

A survival stroke is almost like swimming on your side, with one arm draped across your 'casualty' like a seat belt and your other arm reaching out to stroke.

Armstrong, bless his heart, took the exercise extremely seriously and went as limp as a wet sleeping bag the moment we got in the water. After a great deal of splashing, and what felt like an hour, I managed to flail him and myself across the width of the pool. When it was his turn to move me, his ridiculously long limbs got me across the pool in about ten strokes.

Eventually, after a cacophony of splashing, spluttering and more than a little swearing, everyone in the platoon was standing on the edge of the pool, gratefully sucking in air. Steam was rising from us as the water, warmed by our bodies, met the frigid dawn air. It was now about 0500. Everybody was beginning to get the feeling that it was going to be a long day.

We were gravely mistaken. It was going to be a very long *two* days.

The next task was a mock river crossing. In reality this is something a good commander should avoid at all costs, as they are not only exceedingly dangerous but, even if they do go smoothly, having an entire section or platoon of soaking-wet soldiers usually leads to more problems down the road.

Our river crossing meant sealing up our packs as tightly as possible, strapping our boots to the top and swimming across the pool, pushing our packs in front of us. Sounds easy enough, right? Sure, it would've been – if army packs floated.

The army ALICE pack not only has a metal frame, but is also made of an extremely heavy nylon material that holds an astounding amount of water. As we each slid into the pool after our packs, we quickly realised that they were not going to be the nifty little rafts we imagined. We basically had to resort to a legs-only doggy paddle, keeping the pack above water by holding it with our arms and using the air in our chests. I could see water running into my outer pockets, swirling around the dry bag that held my sleeping bag. If my sleeping bag got wet my pack would sink like a stone (and I'd also likely get yelled at for compromising my equipment). So I kicked and sloshed as hard as I could. I just needed to make the twenty-five metres.

The wake created by thirty other people was threatening my pitiful excuse for a raft, so I kicked harder. By now, my body was acutely aware that I was making large requests of it without any fuel, so with ten metres to go, both my feet started cramping. I grimaced and grunted. My kicks were now only getting me inches of distance at a time. It was slow going. If I'd had a rifle, or food and ammunition in my pack, or if the river had been an actual river and not a swimming pool, I'm certain I wouldn't have made it across.

Somehow, myself and almost all of Ngarimu Platoon made it across without incident. True to form, Wayne started panicking after swimming about five metres and had to be rescued by his long-suffering section mates.

Once we were all out of the pool, looking like a pack of drowned rats, we were given the obligatory words of encouragement from our benevolent NCOs.

'What a sorry fucking sight that was.'

'You cross rivers like old people fuck.'

'If any of you lot ever get deployed, you'd better hope it's to a country with no fucking water in it.'

Really inspiring stuff. At this stage in basic training, this sort of thing didn't even count as insults anymore.

We threw on our boots and strapped on our sodden packs. The chorus of water cascading onto the stone almost drowned out Corporal Green's command to double-time back to barracks. We sloshed down the road as he roared our next set of instructions.

'Once you're in barracks, you will have TEN minutes to hang your kit up, get on a fresh set of field dress and be ready to march down to breakfast. Resist the urge to get friendly in the shower, we don't have the time today.'

Flawless homophobic beratement, as always.

We squelched our way back to barracks. Our packs were dripping a considerable amount of water, which quickly froze as it hit the cement. From above, we must have looked like a dark green slug ambling along, complete with a shiny trail left in our wake.

By the time we had showered and were once again formed up on the parade ground, it was almost 0600. I was absolutely famished. The prospect of breakfast outweighed my trepidation at the trials that lay ahead. We marched towards the mess, beating another platoon by moments. We eagerly skipped ahead of them and commenced our daily crush into the balmy mess hall. The smell of terrible bacon and hundreds of eggs wafted out as we opened the double doors.

When I was a civilian I never ate breakfast. That had changed drastically. On this particular morning I was particularly hungry, but I did eat like this most mornings on basic training:

- two poached eggs on toast
- bacon
- beans on a third slice of toast

- something in the shape of a sausage
- a cup of instant coffee with milk and three sugars.

I inhaled all of this as quickly as possible. If I managed to get it down before the duty corporal had started eating, I knew I had time to dash up to the continental table and load five to seven Weet-Bix into a bowl, douse them all in milk and sugar and smash those down too.

If you're wondering how to gain seven kilos in four months despite filling each day with extreme exercise, wonder no more.

As we were nearing the end of breakfast, I recalled that someone had told me a particularly unpleasant detail about Exercise Warrior. That despite the constant moving around, pack marches, obstacle courses and all manner of general exertion, there was, by all accounts, almost no food involved.

Keeping this in mind, I took the opportunity when I was at the toast station to grab a handful of peanut butter sachets and stuff them into the pocket of my smock. At the time, with a belly full of food, standing in the nice, warm mess hall, I felt like five or so would be plenty to snack on.

With the benefit of hindsight, I wish I'd grabbed twenty of them.

After breakfast we were told to grab our webbing and be ready to head to the armoury to sign out our rifles. It was a bitterly cold morning, and the two-kilometre walk out to the range didn't warm me up as I would've hoped. As soon as we were out past the blocks of buildings that make up the centre of Waiouru Camp, the south-westerly wind cut through us. It didn't let up the entire time we were at the range, either.

We didn't go to the firing range that we were used to. This morning was a little different in that we were using the live firing range and given live ammunition. Real bullets, designed to put holes in human beings. We were placed in our sections and paired up so we could conduct what we called 'pepper pot' assaults. There would be a target, made of either silicone or sandbags, about fifty metres away, standing in a trench. Two pairs of us would be lying down on the mound, ready to go. As soon as the corporal yelled 'LIVE' we would go through the drills that we would use to attack an enemy position. The two pairs went through the same drills, independently. Contrary to what Netflix would like you to believe, you don't win a firefight by firing off a few well-aimed headshots. You win by firing more bullets at the enemy than they can fire at you. Corporals will constantly be screaming at you to 'get rounds downrange'. The logic being, if you're shooting at them, it makes it harder for them to be shooting back at you. It goes a little something like this ...

The 'Enemy' was 'firing at us' so the intention is to keep firing back at them whilst also getting closer and closer to them. I would be lying down, firing at the target. I screamed 'FIRING'. My partner would be about five metres or so to my right. As soon as he heard me, he'd reply with 'MOVING' at the top of his lungs and sprint forward in a low crouch. When training to be in a firefight, you don't jog, or even run, you *haul ass*. You're running towards the enemy as though you've just bunted a softball and your target is home base.

So I would be firing, and my partner would start running towards the target. He'd ideally go far enough to make ground, without going far enough to wander into my firing arcs: about ten metres. As soon as he lay down, he'd start firing at the target and yell 'FIRING', and it would be my turn to dash. You can barely hear anything that anyone is yelling; even less so considering that there are about ten pairs of people shooting and screaming at once. So, in reality, I'd keep an eye on him until I saw him lying down and rounds coming out of his rifle.

We would fire a 'sustained rate', which is about two to three bullets every five seconds or so. This way, you can make a full magazine last about three dashes. Rinse and repeat ten times, and one of you will be able to reach the enemy with their final dash. Whoever that is sprints right up to the (presumably bloodied and battered) target, fires a healthy number of rounds straight into their face and yells 'ONE DEAD ENEMY'.

And that's how you defend democracy, apparently.

If it sounds exhausting, it's because it is. It becomes especially fun (read: excruciating) when you're holding a giant machine gun instead of a rifle. I was the designated machine gunner for most of my career after basic training.

We took our turns on the mound, sweating and hollering. When we weren't doing firing drills, we were going through the loading and firing TOETS for the M203 grenade launcher. These are carried everywhere but rarely fired, because of the massive danger of a propelled grenade in a training area.

When we had all expended all our rounds, and had convinced the corporals that we could fire the 203 without accidentally murdering half the platoon, we got to actually fire the 203.

We were back in our pairs, and a corporal led us up a winding path near the range. We were overlooking a huge chunk of the training area. About three hundred metres away, there were some burnt-out husks of old vehicles: a couple of smashed-up Jeeps, a rusted old blue station wagon, and, at the very edge, almost four hundred metres away, a tank that was missing a turret. To our absolute glee, the corporals handed us each three grenades and let us loose with a 'Bet you can't hit the tank,' or 'Try and wreck that red car.'

As I've mentioned before, basic training isn't all push-ups and verbal abuse. Sometimes it was downright enjoyable.

Of course, this too would pass. All too soon the grenades ran out, and we set to cleaning our rifles with manic energy, lest we incur the wrath of an irate corporal. By the time our weapons were clean enough to stir soup with, it was about 10 in the morning. My stomach rumbled and I quickly sucked down a cigarette to distract myself.

The corporals were all bent over a map and nodding a lot to each other. Clearly something was happening. We were told to get into our sections, and us lads from 3 Section all congregated and immediately started an earnest discussion about who was the best shot with the 203.

Before we knew it, Corporal Henare had stomped over and summoned Dan. Dan wasn't our official section commander or anything, but he was tall and his receding hairline carried a certain amount of respect amongst his younger peers, myself included.

Dan came over and gave us the good news. He knew exactly where we needed to go, no need to consult the map. Brilliant. The bad news? It was all the way back in camp, a brisk four kilometre walk, with all our FSMO.

We stomped along, still in pretty high spirits. It was warm enough and nobody was incredibly hungry yet. We arrived at the designated corner: a stretch of road with a dilapidated building plonked on the side of it. I had just enough time to suck down a cigarette before the corporals came barrelling over. We were to conduct the Army Battle Fitness Test, 'Right fucking now.'

The Army BFT (which was replaced with some other test, sporting a different acronym, shortly after I completed basic training) is a test designed to simulate various tasks that an average solider should be able to carry out in their full FSMO.

It was almost lunchtime according to my stomach; nevertheless, we loaded up our packs with sandbags and rocks and other assorted useless weights to the necessary fifteen kilos, and loaded our webbing to the necessary six kilos. Our section was also provided with two full jerry cans. For the uninitiated, a jerry can is one of those very generic-looking rectangular containers, usually for holding gasoline or water. When they're full, they weigh exactly twenty kilos and slosh like a drunken rocking horse.

The BFT was a six-kilometre walk with seventy minutes to get around it. Not super difficult, but with all the weight and extra hassle added by the jerry cans, you don't exactly have time to fuck around. It basically means you have to powerwalk the whole way.

Despite our other failings, my section was fit. Or at least, fitter than the rest of them. We had several huge farm boys, like Weber and Spike (Spike looked like the picture you get in the dictionary besides the words 'loosehead prop'); and we had a few fast, skinny whippets in the form of Dan, Williams and me.

We huffed and grunted our way around the marked-out course, which was all on tarseal except for the last kilometre, which was gravel.

We finished ahead of every other section, with a good fifteen minutes to spare. Proud of each other, after some high fives and 'fuck yeahs' we dumped our packs and did the only thing there was to do; head back down the road and start encouraging the other sections to finish on time. Not only did we want our mates to pass the test, if we'd been spotted sitting down smoking darts while a fellow soldier was sweating, you can bet we'd be doing the course all over again wearing body armour, or dragging a truck with a chain.

We jogged down the road to the final bend in the track and whooped and hollered as each section came shuffling in. The final section was cutting it terribly fine. They had two members who were absolutely beetroot red in the face. Neither of them had the jerry cans, but nobody was allowed to carry their packs, webbing or weapons for them. This was called a test for a reason and anybody who couldn't pass it before the end of basic wouldn't be allowed to graduate as a soldier.

Amazingly, with the help of thirty people screaming encouragement, the final two stragglers made it across the line with about one minute up their respective sleeves. We cheered and gleefully gulped water from our canteens. The corporals outlined the next part of the test, the dreaded 'battle drag'.

As you may be aware, soldiers in combat do occasionally get injured. Obviously, if you're hurt enough that you can't move, your only chance to survive is for someone in your section to get you out of there. A big part of your rescuer not becoming a casualty themselves is to stay relatively low while doing the rescuing. This rules out the Hollywood 'fireman's carry', where you sling someone over your shoulder and keep firing your machine gun one-handed while throwing out snarky one-liners at the enemy.

Our BFT standard battle drag went a little differently. In pairs, one of you lies on their back, with their head towards the other side of the field, fifty metres away. The standing partner squats down, grabs you by the shoulder straps of your webbing and runs backwards in a sort of goblin-esque crouch. It's absolutely exhausting after about ten metres, and after twenty you feel as though you're dragging a face-down walrus. People's heels always drag along the ground for maximum friction. Obviously, being dragged is no picnic either. You get filthy, often with a decent amount of gravel-rash on your back, and you're clinging onto your webbing harness for dear life because if you let go of it there's a good chance your buddy will lose their grip and drop you like a sack of fertiliser. Just to make things more challenging, you both still have your rifles. So the person doing the dragging will sling their casualty's rifle over their shoulder as well as their own. Ten kilos of metal and ballistic plastic continuously smash against each other and make a marvellous job of throwing off any sort of momentum you might be able to achieve.

Once the battle drag is done, there's a rope climb, straight out of an American high school movie, except, again, you have webbing and a rifle to drag up the rope with you. People lacking in upper body strength (such as your humble narrator) can really struggle with this one. Good technique means that you can get your legs to do most of the actual climbing and just rely on your arms to hold on.

One of the people in our platoon missed his grip with his legs and was clinging on with his hands about ten feet up. We shouted encouragement as we watched, but his grip loosened and the poor recruit quickly became acquainted with the bark-covered (but not exactly soft) ground at the foot of the rope. After checking to make sure none of his bones (and more importantly, his rifle) were broken, he got sent to the back of the line to recover before taking another attempt.

Four people failed the rope entirely. They were told they could try again once more before basic ended, but if they couldn't get up there before 10 December they wouldn't be able to march out.

The BFT continued; a smooth, wooden, six-foot wall had to be climbed without any assistance, and finally a pit had to be jumped across. It was only about six feet across, but all that gear can really restrict your stride length. One more person failed the pit, but everyone got up the wall.

Our platoon had completed the BFT. It was one of those rare moments that needs to be taken full advantage of on basic training, where the NCOs let you bask in a modicum of glory. To put the icing on the cake, a Unimog showed up and one of the corporals emerged from the back with a tray filled with cut lunches. Each brown paper bag – I saw later – contained a muesli bar, a piece of fruit, some juice, and a couple of truck-stop style sandwiches. By no means 'good food', but better than a poke in the eye with a sharp stick.

Fuck yeah! I thought. Although, as the thirty-odd people that comprised Ngarimu Platoon began swarming the truck like an army of the dead, it occurred to me that there were only ten or so lunches in the tray.

No sooner had this occurred to me than Corporal Jones, who was wielding the tray of lunches, barked at the gathering recruits like a farmer surrounded by his constantly hungry and woefully stupid chickens.

'Get out of it, go on, fuck off.'

The space around him widened as disheartened recruits shuffled away and pretended not to look hungry.

Jones handed out a bag to each of the Ngarimu NCOs, leaving eight bags in the tray. Jones looked up and barked an order. 'Section commanders, to me!'

Dan, Callahan and two other recruits materialised at Jones's side. He gave each section commander two bags and they each walked towards their platoon. The corporals had taken their bags without opening them. None of them would take a single bite until the people under their command had eaten. That was gospel in the military.

Dan walked towards us with pursed lips. I wasn't going to like what he was about to say.

Weber, as usual, verbalised everyone's first thoughts.

'Oi, what the fuck?'

Dan sighed. He held up the two bags. 'This is it. This is lunch.'

'But there's ten of us,' moaned Louis.

Dan nodded. 'Yeah, so we'll just split this as best we can.'

I groaned. Figuring out how to do this fairly was going to expend more energy than I was going to get from 10% of the contents of those bags, so I quickly threw my decision-making on the bonfire.

'I don't give a shit. Split it up how you want and save me a bite of something.'

Most of 3 Section felt the same as me. Sometimes, the best way to reach a group consensus is to minimise the number of voices involved. I stomped off and smoked a cigarette with Alisi while Dan, Watson and Wilson began the highly scientific process of splitting four small sandwiches between ten (nearly) grown men. I watched the other sections bickering and arguing with one another. Nearly all the other sections had every member chiming in, trying to work out if a whole apple was equal to a third of a muesli bar, and so on. It looked like agony.

Two cigarettes and a brief shouting match later, I ended up being given a corner of a sandwich and half a wrinkled apple by a very sombre Williams. The food did nothing for my hunger. If anything, it made it worse. Sharpened it somehow. Fortunately, your conniving narrator had secret peanut butter stashed away. Before I could retrieve my fourteen millilitres of hoarded joy, the corporals were bellowing orders to form up into marching order.

Rifles at the ready, we trooped away from the BFT course, presumably back towards barracks for a shower and change of clothes. Right? Right??

Obviously not.

I watched our barrack building loom closer and my internal optimism (which had somehow survived the past three months) swelled. I almost turned into the walkway on my own accord, which would have not only resulted in a motorway-style pile up, it would have earned me a swift crawl around the parade ground. Instead, I watched wistfully as the barracks faded into the distance. We marched past the parade ground, past the officers' 'castle on the hill' and into the great beyond of the Waiouru training area. Once we were officially out of camp, about two kilometres from the BFT track, we stopped for a moment. The corporals ordered us all to fill our canteens from a nearby tap (literally just a rogue water pipe and valve sticking out of the ground, no other structures in sight). The section commanders had their destinations pointed out to them on the maps and the corporals leapt into the 'mog and sped away, leaving us all covered in a fine layer of dust.

Once they were gone, there was a frustrated silence.

'Great,' said Spike. 'Just fucking great. What bullshit is there at the other end then?'

'Probably cancer,' grumbled Dan.

The other sections were whining with equal enthusiasm.

'Don't worry, bro,' chimed in Weber. 'At least—'

'Don't say it,' I snapped.

'Shut up, Webs,' warned Louis.

'—it's not raining,' finished Weber unflinchingly.

As one, we all looked up at the menacing black clouds that had seemingly leapt out from the horizon as Weber finished his sentence. Before we had finished forming back up, the first angry droplets began stinging my face.

We trudged along the gravel road, thirty-odd members of Ngarimu Platoon, already exhausted by the day's activities. It was just after 1100. The wind picked up and the cold began attacking my ears, nose and fingers. You are always taught to have your index finger (or trigger finger) resting outside of the trigger, ready to move should you need to fire your weapon. A great tactic for adding an extra layer of safety to your weapon. People who strut around with their fingers on the trigger (even with the safety catch on) just look like clueless fools. But a drawback of this is, if it's October in Waiouru and you've been walking for five kilometres with no food, your exposed index finger is being pummelled by snow that's disguised itself as a cold, fat raindrop specially imported from the South Pole. The knuckles on my index and middle fingers on my right hand went red, swollen and numb. Even as I write this now, eleven years later, they remain visibly larger and less sensitive to touch than the rest of my hand.

We crested yet another hill and began stomping down the road into a wide valley. The rain continued to fall with an unrelenting consistency and the wind cut through us with a force that could only be described as cruel. I spied the corporals' Unimog and saw three of them huddled in the cabin. As one, the platoon began numbly stumbling towards it.

At first, we failed to hear the voice coming out of the trees to our left.

'OI! DICKHEADS!'

I was near the front of the procession, so I was one of the last to react. Callahan grabbed my shoulder and spun me around. I looked and saw Corporal Arapeta and a portly corporal (whose name I couldn't remember) from another platoon. They were wearing raincoats and standing at the edge of a copse of pine trees about thirty metres away.

Arapeta stepped forward and said just three words, before turning around and disappearing into the forest. 'Males, with me.'

We barely had the time (or the energy) to exchange confused glances before the twenty-eight male members of Ngarimu Platoon shuffled into the woods after the receding figure of Arapeta. He and the other corporal led us silently into the woods. The rain was less steady in there, but it ran along the branches, where the droplets converged, devised a plan and then launched themselves down the backs of our necks with unnerving accuracy. I was only marginally drier than I had been when we were swimming in the pool that morning, which now felt like days ago.

After about a hundred metres, we reached a small clearing where we could see Hinton Platoon. I didn't know any of them by name, but I recognised a few characters. There was a loud but generally well-liked guy who always had a quip when the four platoons all gathered together for whatever reason, and a freakishly tall ginger who looked almost exactly like Beaker from the Muppets. They were just as soggy as we were, standing and kneeling in a rough semi-circle around an ALICE pack. They'd left room for us to stand across from them.

The two corporals stood in the middle.

'Alright, boys.' Arapeta's voice was uncharacteristically calm. 'The name of the game is king of the ring.' He reached into the pack and produced two sets of boxing gloves. 'You'll spend two minutes in the middle, one minute fresh, one minute spent. Stay on your knees, no elbows, no headshots. If someone falls down, the fight is done. Got it?'

We nodded numbly. Nobody had any idea what we were supposed to ask.

We gathered into a tight circle and began stripping off our packs, webbing and excess kit. The corporals solemnly handed out the two sets of ancient boxing gloves to someone from each platoon, and it began.

The first two got on their knees, scooted towards one another and gingerly touched gloves. They knelt there, gloves up to guard, but neither of them moved.

Hinton's corporal got the ball rolling. 'The fuck are you waiting for, HIT HIM!' he bellowed.

His recruit wound up and threw a rushed hook at my platoon mate. It barely connected, but it didn't matter. The fight had begun. As soon as the fists started flying, we all started screaming encouragement. It was eerily like watching a schoolyard fight back at high school, except everyone had an automatic rifle slung over their shoulder. So, maybe more like high school in Texas.

The two on the ground swung furiously. Very little effort was being made to block one another's blows. After a minute that was at least three minutes long, Arapeta grabbed our recruit by the scruff and the sweating, battered guy quickly stripped off his gloves and gave them to Dan. His adversary on the ground took several ragged breaths, knowing he was about to fight a fresh opponent. Dan donned the gloves in a flash, dropped to his knees, charged in and went for an uppercut without waiting for an invitation. I could tell he wasn't a boxer, but Dan always threw himself into every task like a Russian conscript defending Stalingrad.

Another minute passed and then Dan was fighting off a fresh Hinton recruit with arms like oak trees. Dan's narrow upper body was pummelled from side to side for what seemed like an age.

At some point, the weather worsened. I didn't notice until water was running from my hair into my eyes; I was so fixated on the fight and trying to mentally track how many of Hinton Platoon's largest members had already gone through. Finally, as the rain increased from a downpour to a sloppy deluge, I felt the gloves being shoved into my hands.

They were hot, and just as wet with sweat on the inside as they were sodden on the outside with rain (and a few sticky drops of blood).

I hurriedly got onto my knees and sized up my opponent. He was about my size and looked exhausted. I threw a hurried feint with my left, which he barely blocked. I went to throw a haymaker with my right and lost traction on the mud beneath me, which was covered in a thin layer of pine needles. I fell flat onto my side and my opponent started punching me in the ribs, stomach and upper arm.

Several sets of friendly hands hauled me up and I heard Louis bellow in my ear, 'Fuck him up, bro!' He punctuated this with a light slap on the back. I was injured, and a little embarrassed. Perfect fuel for a counterattack. I growled and launched a straight punch into my opponent's sternum. We went back and forth, but after ten seconds or so, my rage and my freshness overcame his fatigue. The minute ended with me repeatedly punching his gloves, which were up in a feeble guard. The guy was so tired that his arms couldn't hold their position, and my blows were driving his gloves into his face. He was pulled out of the muddy pit that was forming.

I took long gasps of air as I was slapped on the back and a ragged cheer went up.

I tried to use my sleeve to wipe my eyes and when I brought my hand away, I saw a giant before me. This guy looked like he had weighed a hundred kilos before starting fifth form. He knelt down and was still a head taller than me. I was supposed to fight him? He looked like the only thing that could take him down was coastal erosion. I cringed and held my gloves up. He bobbed in and delivered a surgical jab to my exposed kidney that made me see stars. I swore and hit him in the shoulder, trying to put him off balance. Punching a wall would've hurt less, I'm sure.

The following minute was savage. Each strike from this guy was precise, lightning fast, and left a wide, deep-red bruise on me that formed almost immediately. Not only was he twice my size, he definitely knew how to box. I was hilariously outmatched. I managed maybe three punches in return, which he may have mistaken for large raindrops. Finally, I was allowed to escape my own private gauntlet. My arms were so battered I couldn't take the gloves off myself.

I staggered to the outside of the circle and flopped to the ground. I looked around and saw I wasn't the only casualty. There were only five or so more fights to go. Everyone was soaked and hoarse from yelling. I needed to smoke.

I patted my breast pocket. Of course, my fresh pack of cigarettes was still there, now bashed into a soggy wet ball of tobacco, paper and cardboard. Utterly useless. Great. I sat on the ground and managed two puffs out of a broken stub, held with shaking hands.

What happened next was even more tiring, and slightly more painful.

We shrugged our packs back on, picked up our weapons and shuffled, battered and bruised, back towards the road where we had entered. I spotted the women from our platoon and a few others emerging from the treeline just down from us. They also looked like they'd been beating each other into the mud for the past hour.

The rain eased off, but before any of us dared to enjoy the respite, a corporal (I don't know who; after a while they all start to look and sound alike) declared that we were in enemy territory and needed to get into a platoon harbour, with shell scrapes.

Oh yes. Shell scrapes. You see, your enemy will definitely try to kill you through traditional means, like stabbing you or shooting you in the face with the biggest bullets they have on hand, but they can avoid all that hassle if they can drop something on you from far away. Things like mortars and long-range artillery, for example (known as IDF: indirect fire), save them the risk of getting shot in return. A hostile platoon of infantry can be a real hassle in wartime. If you know where that enemy platoon is, and can drop several kilos of explosives into the middle of them from a great height while they sleep, that platoon quickly ceases to be a problem.

Obviously, as the protagonist of this particular infantry platoon, I didn't want this to happen.

Modern warfare requires modern solutions. The general tactic is to arrange yourself into a defensive triangle, and each man digs themselves a hole. The hole should be as long and as wide as they are, and about two and half feet deep. The principle being that, if mortar rounds are landing all around, and you're in a hole, the shrapnel, debris and pieces of your friend who was unfortunate enough to be taking a shit will pass straight over you, instead of ripping through you like rocks through a wet paper bag.

Should you be unlucky enough to have a mortar round land directly *in* your shell scrape, at least you're already in a neatly dug grave. This is what's known as a 'win-win' situation.

We arranged ourselves into our harbour and pulled entrenching tools out of our packs. These are small, collapsible digging tools (spade is too generous a term). They look cool, all black and folding out. But the reality is that using one is like digging with a pretty big spoon.

Anybody who's spent a day digging holes will tell you that it's exhausting, backbreaking, pretty shit work. E-tools, I'm fairly certain, were designed by physios and chiropractors as a means of generating additional business.

It takes slightly less than an hour of aggressive, manic digging to knock out a shell scrape. There's no particularly refined technique. Once you've taken off a few pieces of turf (to be carefully replaced when you leave – 'leave only footprints' is not just a tourism catchphrase) you really just have to attack the soil like you've caught it in bed with your girlfriend.

I was never any good at it. Having a lot of stamina didn't count for much when my thin, noodly arms could only excavate what chefs would describe as 'a pinch' of dirt with every hack of my spade. Nevertheless, I persevered. My bruises hurt. My legs hurt. My back hurt. I was soaked through. I was hungr—

I quickly leapt into my hole, whipped out my second-to-last peanut butter sachet (why oh *why* did I not grab more?) and ate it with a vigour that would've made a stray dog cringe. It did nothing for my hunger, but I liked to pretend I could feel a surge of energy from the meagre influx of calories it gave me. I was nearly done with my hole, anyway. I probably had less than ten minutes of digging left and then I could finally, *finally* get some rest.

Of course, you know where this is going.

Corporal Green stalked across the harbour, the bearer of bad news, the harbinger of doom.

'The enemy has moved! Abandon your shell scrapes, into marching order. GO!'

We looked around in disbelief. Surely not. But when Green stood there, eyeballing anybody who dared to glance his way, we knew he was serious. We started clambering out of our holes. The digging had covered everyone in deep, dark dirt that became a layer of caked mud as it sat on our waterlogged uniforms. We began packing away our E-tools and shrugging our packs on. But just as the first few people made it to the road, Green was back to bellowing.

'The fuck are you doing? Are you just going to move off and leave all this sign behind?' He was pointing at the thirty half-dug holes and mounds of fresh earth piled high all around us. 'Fill them in and get a fucking move on. We'll see you at the next location.'

He turned on his heel, leapt nimbly into the Unimog, and thirty seconds later he and all the other corporals were gone.

Everyone sighed and began filling their shell scrapes back in. The especially bitter pill to swallow was that those of us who had dug the hardest and the fastest of course now had the most work to do. I noticed Wayne absently kicking dirt back into his hole, which wouldn't have been deep enough to bury a cat in. Bastard.

I lit another one of my battered half cigarettes and started heaping soil back into my shell scrape. It was still overcast and now well and truly into the late afternoon. The one stroke of good fortune was that it didn't start raining again for another half hour, by which time almost everyone had filled in their holes and replaced the pieces of turf. Of course, the entire area looked like thirty people had attacked it with shovels. But the returfing isn't for people on the ground. It's only supposed to stand up to aerial observations. So, hopefully, that was good enough.

We trudged along the gravel road, yet again. Nobody joked, nobody talked. We all had our hoods up against the stinging, horizontal rain, and were trying not to drag our feet in boots that had become impossibly heavy with mud, water and overall exhaustion.

After what might have been two kilometres, or twelve, I saw the roof of the Unimog. I wasn't thrilled to see it, as it meant more digging, but at least my mood didn't deteriorate.

The rain had reduced to an inconsistent drizzle of the worst kind, the kind that doesn't get you wet enough to stop trying to get dry, but regular enough that you never actually started the process of drying out.

Corporal Green didn't even get out of the cab. He took a long sip from his Thermos and merely pointed at the large expanse of mostly flat ground to the side of the road. That was our new harbour then.

'Merry fucking Christmas,' said Jack, as he threw his pack to the ground and fished out his E-tool.

It was after 4pm now. Everyone was absolutely ruined. We started digging our shell scrapes with about as much enthusiasm as … well, as much enthusiasm as an exhausted, hungry, wet and miserable person would have for digging a hole in the ground to sleep in.

I could tell everyone was fading. I resolved to be the voice of encouragement. 'Come on guys, the sooner we finish this, the sooner we can lie down.' Nobody responded. Everyone was in their own personal hurt locker, suffering in silence.

I abandoned my hole and jumped across to Jack's. He had barely made a dent in the tough, root-ridden earth. 'Come on, mate, pick it up.'

I spent five minutes with him, attacking the large clumps of soil, and the two of us made significant progress. I slapped him on the shoulder, repeating my mantra. 'Sooner you finish, the sooner you're finished.'

I strolled past Weber who, despite having to dig a significantly larger hole than the rest of 3 Section, was already knee-deep and actually humming to himself. I shook my head and moved on.

I helped Dan for five minutes. He only had enough steam to gasp a thank you. I was starting to help Evans when Corporal Green poked his head out of the Unimog.

'That's it! Enemy has moved, replace the turf and move on.'

We looked around in disbelief. Surely not, this had to be some kind of sick joke. Jack and Louis stood with their mouths agape. I was still standing in Evans's hole, holding my E-tool.

'MOVE!' barked Corporal Green. The Unimog engine started up, and that was that.

'Sooner we finish, the sooner we're finished,' Evans quipped at me as we started shovelling mounds of dirt back into his hole. I didn't say anything, I had run out of encouragement, or even a semblance of positivity.

As I stood and flung more dirt back into my hole, I thought I could hear something, like someone yelling, far in the distance. It was faint, but it sounded like, '—uckling!'

I looked over at Jack, who had also stopped digging and was looking around like an anxious meerkat.

'Dario,' he murmured. 'Is someone yelling about being in a hurry?'

Evans chimed in. 'You mean the guy yelling "no worries" over on that hill?' He pointed with his E-tool. Like an entire mob of meerkats, the rest of us followed Evans's direction. Sure enough, at least a kilometre away was a tiny figure on top of a hill. He was in full DPM, like the rest of us, but his silhouette stuck out against the grey clouds and made them extremely visible. Skylining, in full effect.

Several other platoon members had stopped to watch now. The wind had shifted and it was obvious to everyone that this individual was yelling the same thing, over and over. None of us could agree on what it was, however. I definitely heard the word 'duckling' over and over again. He was also, it appeared, jumping up and down on the spot.

We watched him for another minute or so. When it became clear that no further developments were occurring, we went back to the task at hand. The figure on the hill was still leaping into the air when I packed the last square of turf onto my mound.

Since I had barely started my shell scrape, it didn't take me long to refurbish it. Ngarimu Platoon made a very sorry job of returfing our second harbour, and trudged on down the road, without any sort of formation or patrolling happening. The only thought now was to push on.

Just before we set off, we saw the man from the hill abandon his post and start a stumbling run down towards one of the other platoons. Our curiosity was at an all-time high, and finally satiated when he came down the track towards us. I recognised him as one of the boxers from Hinton Platoon. He ran through our cluster in an effort to get back to his own lines.

We pressed him for details.

'I'm the section medic,' he gasped, as he took the water canteen someone offered him. 'I left the med kit at the last platoon harbour. Bombardier Cooper found it next to my shell scrape.'

Everyone winced sympathetically. Leaving behind the platoon's supply of bandages, tourniquets and morphine was most certainly a party foul, and Bombardier Cooper was about as forgiving as a tree can be to a drunk driver at 150 kilometres per hour.

Newark asked the million-dollar question. 'So what were you yelling?'

The guy's face fell. 'When he first hit me up, I told him I was sorry for leaving it behind. He told me to make sure everyone knew how sorry I was. He made me run all the way up that fucking hill and do star jumps while yelling, "IM FUCKING SORRY."'

Everyone was sympathetic, but we also all laughed. It was a textbook punishment for a moment of absentmindedness. The guy handed back the water canteen gratefully and started jogging back to his platoon.

We had all enjoyed the brief respite from our personal miseries, but now they were firmly back with us.

The rain had finally stopped, only to be replaced with a fierce, gusting wind that definitely felt worse. The great gusts pushed my wet, clammy uniform onto my skin from different angles that made me flinch each time. I was actually grateful when, after a kilometre of shuffling, we were rewarded with the sight of the Unimog, and Corporal Green's all-commanding finger pointing at our newest harbour spot.

For the next ninety minutes I'm sure I was on autopilot, because I have little to no memory of actually digging. But at some point I looked up and saw the sun dipping behind the hills in the distance, and I was unfurling my damp sleeping bag into a shell scrape I had somehow dug.

Corporal Green emerged from the Unimog. We all tensed up, waiting for him to utter the dreaded words, 'Enemy has moved.'

But he didn't. Instead, he moved into the middle of the harbour, looked around, nodded to himself and told us what would happen next.

'The enemy in in our vicinity. That means noise discipline, smoke discipline and light discipline are in effect. Get some warm kit on, get beside your shell scrapes and face out. It's going to be a cold night.'

He paused for effect.

'If at any point you feel like you've had enough – if it's too hard, and you're a bit cold, and a bit hungry – come visit the Unimog and we'll give you a hot brew and drive you back to camp for a shower.'

He let that sink in. Every single one of us was imagining how good it would feel to sit inside the sheltered canvas of the Unimog, with a warm drink between our numb fingers. Corporal Green let that collective vision sit in our heads for just a moment, before he dropped the hammer.

'And in the morning, you'll be on the first bus back home, I promise you that.'

He didn't wait for a response before turning and marching back to the Unimog.

So, that was that. As I looked into the fading light, I noticed that the wind had blown away the clouds that had sat above us all day. The night would be a clear one; the temperature was already plummeting. I dived into my pack and threw on everything warm I could find. I laid out my ground mat right next to my hole, lay down on it and gripped my rifle, staring directly ahead. I was grateful to no longer be marching or digging. But that gratitude only lasted about ten minutes.

The temperature didn't drop so much as hurled itself off a cliff. I lost the feeling in my toes. I told myself I was wiggling them in my boots, to keep the blood flow going, but honestly, I couldn't tell. Weber checked his top-of-the-line G-shock watch and informed us in a cheerful whisper that the temperature was now three degrees Celsius. It occurred to me that if there was a working fridge nearby, I would actually be slightly warmer inside it. Brilliant.

We kept staring straight ahead. Waiting for an enemy that we knew (probably) wasn't coming. I looked at the hill in front of me. Even now, I remember every feature of it. The slightly crinkly way it veered off to the right, the large, sand-coloured clump of tussock about halfway up that looked like a sleeping bear. It looked like every other hill in Waiouru, except that I had all the time in the world to study it.

We lay there until 2300. It was utter misery, I can tell you. It got much, *much* colder. Well below zero. Weber kept giving us updates at first, but after he announced that it was six below zero, Dan threatened to slice him open like a tauntaun and climb inside of him for warmth.

I must have drifted in and out of a semi-conscious doze, because I'm certain that six hours of staring at the same spot would have driven me utterly insane otherwise. I thought about my last peanut butter, from time to time, but I held off from eating it. 'When you're in your sleeping bag, you can have it,' I said to myself. It was something to look forward to, something to keep me focussed on the task at hand. During the course of the night, I saw four people get up, holding their rifle, and do that miserable shuffle that cold, wet people do, over to the Unimog. After a brief talk with the corporals inside, one of them returned to his position. Three of them got in the 'mog. I didn't see them again.

Finally, we were allowed to sleep. If you can call it sleep. We collapsed into our bags, too tired, wet and cold to even attempt to get undressed. I didn't take my boots off because I was worried that we'd be shouted awake within minutes of falling asleep. My hands were shaking violently, but I managed to extract my last sachet and lick/chew the tablespoon of now rock-solid peanut butter. It helped, a little. I closed my eyes for what felt like thirty seconds, and then Louis was poking me.

'Get up, we're moving.'

My thought process went: *What? How? Shit. Shitshitshit.*

It was dawn, barely. The morning was as cold and crisp as the night had been, but somehow far less depressing. As I was admiring the scenic view of the hill I had come to loathe just hours before, I looked around and saw that some people were already filling in their holes. *Fuck.* I leapt to my feet ... and immediately collapsed. My legs were completely numb below the knees. An aching, intensely uncomfortable type of pins and needles ripped through my calves. My wet feet had spent too long being cold, it seemed.

I crawled out of my hole on my hands and hobbled over to my pack. As I fished out my E-tool, I caught a whiff of cigarette smoke. Sure enough, I saw Callahan and Alisi sharing one of Callahan's roll ups. *Good*, I thought to myself, *I can have breakfast at least.* I fished into my chest pocket and rummaged around in the sodden, tobacco-filled mess until I produced a cigarette. This one was stained brown with wet nicotine, but it was almost three quarters of a whole dart. It may have been fatigue, or delirium, but I was practically humming as I lit it and started stuffing my mud-caked sleeping bag into my pack. I was even able to endure Weber's never-ending supply of good cheer.

'You alright, bro? How'd you sleep?' he quipped as he flung scoops of dirt into his hole faster than a team of mobsters burying a dead snitch.

'Not bad, not bad,' I replied. 'Bed was comfortable, but the room service never arrived. I'll be speaking to management about that. You?'

Weber executed a tactical version of his characteristic, booming laugh. It sounded like a ute engine trying to turn over with a dead battery.

'Ah, you know, bro. Usual. Couldn't get to sleep at first, so I had a good wank and then boom, I was out like a light.'

I stopped shovelling. So did Evans, Dan and Louis, who had overheard the exchange.

'You what?' asked Dan.

Weber looked confused. 'You know, I just a had a quick tug and went to sleep.'

Louis looked flummoxed. 'But, *how*?'

Weber, looking equally flummoxed, held up his hand and made the appropriate motion. 'Just like this, you need a lesson or something?'

Evans started laughing. Dan followed suit, and soon we were all giggling like nine-year-olds.

'Un-fucking-believable,' said Dan, shaking his head.

'Wish I'd thought of that,' said Jack.

Weber had finished his hole and was bounding between the rest of us, helping us all like a foul-mouthed Mother Teresa.

'Piece of piss, boys. Let's get rolling, eh?'

The rest of the platoon finished within the hour, and we had all gathered on the road in marching order. Most of us were bleary-eyed, about one in three people were continuously sniffing through runny noses, and absolutely everyone was caked in a combination of wet and dried mud.

Recruits are herd animals. Like any good livestock, we walked until we were told, or barked at, to stop. As a platoon, we walked the almost ten kilometres back to the front of camp. It was about 0800 and the air was still biting cold from the night before, although my legs had finally stopped cramping and were a soggy, crusty sort of warm. We rounded the corner to see Corporal Arapeta standing next to a truck. He was surrounded by jerry cans.

'Fill up your canteens and move over there.' He pointed vaguely to an ominous gap in the shrub that flanked the side of the road. Naturally, nobody questioned his order, we just did it.

The gap in the shrubs led to a downward slope where the grass gave way to churned-up mud. I could see dozens of boot prints around me. The night had been cold enough to frost, and the way the rich brown mud crunched under my feet reminded me of chocolate mousse.

Shit, I shouldn't have thought about food. My stomach made a rolling, gurgling noise best described as a snarl of hunger. There was no peanut butter to save me now.

'Line your packs up here, grab out your barrel protectors and form up in your sections with your weapons and webbing on.'

I couldn't see Corporal Green, but his voice emanated from the trees. I did as I was told.

The barrel protector is sort of like a plastic condom that goes over the end of your barrel. But unlike a condom, its primary function is to prevent things *entering* your bangstick; it wouldn't do much to prevent a bullet leaving the barrel.

'What do you reckon it'll be now?' asked Louis as he knelt beside me and fitted his BP.

'Storytime? Maybe with a hot chocolate?' I ventured.

'KFC run, surely,' chimed in Jack.

We sniggered with the callous despair of those who know the worst is yet to come.

'Assault course,' whispered Dan, without smiling.

As one, we turned to look at him. None of us had ever seen the Waiouru assault course, not in full, but there definitely was one. You could catch glimpses of the obstacles if you looked out of the Unimog at the right moment when passing by this side of camp. We knew at least part of it ran through a creek, because there was a series of photos on a wall of the bar that had various pictures of muck-splattered recruits climbing a rope to escape the muddy banks of a creek.

'We're on the right side of camp, the creek runs right through here and the ten-foot wall is just up around that corner.' He wiggled his BP for effect. 'And these? Things are about to get real dirty.'

Before any of us could respond, Corporal Green was talking.

'Three Section. You're up first. Form up, 2IC in the rear.'

We scrambled to our feet and stood in a ragged line. Green spoke again. 'As a section, you will navigate these obstacles. Your rifles will not be slung, they will be *carried*. Understood?'

'Yes, Corporal,' we droned in automatic response.

'Three section, you're up. Get in over there.' He jerked his thumb towards the bushes over his shoulder.

As the sig, I was fourth in line. Watson was at the front. I saw him disappear into some flax ahead of me and then I heard both him and Spike exclaim as one.

'Oh, fuck me!'

Seconds later, my curiosity was answered. They had found the start of the assault course.

It wasn't so much a creek as it was a pond. The muddy, grassy bank quickly gave way to an expanse of water wider than a basketball court. It had that slimy, life-filled stench that thick mud always carries.

Further ahead, I vaguely saw some tangled wire and vertical logs sticking haphazardly out of the water. But what I specifically saw, what really jumped out as immediately obvious, was that the creek wasn't moving. It was covered in a layer of ice.

Weber paused for a moment and looked back at us, uncertainty etched across his massive features.

'What the fuck? What do I do?' he hissed.

'Fucking GO,' said Spike, giving him a prod.

Weber shook his head, took a deep breath and took a step off the edge of the bank. The ice layer was no thicker than the glaze on a cake, so there wasn't a deep, crunching noise or anything like that.

'Jesus mother fucking holy shit fuck *cunt* that is cold!' bellowed Watson, holding his rifle aloft. With that asserted, he turned and started sloshing his way towards the wire.

When I entered, there was no ice to kick through, but the water felt like it was still frozen. It was the kind of cold that didn't just take your breath away, it punched you in the face and mugged you for it.

The cold, damp unpleasantness of my nearly dry pants getting soaked through was replaced by the deep, aching sensation of near-freezing water on my bones. My balls were somewhere up in my chest as I waddled forward, trying to keep my arms close to my body. After ten steps or so, the ground dropped away and I was up to my collarbones in brown water.

The wide entrance narrowed from a pond to a more conventional creek shape up ahead, where I'd seen the tangled barbed wire. We sloshed forward as fast as we could. It was easy enough to duck under the scraps of wire, but then we came across four logs, horizontally stacked across the creek at around chest height. That meant submerging completely and bobbing underneath them.

We slogged through that, although I smacked my head on the last log coming up too quickly. Despite the sharp and immediate headache this gave me, I was starting to feel better. It wasn't as though I could get any wetter now. The cold had settled in to the extent that I wasn't wincing with every step. And this was an assault course, I was *good* at assault courses. I was skinny, I was fit and I have strong hands. I've always found clambering up a wall using a rope or swinging from bars to be quite easy. They had been my favourite part about the Skill at Arms cadet competition, which by now seemed like a very, very long time ago.

Our section saw a huge open pipe that led up and out of the water to another bank, so we crawled in on hands and knees and immediately spied a ten-foot wall. We flung each other up and over it like we had done many times before on the CFT track. Then there was a low net staked to the ground that we had to crawl under on our stomachs. It wasn't so bad, but I knew that the second and especially third sections would be sliding though slick mud instead of wet grass.

The next obstacle was a corporal, whose name I didn't know, just standing there, pointing to his right up the steep slopes of the valley that the creek ran through. About fifty metres up was a red rag tied around a bush.

'Up and around the flag,' he droned as we stumbled towards him.

It was about halfway towards this flag that I realised how tired I was. Not just from this run, but from everything that had happened in the past thirty hours. I was shattered; even my eyelids felt fatigue every time I blinked. My breath was ragged and my legs wouldn't move beyond a feeble sort of stumble. We all moved like decomposing zombies; a few of us even groaned. The last ten metres to that cone were like scaling Everest. I so desperately wanted to just *sit down*, for a minute. I willed my legs to move faster. My foot caught on the ground and I stumbled. My rifle jarred painfully into my side and my palm scraped along the rocky, muddy ground. I took a breath and the beginnings of a sob escaped from my chest. I began to panic. No way was I going to cry, I'd never hear the end of it. I was supposed to be a fucking soldier, wasn't I? Desperate, angry frustration boiled up inside of me. I was fucking *over it*.

But then, something happened. From the moment I passed the cone and began to stumble back down the hill, energy came back. It felt as though my legs had finally defrosted from my night in the freezing mud. My breath was less ragged. Someone slapped my back encouragingly and I let out a whoop. So did Jack. Weber roared like a Spartan and 3 Section began charging towards the next obstacle like a phalanx of Roman legionaries. We were going to smash this.

The rest of the obstacles were laughably easy. Not because they were any less challenging, but because 3 Section had found our second wind. We were exhausted, hungry and cold, and we were still going. Nothing short of actually being fired upon at this stage would've stopped those ten, mud-covered, ragged recruits. We not only finished the assault course in record time (according to the corporal holding the stopwatch), we all went back and hauled the other members of Ngarimu Platoon over the larger obstacles, which were fast becoming incredibly slippery.

And all of a sudden, Exercise Warrior was over. It felt surreal to be back in barracks, under a hot shower, and then outside, scrubbing mud out of our packs and boots. Meticulously cleaning our rifles, which so often felt like a gruelling chore, was now a moment of serenity and reflection. All of 3 Section, already good friends after months of shared suffering, had become even closer.

Inexplicably, it was the day after Exercise Warrior that Jackson, a member of 3 Section since day one of basic training, told us he was quitting. He didn't want to be a soldier. We were stunned. He'd been there for almost four months. Warrior was over, the most gruelling part was *done*. And yet, he said he knew now that being a soldier wasn't for him.

I didn't understand at the time. I still don't, really. But it was his choice to make. He was gone by that afternoon, and that was that. The first and only member of 3 Section to not make it through basic training, gone by his own decision.

There was less than two weeks until March Out, the final parade and the end of basic training. The two biggest tasks that lay ahead of us now were to learn the drill for the big day, and (cue drool) *finally* unwrap and shape our berets. The mark of real soldiers.

MARCH OUT PARADE

OUR MARCH OUT PARADE, in early December, was akin to a graduation ceremony. Those of us who had passed every mandatory test on basic training would cross the parade ground in our finest ceremonial dress (the unmistakable olive-green suits) and be presented to our families as soldiers. We spent weeks practising our drill formations, getting the creases in our trousers crisp enough to slice through bread, and generally fretting about the grand ceremony of it all. There were awards for best platoon, top recruit, and all other manner of trivial measures of achievement. In two short hours, it was all over. We had passed, and now we were soldiers.

One of the most prevalent lessons driven home during basic training is that of teamwork – helping out your mates, looking out for each other to achieve a common goal are all good stuff that translate over to civilian life and, in my opinion, make you an all-round better person. Of course, this can be a double-edged sword. Such was the case of Wayne. I've detailed his uselessness at length already. His long-suffering section mates became so adept at covering his ass over the course of basic training that he too was able to march out with the rest of us.

My mother, sister and grandfather made the journey down from Auckland. Once everyone had met and hugged their families, Corporal Green summoned us to address Ngarimu Platoon one final time.

'Well done to you all. Reaching today is a big achievement. Now you'll be off to your units, to do the jobs you signed up for. Just remember, if you're the top recruit, or from the top section, or whatever: nobody outside of this base gives a flying fuck. As of right now, you're all just soldiers. The playing field is completely level again. These are not laurels to rest on, trust me.'

He stuck around to shake our hands, and that was that.

The twenty-something remaining members of Ngarimu Platoon gathered in the corridor for one last time. We knew we'd likely be seeing each other again over the years to come; the NZ Army is a small organisation. But even so, it was the end of an era. We had entered this building as timid civilians. We were leaving it as beret-sporting soldiers. I felt a genuine sense of pride and achievement. The pain and suffering of the last four months only made me feel stronger for having endured, especially thinking of the people bigger than me, or fitter than me, who had thrown in the towel and were now sitting at home.

I wasn't even mad at the corporals who had filled our days with insults and menial tasks. They were doing their job. I saw that the point of beasting people ('drop and give me fifty, you useless maggot', etc.) isn't to 'break you down' or any of that nonsense. It's a pressure test. If you can't handle being yelled at – or made to clean something that you've already cleaned, or any of the other thousand frustrating tasks that were set before us – if you can't handle that level of stress without losing your cool, how are you supposed to handle being shot at? Or having grenades fall around you?

It's not for everyone. That's the short answer. Just like being a surgeon or a professional footballer isn't for everyone. It's a job that only some of us can do. And I knew now, beyond a doubt, that I could do it. It's difficult to have imposter syndrome when you've been through an ordeal like basic training. People don't make it through four months of that by accident. Of all the lessons I had learned on basic training, from firing a rifle, to laying a mine, and all the hundreds of other small soldering skills around teamwork that went with them, one stands out as the most enriching. I learned that I was much stronger and tougher than I had ever thought possible. I was capable of walking past the point of exhaustion. I could endure without food or sleep. It wasn't pleasant, but I could do it. Most people (myself included) went through life thinking that being tired meant you needed to stop and rest. Not so. If you need to, you can always go a little further, and dig a little deeper. But it's a lesson we all have to learn for ourselves, in whatever crucible life throws at us. My trial happened to be the tundra of Waiouru. I am forever grateful for that rare self-discovery that few people experience.

PART 2

CORPS TRAINING AND BEYOND

DEPOT TROOP'S PROMISE

ONCE WE HAD FINISHED basic training, there was a period of about a week or so before we were due at our unit. Most people, of course, elected to go home. I did not. Not only did I not have a car, but I actually didn't have a room to stay at in Auckland. Since my new posting at Palmerston North was less than a two-hour bus ride, and Auckland was over seven hours away, I took the army bus straight to the barracks the day after I marched out.

I shuffled into the 'newbie' barracks, which were significantly older and more disused than the rest of camp. I didn't care. I was given a key and told to be at morning parade at 2 Signal Squadron building in exactly six days. I opened the door to a tiny grey-and-brown room with a single bed, a tiny square of window and a stained sink. I was chuffed. It was the first time in my entire life that I had a bedroom all to myself.

I spent the next six days wandering around camp, eating at the mess and watching every season of *The Inbetweeners* on some unmarked DVDs I found in the abandoned common room.

People started coming to base a few at a time. Each morning a few more doors in the hallway would be open than had been the day before. By the Sunday night, there were five of us outside, smoking and exchanging that awful false bravado that young men subsist on. We were soldiers now, true. But none of us had any idea what Signals Corps training would have in store for us.

There were around twenty new signallers at Linton camp now. We were being placed into a newly designed squadron named Depot Troop.

The revolutionary idea behind Depot Troop was to focus exclusively on getting us as close to 'operational readiness' as possible, so that we could show up to our parent units ready to deploy, if need be. The premise was that the usual four months that corps training took would be extended out to six, and by that time, not only would we be qualified signallers, we'd also have our heavy vehicle licences, our security clearances would be squared away and we would all be deemed dentally fit.

(What's dental fitness, you ask? Simply put, the army won't deploy anybody to a foreign country if they still have wisdom teeth in. The logic being that if you're in some foreign country, surrounded by insurgents and 3,000 miles away from the nearest dentist, and your wisdom teeth suddenly start coming through, you'll be as useless as a one-legged man in an ass-kicking contest, so to speak.)

Standing there, on that first morning, being told the great visionary efficiency of this plan, we were all pretty chuffed at the idea. The reality was, those six months became nine months, and not one of us got a heavy vehicle licence. A handful got security clearance, and I got my wisdom teeth out.

THE BAGGIES' BAR

IT HAS BEEN SAID that soldiers like to drink. I can confirm that this is true. A recurring problem that commanders the world over have found is that, when their soldiers drink, they quickly become a problem for any civilians, breakable objects and, most often of all, each other. A solution was devised: for as long as anyone can remember, most Western military bases have their own bar.

In the NZ Army, each camp has several bars. The officers have a bar, the sergeants and senior NCOs have a bar (known as the Stripey's) the lance-corporals and corporals have a bar, and finally, there is the 'baggies' bar, which is for anyone without rank. Privates, sigs, sappers and so on. This bar is understandably the largest, most frequented and most battered of all the bars.

Why have so many separate bars, you ask? The reason is simple. Even during peacetime, even when you're not out on exercise, the military can be a very stressful place to work. The purpose of separate bars is so that, after you've spent a day being grilled by your corporals for not doing a good enough job, you can saunter into the bar, drown your sorrows and start complaining about the twat in charge, without being worried that he's sitting at the next table taking notes on every dirty word you just called him. The corporals have their own bar so *they* can finish work, enjoy a beer, and bitch about the useless pack of cunts under their command without being overheard by those very same useless cunts.

There were many, *many* nights spent in that bar. Playing pool on the badly scratched table, drinking $4 jugs of beer (thanks, taxpayers) and eventually stumbling the 250 metres back to our barrack rooms to be up at 0645 for morning PT. We did that six nights a week, on average. It would have been seven, but the bar was closed on Mondays, presumably to restock the Olympic swimming-pool's worth of alcohol we annihilated each week.

LAYING CABLE

MUCH LIKE EVERYONE ON basic training learns to be an infantry soldier, regardless of which corps they are going to, every signaller on Signals Corps training learns to be a basic radio sig, regardless of trade. Trade training comes later.

Communications Systems Operators (CSOPs) are commonly referred to as 'radio monkeys' by the Signals Corps. Their job is largely setting up and maintaining radio networks for field deployments. There are dozens, arguably hundreds of different means and configurations this can take. CSOPs need to know how to do everything from carrying and operating the section radio for a ten-man patrol, right up to connecting to a satellite network so a brigade commander can talk to other countries while fighting in Afghanistan.

But it doesn't stop there. Forward Operating Bases (FOB), temporary military installations overseas, are so vast that they need internal communications too. It's hardly practical for someone to run three or four kilometres across camp each time they need to check with a different unit about something. Cell phones are a terrible solution for this, as they can be tracked and are often unreliable.

As is so often the case with technology, sometimes the most secure solution lies in the past. In an FOB that isn't going to move for several months or years, an internal phone line can be set up. It's essentially a series of thin, copper cables, all connected to each other, and then a handset (it looks exactly like an old landline phone, except in army green) is connected to the cable somewhere in each unit's HQ. If you need to talk

112

to other units, you simply pick up the phone, press the number assigned to any unit or units you want to talk to, and their ugly green handset starts ringing. This is virtually impossible to intercept, because unlike radios, the signal in a cable never travels through the air. There is a miniscule amount of signal that actually emits from the cable, a matter of inches either side of the live wire; we call this signal bleed.

It all sounds very nice and secure and convenient, doesn't it? But, of course, some poor bastard has to go around the entire camp, running out kilometres of cable from a spool, and then *bury* it, so that it doesn't get run over or tripped over or snipped out of sheer spite. In the sigs, we call this 'laying cable' (hah-hah). So for two weeks of corps training, we reported to the dreaded Depot Troop sheds and ran cable all around camp. We climbed on roofs and we crawled through drainage ditches. We dug and unearthed cable for eight hours a day. It was exhausting, dirty work. Once I left corps training and moved to Electronic Warfare (EW) Squadron, I never saw another cable line again, and I couldn't be happier about it.

DOING IT WRONG WORKS BEST

RADIOS HAVE BEEN AROUND since the end of the 19th century. They've come a long way since then, especially when you consider that things like cell phones, laptops and smart TVs are also basically radios operating on different bandwidths. Sure, an iPhone 15 is a bit of a step up from transmitting morse code, but they're not infallible. What you really need with radios, a lot of the time, is somebody who knows what they're doing.

And sometimes, that's exactly what you don't need.

We spent a great deal of time just learning how to set up and establish communications between two radios. We'd do it at short distance, long distance, low power, high power, during sunny afternoons and in the middle of the night in pissing rain. The basics get hammered into your head. Have the right antenna for the job, position it correctly and, if all else fails, the simple tenet of 'higher, higher, higher'.

This basic principle stated that if you couldn't get a signal, the easiest troubleshooting was to get your antenna higher up (either by moving the antenna itself or, more often, repositioning the radio and yourself to a higher elevation). You could also transmit on a higher frequency, which makes your signal 'louder' to receive antennas, or find a way in transmit on a higher power. Higher, higher, higher.

One night on exercise, we were stuck out in some field somewhere, tasked with getting comms back to Linton Camp using a standard radio setup of a patrol radio in a Pinzgauer all-terrain vehicle and a large whip antenna set up outside. It didn't happen. The day's work being done, the gist was that as soon as we had established comms everyone could go to bed and just take turns doing a two-hour stint on radio shift. But, because we couldn't hear the other side, what happened was that at least ten of us were there moving the antenna around in every conceivable position in the lashing rain, screaming 'Try it now!' and 'Anything?' for several hours, to no avail.

Finally, as midnight was approaching, one of the corps training corporals felt sorry for us and told us to turn in. We had tried virtually everything and even the staff had been throwing us suggestions for the last hour or so. It seemed that the gods of the electromagnetic spectrum were displeased with us, for every time we sent out a radio check to Linton, we received only the ghostly hiss of static. We assigned shifts to people anyway, and Corporal Davies told us all to 'keep trying', even though it was futile.

We woke up early the next morning, damp, cold and disheartened by our failure. It was still dark, but in the gloom we were surprised to see Roto, the guy currently watching the radio, cheerfully sipping an instant coffee as he walked back to the wagon.

We were all thinking the same thing, but Davies beat us to it.

'Why aren't you manning the fucking radio?'

He blinked. 'I was, just did a radio check ten minutes ago so I thought I had time for a coffee, Corporal.'

We were stunned.

'You got comms?'

'How?'

'What did you do?'

Roto looked surprised.

'I don't know … It just started working like an hour ago. I wrote it in the log book,' he added, helpfully.

'Fuck the log book,' said Aaron. 'Where's the whip?'

We had moved the antenna around so many times last night, nobody could really remember where it had ended up, so we ended up following the cable from the radio in the wagon, like detectives in a children's TV show.

Ten of us huddled around the black wire and, resembling a gaggle of camouflaged, cigarette-smoking ducklings, we traced its path through the morning twilight, straining to see where it went. We had attached the longest cable we had, in our efforts to place the antenna anywhere it might possibly get off a signal.

Finally, fifty feet later, we came across the antenna. It lay flat on the ground. It had fallen over in the night, and there, on the wet grass, it had defied every textbook we had studied and proceeded to establish crystal clear comms between us and Linton Camp, some sixty kilometres away.

This was a good, humbling reminder to all of us entering the world of signals, that despite all the technical knowledge and years of experience we had to learn from, radio waves are still relatively new technology to humans, and sometimes they just do as they please.

We left the antenna exactly where it was, agreed to not tell anyone about how we had established comms, and started working on our story for the sergeants back at base about why it had taken us most of the night to get a radio check going.

TRAINING AND MORE TRAINING

BEING MORE INTELLECTUAL THAN most (and less intellectual than some) trades in the army, Signals Corps training was very heavy on theory. Our days were always filled with lessons. I had joined the army to avoid going to university and lectures, and yet here I was in classrooms, sometimes five days a week, learning from textbooks and spending my nights studying for tests.

One afternoon, without ceremony or pomp, the instructing corporal snapped shut the binder he was reading from and announced that the very last module of Signals Corps training was now complete. Jordy, Andrew, Aaron, Reid and I had done it. We had finally finished corps training. We now supposedly had the skills to be a New Zealand Army signaller, with none of the licences or security clearances we were supposed to have, seven ex-girlfriends between us and a long list of senior soldiers who looked as us like a streak of shit on their favourite rug.

Nevertheless, we were absolutely rapt to be leaving 2 Sigs Squadron and, more importantly, Palmerston North. There was a gathering at the 2 Sigs hangars, where our fearless staff sergeant bade us farewell before we flew the coop to head down to Burnham and get amongst 'that secret squirrel shit they get up to down there.' It was a vague and confusing introduction to a job that none of us really knew anything about, despite the fact that my paycheck had read *D. Davidson, Electronic Warfare Operator* for over a year at this point.

Writer's note

Due to security reasons, I have been relatively vague about what my trade, Electronic Warfare, actually does in the army. But I can tell you this much. After four months of basic training and almost a year of corps training, I finally arrived in Burnham to be told:

'You will detect, intercept, collect, identify, analyse and exploit electronic emissions contained within the electromagnetic spectrum.'

Make of that what you will, dear reader. I cannot elaborate beyond this, except to say that most of my time in 3 Signal Squadron was spent climbing very large hills wearing a

very large pack carrying equipment I am not at liberty to
name or describe.

I was still pretty clueless about the position. The interactions
I'd had with 3 Sigs personnel at this point were few and far
between. On the rare occasion that one of the elusive members
of that most secretive sig platoon would venture north from
Burnham camp, they looked at us with only a shred less disdain
than they gave the other corps trainees. Because we were still
corps trainees at the time, we were regarded basically as recruits
in the wild, much like a pet chihuahua that was trying to pass
itself off as a sheepdog. If we ever did manage to corner one of
these EWOP corporals and ask them, 'So, what is it that you do,
exactly?', we always got a different version of the same answer.
'Can't tell you until you have a top secret security clearance and
get to the squadron.'

Great, very helpful.

The speech was delivered, we shook hands with the sergeant-
major and she gave us a heartfelt 'Farewell, and fuck off.' After
nearly four minutes of non-stop talking, everyone was parched.
And so the beers were brought out. In true army fashion, people
began drinking like booze was about to become illegal.

We had a ferry to catch, so we left them to start enjoying
our absence early and jumped into our respective cars to begin
the pilgrimage down south.

We spent the night in Wellington, with Andrew's family,
and spent the whole next day in the car. Between the ferry ride,
stopping for lunch and the distance from Picton to Burnham
(not to mention our late start) it was well after dark on Friday

when we arrived at Burnham Military Camp. I had never been to the South Island before that day.

Compared to Linton, from the outside the camp looked dark and abandoned. Once we got *inside* the camp, I decided it was most definitely dark and abandoned. The duty corporal looked like we had interrupted his nap. He was irate as he plodded along ahead of us to show us to our new barracks. These were basically the same design as Linton base, so we figured we would dump our bags in our rooms and wander down to the common room to see who was about.

On any given night in 2 Sigs barracks in Linton, the common room would be inhabited by anywhere between two and forty-two people. There'd be people watching TV or playing Xbox on the huge screen, people shooting pool and people in the kitchen trying to figure out how to microwave an entire chicken. There'd be music and beers and a general homely vibe that we had all come to find comfort in within the place we called home.

The Burnham common room was completely empty.

Well, not exactly. It had occupants, except they were nearly all of the eight-legged and scuttling variety. The lights were out and there was the outline of a pool table with only two legs. The room was only visible due to the glow from an ancient vending machine that stocked drinks I had only seen in old Sam Neil movies.

Jordy exhaled loudly. 'What a shithole.'

He had a point.

Slightly miffed at the lack of any sort of reception, we went to our respective rooms to get ready for our first morning at our home unit.

I had joined the army in 2011 and it was now late 2012. I had been in the army for over a year. I was only now going to learn what being an Electronic Warfare Operator was actually about.

The next morning we rose, shaved and showered like we had every day up in Linton. We formed a small squad of five outside, and marched towards what we hoped was the meeting point for 3 Signal Squadron.

We saw signallers walking around, but they largely ignored us. We settled for standing outside of a large hanger with a three-headed dog crudely spray painted on the side. As far as we knew, Cerberus was the 3 Sig emblem, so we figured it was a good a spot as any.

Eventually, a face we recognised appeared. Lieutenant Wright had been one of the members of EW who had stopped by Linton during corps training. He hadn't said much, but he'd shaken our hands and said 'see you boys soon' in a conspiratorial tone that made us tingle with suspense.

As soon as I saw him, I went through the appropriate army etiquette for a group of soldiers seeing an officer for the first time that day.

'Standfast!' I barked. My four comrades snapped to attention. I crisply flicked my arm up and snapped off a salute that would've given Captain America a hard-on. 'Morning sir!' I chirped.

Lieutenant Wright didn't even break his stride. He lazily threw a salute back at me with an arm seemingly devoid of any bones. 'Morning gents,' he responded.

The other signallers wandering around the compound were sniggering.

Lieutenant Wright got closer and lowered his voice. 'Look guys. I know you're fresh from Linton, but we don't really do that whole ... thing here.' He waggled his arm in a parody of a salute.

'Just a "good morning sir" will do. Alright? You're in Mexico now. Follow me.'

And with that, he turned on his heel and lead us across the compound. The boys and I exchanged glances. No saluting? Had we come to Neverland and joined the lost boys? What was this?

CONFINED TO BARRACKS

PEOPLE OFTEN WONDER HOW punishments work in the army. Such a strict and regimented place must surely have some hefty penalties in place for those who don't comply, right?

There is a system in place for infringements. When you make a serious mistake in the army, you will be 'charged'. It is run much like a courtroom, with your commanding officer acting as a judge, a senior NCO acting as a prosecutor and an assigned senior NCO to defend you, or at least try to mitigate the hefty book about to be thrown. People get charged for all sorts of things, accidentally firing their weapon (known as an Unauthorised Discharge), falling asleep on sentry, being too drunk, and so on.

I was charged only once during my enlistment. I was late to a Corps Training class. It was somewhere between one and two minutes, depending on who you ask. I argued my case: 'the instructor wasn't wearing a watch, I was' and other such arguments fell on deaf ears. I was given a typical punishment for a soldier of my rank, being 'Confined to Barracks' for a week.

Let me tell you, CB is the absolute pits. You go to work normally, but effectively, every single shred of your spare time is taken away from you. You report to the duty sergeant every morning at 0600, just like being back on basic training. You then have to wear a bright orange vest that says 'DEFAULTER' across the back in huge letters. This tells everyone who sees you that you have failed in your duties. The duty sergeant then has to spend all morning giving you menial tasks around camp to perform. Mostly picking up litter or polishing something.

You get to leave for work, but for your lunch hour you have to report back to the duty sergeant. Lunchtimes are the worst: they march you and the other defaulters out to the parade square, in full sight of everyone, and make you do double-time drill. It's ridiculously fast and leaves you gasping for breath after about five minutes.

You go back to work, sweaty and humiliated. Once your work day is over and everyone else heads back to their barracks or their homes and families, you have to report back for more menial tasks. You will rush around camp, picking up cigarette butts, emptying bins and so on, until about 2200, when you are finally released to bed, to be ready to do it all over again the next day. While you are on CB, you aren't allowed to leave camp for any reason. People who live off base with their families actually have to move into barracks when they are sentenced to CB.

Needless to say, I made every effort to never wind up on CB again.

PT: GOOD FOR YOU, GOOD FOR ME

A LOT OF PEOPLE are curious about what sort of physical training we get up to in the army. Yes, we do obstacle courses, yes, we run around with packs and body armour on, and yes, naturally, we do many, *many* push-ups. Regular PT sessions are more or less what you're probably picturing. There are other, less typical but equally gruelling ways we get our exercise in.

The army is big on sports. They facilitate teamwork, competitiveness and cardio, and they generate good, healthy doses of testosterone. Army physical trainers are extremely dedicated. They take their job seriously, and their passion shows in every gasp and drop of sweat that comes out of the soldiers in their sessions. They create circuits, dedicate time to stretching and aerobic exercise and, occasionally, invent whole new sports. One such sport is what we called murderball.

I've always been of the opinion that modern sports are watered-down versions of battle. Murderball, as we played it, is less watered-down than most.

You'll need anywhere between eight and twenty-eight people. Divide them into two even teams, put them on a basketball court and give them a basketball. Then, give everyone a boxing glove and a mouthguard.

The rules are the same as basketball, except you can punch anybody you like, provided you use your gloved hand. It's madness, absolute chaos, and it *hurts*. But it is, oddly enough, a lot of fun.

The games were always very low-scoring. It's hard to shoot one-handed, especially when you're getting punched in the face by five people at once.

Other fun PT games included king of the ring, which involves a rope being laid on the grass in a vast circle, ten metres in diameter. Twenty or so people get in the circle, on their knees, and the PT blows the whistle. The last person inside the circle wins. The prize for winning usually means you get to sit and watch while the rest of the class goes for a run around the immense sports field, so competition to stay inside the ring is fierce. Being smaller than almost everyone in my squadron, my usual technique upon hearing the whistle was to dive into the middle of the dog pile that would immediately form in the centre, and latch onto someone heavy. This would allow me to survive the first initial cull, as lighter people would quickly be dragged out by the heavyweights, grinning wolfishly.

A few rounds of king of the ring would ensure that everyone was filthy, bruised (possibly bleeding) and exhausted. I maintain that out of all the exercises – running, circuit training, F45, CrossFit, whatever – the most rapidly exhausting thing you can do is wrestle with someone. Less than a minute of vicious grappling will have you gasping for air like you've just run a mile. Grappling with five or more people at once is even more bone-aching.

We did this sort of thing each morning, five days a week.

UP, UP AND OH SHIT

MY FIRST EXERCISE WITH 3 Sigs came towards the end of 2012. I had not learned any of the equipment, the patrol orders or even the names of everyone in the squadron. Nevertheless, with the current rotations of troops going to Afghanistan and the huge number of injuries that EW work inflicted on the human spine, Squadron Operations couldn't pass up five young, healthy soldiers arriving less than a month before a large-scale brigade exercise.

This is where I first met Sergeant Tim Collins, AKA the Silver Fox. Tim Collins was a 'lifer'. He had joined the army just out of high school and, now in his late thirties, had helped to form the modern 3 Sigs unit. He was an EW guru, field operator and three-time Afghan veteran. He was also short, handsome and extremely likeable. He had silver spiky hair and, since his ugly divorce a year earlier, he never dated anybody over the age of twenty-five, hence the Silver Fox moniker. He was also the troop MacGyver. He was always pulling pieces of equipment apart and reappropriating pieces of tech to suit his vision of EW operations.

With only a few weeks before the start of the exercise, myself and the other EW newbies were sorted into the existing detachments like fat kids into sports teams. None of the current operators looked particularly keen on having fresh meat in their detachment.

The standard layout of a four-man recon detachment (called a det) is a det commander, a 2IC, a signaller and a gunner. If we were lucky enough to have a five-man detachment, this would also include a scout. The equipment and responsibilities were pretty much standard for all exercises.

Det commander: Lord commander of the detachment, the det commander makes all the decisions, including patrol route, what antennas to take, place to position the LP (Listening Post). Everything begins and ends with the det commander. Usually they will be a full screw (corporal) or senior lance-jack (lance corporal). They carry the most sensitive equipment, such as orders, maps and encryption keys. Armed with a standard-issue IW Steyr, they walk either in front (four-man det) or just behind the scout (five-man det).

2IC: The hardest-working person in a detachment is the 2IC. Most of the actual work falls to this position, while the det commander tries to navigate the hierarchy above. Usually they will be a lance-corporal. They will write shift rosters, check up on the det members and triple-check that every order given is actually being carried out. They will carry an IW Steyr fitted with a 203 grenade launcher and patrol at the rear to make sure that the det isn't leaving too much sign when they pass through dense bush. In case of a contact, standard operating procedure is to fire 203 grenades *over* the detachment into the enemy while the det gets into firing positions.

Signaller: Usually a senior baggy (private), and unofficially the 3IC. They carry the patrol radio (a seven-kilogram block of copper and steel) and a few spare batteries, and are tasked with checking in with HQ and finding the best location to position antennas. They'll have the heaviest pack out of anyone and need to be on the ball when it comes to having shit together.

When you're patrolling with thirty-five-kilogram packs, moments of respite are extremely therapeutic. While everybody else gets to sit for ten minutes, the sig has to whip the radio out of their pack and hustle up to where the det commander is and relay information back to HQ under their direction. It's a tough gig. They are the link to the rest of the force when out on patrol. The most competent soldier should be the detachment sig.

Scout: If there is one, the scout patrols at the front of the det and carries a map and some of the listening equipment. They choose the specific route under the guidance of the det commander. The scout will walk further ahead of the det in order to explore possible routes and identify unpassable obstacles, which means they end up walking further than everyone else and have to bush-bash through thick undergrowth. They also do by far the most running in a Break Contact Drill (BCD). Ideally, the fittest person in the det should be the scout (Taylor was always the scout when I was on patrol with him for this exact reason). They carry an IW Steyr.

Gunner: The gunner carries the detachment machine gun and extra rounds. This task is part of being caretaker for the machine gun, which is the centre of every small-scale firefight. It can fire more rounds per minute than every other rifle in the det *combined*. It is often described as 80% of a detachment's firepower, being wielded by ONE person.

Being a gunner means knowing where to position yourself for maximum output and ensuring that your gun is constantly firing during a contact. On the daily, it also means maintaining and cleaning a large, complex piece of weaponry. For perspective, the IW Steyr, a standard (if somewhat outdated) assault rifle, field-strips down into approximately fifteen pieces. The C9 light support weapon (which was the standard-issue gun when I joined) breaks down into nearly sixty pieces. Put simply, it is a motherfucker to clean. Technically, it is the responsibility of everyone in the det to help clean and maintain the gun, but the reality is that the gunner takes care of it. At the end of an extremely long day, when you're deep in a pine forest and the Sig is trying to find a radio signal, the scout is laying out trip flares, antennas and such, the det commander is scanning frequencies and the 2IC is doing a thousand other small things, the gunner probably won't feel like asking around for help with their one job. The C9 is a heavy gun. It weighs eleven kilograms with a 200 round box attached, and it's long. It fires 7.62 ammunition, which weighs a shitload more than 5.56.

I was given the gun on my first few exercises and carried it right up until I became a det 2IC. Originally, I hated that fucking gun. It weighed twice as much as everyone's rifles and would get caught on every branch and vine as I tried to move silently through the bush. But the more I carried it, the more I became enamoured with mastering it. I spent a lot of my early days in 3 Sigs carrying the gun on exercises and practising contact drills with it in the training area. In less than a year, I went from dreading the sight of that machine gun to being one of the few people in the squadron who could actually reload it while running. For a weapon designed to be reloaded while lying down, this was a big accomplishment.

I will take this moment to blow my own horn. I was a good gunner.

I used the C9 so much that I actually failed my rifle test one year because it had been so long since I had used one. I tried to reload my rifle like a machine gun and used my right hand to pull the magazine (like opening the top cover to sweep the link away).

A mere two weeks after my arrival at 3 Sigs, it was late afternoon in Waiouru and I was standing in front of a stationary

NH90 helicopter. The blades were roaring as I swayed slightly from the enormous pack on my back. I had never carried anything so heavy in my life. It was almost exactly half my weight. I was periodically leaning forward, almost doubling over to try and take some of the strain off my spine. Every time I took a step, I felt my vertebrae wobble. I should've guessed it then, but this would be the start of years of back strain and injury for me and my friends in the squadron.

I wore full DPMs, a J-hat and a buff wrapped around my neck. My face was smeared with cam paint. As soon as that pore-clogging sludge touches your skin, you know two things for certain. You're going to develop a pimple within the next ten minutes, and it'll be the only thing you can smell until your next shower. Which, on average, will be about three days away.

We were all lined up about twenty metres from the helo (helicopter) and being given a quick rundown on how to dismount when we got to the landing zone. The other three members of the detachment were all EW veterans. They'd done countless exercises and each of them had been to Afghanistan at least once. Walker was in command, with Daniel Knight and White acting as sig and 2IC.

I got lumped with the machine gun for the first time. I knew how to operate it from my time at Depot Troop. But mostly I just thought of it as a stupidly heavy piece of kit. I tried to nod as the air force sergeant in charge of deploying us safely out of the helicopter gave us rapid-fire instructions, but I was distracted by the Christmas tree of blinking lights inside the gunmetal-grey helicopter and the roar of the rotor two feet above my head.

'All good?' The sergeant's question snapped me back to reality. I shrugged, and the rest of the detachment began piling into the helo, awkwardly shoving their immense packs into the small storage area in front of the bench seat. I went to shrug off my pack and get in with them, but the sergeant placed a hand on my chest.

'Wait up, buddy. You and your girlfriend get a window seat.'

It took me a moment, but I realised he was talking about the metre-long machine gun I was cradling. I nodded and waited for everyone to be seated, trying not to show the strain from standing still with my impossibly heavy pack. Walking with a heavy pack is very tiring, but surprisingly, so is standing still. After about two minutes, you begin to feel your knees sliding laterally in their sockets. Then, your spine starts to wiggle. After an eternity of testing all my most precious joints, the crew sergeant gave me a nod and I shrugged off my pack and clambered up into the helicopter. It took off almost immediately. At first, I was so glad to have my pack off my back that I didn't even watch the ground floating away from me. It was a smooth ascent, kind of like being in an extremely loud lift.

As we got higher, I began looking at the flight sergeant to see if he was going to close the doors or if I was supposed to do it. I was less than an arm's length from a drop into empty air and the 'seat' I was on was basically just a bench with a lap-belt. We were at least five storeys up at this point. The trees that had towered above me moments before now looked like shrubs. Just as I was about to lean forward and start looking for a door handle, I realised with a lurch that this helicopter *didn't have doors*. I gripped the machine gun so tightly my knuckles went white.

Not a moment too soon, because without any warning the pilot dropped the nose and we started hurtling forward at what is known as 'cruising speed', a brisk 220 kilometres per hour. With no windows, you really get a feel for just how fast that is.

Just as I began to calm down a bit, the pilot began descent, taking huge, sweeping turns and following a large river. I was later told that this style of flight was practised to make any anti-air weaponry harder to aim. It meant following the natural contours of the land. A pilot needs to be highly skilled to do it with the sunset glare shooting scarlet beams of light up at them. Because I was in a window seat, whenever we banked left, I could see nothing but a view of the purple sky as I slid into Daniel Knight. The banking was so sharp that I was basically lying on top of him each time this happened. When we banked *right* for the first time, I nearly pissed myself. I was looking below, admiring the riverbed, when suddenly I was dangling over empty air at twice the speed I had ever travelled in a moving vehicle. I was holding a very heavy, very expensive machine gun, and the only thing holding me inside the helicopter was a strap across my lap that was slightly thinner than a seatbelt. My right leg was completely outside the helicopter. My chest did that swooping vertigo backflip, and I couldn't help but let a loud 'WOOOOOOOOOAAAAAAHHHHHH SHIIIIIIIIT!' escape my lips.

Knight must've heard me over the noise of the engine because immediately he and Walker began laughing. I let out a nervous laugh too. After that, I began to really enjoy the ride. As a rollercoaster fan, this was better than *anything* that the Gold Coast had to offer.

We flew over the Waiouru training area for nearly half an hour. It was at this point that I saw the single most memorable image I had ever seen in my life to that point, or since. I will attempt to do it justice, but sadly, whatever I describe will fall utterly short of capturing this moment.

Waiouru is a collection of rolling hills, both rocky and grassy, covered with tussock and scrub. The river was a chalky light blue and the rocks that lined the bank were as pale as ash. The sun was on my side of the helicopter; about a quarter of it had dropped behind the hill. It was that perfect part of sunset where the light begins bouncing off the underside of the clouds, sending that warm, reddish orange into the sky. The horizon was touched with the start of the night's darkness, making it slightly purple. The river was flanked by large cliffs at this point, so we had to climb slightly to get over them. As we banked right, I turned my chest so it was as though I was flying through the air. I felt the freezing wind at my exposed neck and wrists.

On top of the hill, with the fading sun behind them, were three wild horses. They were sprinting across the top of the hill, and I was about thirty metres above them. They were running from the immense noise of the engine, obviously. They were Kaimanawa horses, light brown and massive. They galloped across the hill and disappeared from sight.

I truly hope to keep that image in my head until the day I die.

I was still daydreaming out the window when the huge air force sergeant in the back of the helo with us slapped my arm suddenly. I jerked back to reality to stare into his huge, clichéd aviators. I was expecting him to tell me something important, maybe relay something from Walker.

'TWO MINTUES!' he screamed, an inch from my face.

Two minutes? Shit, I remembered this meant something. Before I could turn to ask Knight, his freckled nose was nearly touching mine and he screamed it too.

'TWO MINUTES!'

And again down the line, Walker and White yelling emotionlessly into nothingness.

'TWO MINUTES!'

'TWO MINUTES!'

Without hesitation, my basic human instinct to conform and fit in joined hands with my newly acquired military herd mentality.

'TWO MINUTES!' I also screamed.

I waited, but nobody did anything else.

After thirty painfully long seconds, White picked his nose. He seemed pleased with the yield.

After what felt like five minutes, the helicopter began to descend, rapidly. I felt my organs trying to remain where the helicopter had been while the rest of me was dragged downwards, much, *much* faster than any lift. It was at this point that I remembered what 'two minutes' meant. Two minutes until descent, time to get ready.

By this stage, the sun had properly set and our eyes were still adjusting to the gloom. The gigantic sergeant tapped me on the shoulder as soon as the skids touched the ground. The rotors were still 'whup-whup-whupping' just above me as I clumsily undid the lap belt with one hand while I clung to my machine gun with the other. I looked back up and the sergeant barked 'GO!' straight into my face.

This part, at least, I had practised.

Treating the area as enemy territory meant covering the det with the huge gun I was holding. I jumped off the helicopter and tried not to flinch as I imagined the rotors slicing the air just inches over my head (it's more like a metre). I quickly scanned around and saw a patch of grass that was slightly elevated. Perfect. I jogged over, extended the gun's bipod and lay down, scanning the section of road nearly a kilometre away. Behind me, one other person would be covering my back, while the last two members of the det unceremoniously tossed our colossal packs into a rough pile directly outside of the helicopter. Don't ever bring anything into the field that can't withstand a severe crushing.

The helicopter took off behind me. The grass rippled in the grey light of dusk as the final gusts buffeted my back.

I was already getting cold. In Waiouru, the cold lurks in every patch of shade and behind every tree until the moment the sun disappears. Fortunately, one of the only good things about walking with a pack is you can't get cold.

Walker kicked my boot and we jogged back over to where our packs were. I sat on the ground and wiggled my arms into the straps. Then, the only thing to do was to hold out my arms and have two of the guys yank me to my feet. My back ached almost immediately. To complete the misery, White thrust the dreaded machine gun back into my arms. I pictured myself actually sinking into the ground like a ute on soft sand. Walker slapped my shoulder and, without saying a word, directed me back to my little hill.

I waddled over, no doubt looking like a toddler in snow gear, and eased myself onto one knee. With a pack on, this is basically the only alternative to standing that you have available. I stared back out into the hills, focussing on dark patches to build up my night vision as quickly as possible.

A lot of people don't realise that humans actually possess the ability to see quite well in the dark. It just takes time to 'activate'. Most people, in their day-to-day, never spend more than a few seconds looking into darkness. As soon as the lights go out, they assume that the lack of visibility is permanent and immediately find a light switch or turn on their phone. If you wait even just a few seconds, you'll notice that things will look clearer almost immediately.

There's a compound in your eyes, called rhodopsin, or 'visual purple' that converts light into electrical signals your brain can interpret. Too much light will 'bleach it' and cause it to disappear. So, in low light, it needs time to build up, and the only way to get it to accumulate is to stare into darkness. It takes a good five minutes for 90% of it to build up. And closer to twenty minutes for another 5%. The last 5%, the absolute best you can hope to see in the dark, takes roughly an hour. If you look into any source of strong light during this time, it'll destroy the visual purple and you have to start all over again.

I knew without looking, that each time Walker or Campbell were checking the map, they'd use red light (which is less intense and harder to see at a distance) and more importantly, they'd be looking at the map with one eye (their dominant eye) firmly closed. This meant that they were preserving as much visual purple as possible.

At any rate, they didn't need long with the map. The terrain was largely just tussocky hills and our bearing wasn't so much a compass point as it was 'upwards'. Walker gave the hand signal for patrolling in open country: palm flat like a karate-chop, dragging his fingertips through the air in a straight line. That put Walker at the front. As the det commander and the scout, it was up to him where we were going and how we would get there. I was about ten metres behind him, ready to sprint forward and get to work with the machine gun in case we ran into any territorial soldiers roleplaying as OpFor (opposing forces). Knight was behind me: as the signaller he needed to be close to the centre of the det. And bringing up the rear was White, lugging the 203 grenade launcher, which was, of course, empty.

We walked with a good ten metres between us. The reason being, if you're in open country and you hit a contact, you don't want anything explosive to take out multiple members of your detachment at once.

The most memorable thing about that infil (infiltration) was just trying to tackle that hill. I was supposed to be looking up, scanning left and right, keeping a vigilant eye out for enemy forces.

All very top-notch soldiering, in theory. Hyper-alert and ready to fight the Huns at a moment's notice, without missing a beat. In reality, when you have that kind of weight on your back, and the ground beneath you is more rabbit holes than ground, 'patrolling' in that sense isn't really possible. I looked up maybe one step in ten, just to make sure than the outline of Walker's pack was still lumbering along ahead of me. My calves started burning before we'd gone a hundred metres. Another hundred metres after that, my shoulders joined in. At half a kilometre, I felt like someone was hanging onto my pack and dragging me down as hard as they could. I gasped and swallowed dryly. Nervous that I had made too much sound, I risked a look behind me. Knight's head was bowed as he plodded along under the immense weight of the Sig's pack. As I looked ahead of me, I could see that even Walker's huge strides were laboured.

This was 3 Sig dismounted operations. Each man shut inside his own personal hurt locker. I didn't know how far we had to go. I vaguely remembered that Walker had thumbed along a couple of grid squares in our orders and grunted, 'We're going this way.' *How many kilometres was that?* I thought. *Three? Four?* It couldn't be very far, surely.

A five-kilometre walk through town or along the beach can take as little as fifty minutes, if you have a good pace and don't stop. But throw in a hill, that slows you down; make it dark, that slows you down more. Add the weight of a bass guitar amplifier on your back, and now your brisk, one-hour jaunt can take half the night.

I was sweating. My back ached and I tried to stand up straight and let my shoulders slide back. The muscles in my back weren't up to the task. Every time I tried to straighten up, the weight of the pack would threaten to pull me over backwards and I risked tumbling down the hill, à la Samwise Gamgee during the hobbits' shortcut to mushrooms. This meant I had to bring my shoulders forward and walk along in a hunch, looking for all the world like a question mark holding a gun.

The hill kept getting steeper. The ground was bathed in starlight and the grass was smooth enough to be slippery underfoot. I managed to avoid stepping in any significant holes, but each step was harder than the last. It was like when you're holding an immensely heavy shopping bag, the muscles in your forearms screaming at you to put it down, but you need to reach the front door. Except instead of just my forearms it was my forearms, legs and back. I cradled the immense gun and extended my left arm. My elbow had been bent for far too long and the relief I got from that tiny little stretch did nothing to distract me from the misery in my quads, calves and glutes. Each step was a weighted lunge. I didn't know how many steps I had taken, and I had no clue how many there were to go.

Lost in my world of woe, I almost collided with Walker. I saw his huge boot just moments before I would have walked into his pack. He was standing and peering through his rifle scope up the hill. He scanned left and right, either looking for movement or maybe just trying to figure out the best route uphill, I couldn't tell. I wasn't sure what to do here. If he'd taken a knee, that would've been my indication to keep my spacing and do the same. He didn't have his left hand up, so I couldn't tell if he wanted me to cover him, join him or stay put. Keeping my eyes fixed on Walker in case he did make a gesture, I opted to quietly start walking backwards a few steps, to try and maintain the ten-metre gap. I wasn't in the mood to be called a stupid newbie fuck for not following unit protocols. I still wanted to impress these guys.

I walked backwards right into Knight.

'Oi,' he hissed in a harsh whisper. 'You stupid newbie fuck; watch where you're fucking going, cunt.'

Before I could stammer a response, Walker's head whipped around. He saw the two of us, upright and virtually entangled. Even in almost total darkness, I could *feel* him roll his eyes.

Walker made a quick decision and whispered to us.

'Alright, let's take a ten.' As we moved around him to make an outward facing cross, I heard him add, 'Assholes,' under his breath. We each slowly got onto one knee, facing outwards like the four points of a compass. Then, one by one, we eased ourselves onto the ground, trying to make as few collapsing sounds as possible. Once we were all seated, everyone had a sip of water and I noticed something that made my day. Everyone in the det was as tired and strained as I was. They had sweat on their faces, and they sucked down huge gulps of air as quietly as they could. Knight rubbed his shoulders and White was retying his boots. It occurred to me that the real strength of a detachment came from the collective stubbornness of its members. Alone, it would take me all night to carry all my gear up that hill. The detachment did it in less than two hours.

They didn't carry a single gram of my kit, but the presence of the other three kept me placing one foot in front of the other. If they could walk without asking for respite, so could I. Nobody wanted to be the person who said, 'Stop, I can't.' In essence, this is the secret behind our success as a dismounted force. Every man holding out stubbornly, bitterly, despite every screaming muscle and gasped breath.

We finally made it to the top of the ridge. The ground had a small, flat shelf before the actual crest of the hill, which gave us a perfect little hollow to congregate our gear and sleeping mats. We are always told to avoid the top of a hill or a slope. If you poke your head, or even worse, walk over the top of a hill, you become clearly visible at huge distances, even in the low light of dusk. It's known as skylining yourself and is regarded as an extremely rookie error to make during any sort of patrolling manoeuvre.

We set up our antennas, radioed back to HQ and began our overnight surveillance. If we crawled along the shelf and stayed on our stomachs, we could actually see across the valley and had great visibility of the rough road. This was rare: quite often we had no view at all of the enemy and relied on what we could hear alone. The OpFor were supposed to be moving around this area, and the specific force we were targeting was an enemy armoured unit. We slept in shifts and made sure that someone always had eyes on the road.

The rest of the night passed without incident, and we began to pick up some chatter about plans to move the entire 'division' down the road we could see within the next 24 hours. (A division typically has close to a hundred tanks. The NZ OpFor had to make do with a handful of vehicles and the power of imagination.)

We eagerly relayed the intercept back to base and got our usual round of 'well dones' and assurances of a big gold star when we got back to camp. We were told to remain in place until the following day, and to keep relaying as much information as possible about the enemy forces. We did so diligently. Later that day, we watched the entire 'division' (about ten vehicles) moving down the road. We reported it and were informed that

HQ were planning an artillery strike to catch the enemy when they were concentrated.

To avoid blowing friendly forces to shit, these sorts of decisions are made with a huge amount of detailed planning and involve several senior army officers knowing where all their actual soldiers are so they can pretend-murder each other. However, when the focus is on fifty men and ten vehicles, it can be easy to forget about four camouflaged recon soldiers on the side of a hill. So we knew that artillery was planned at some point, but we didn't know *when* it would be.

Therefore, the first warning we received about the artillery strike was when the valley we had been looking at for two days started exploding before our eyes. I woke up to the scream of shells passing over my head and thumping into the hill where the 'enemy' was supposed to be. It was violent, it was intense, it was *loud*.

But this was my first exercise with 3 Sigs; I didn't want to look like a bitch. I tried to look nonchalant, though my ass was clenched so tightly you could've opened a beer betwixt my cheeks.

Walker had no such pretences. He jumped straight on the radio and started bellowing our current position to anybody who would listen. He knew this was a mistake, we were well inside the minimum distance for friendly ordinance to fall. Although the shells were landing nearly a full kilometre in front of us, the guns they were coming out of were over ten kilometres behind us. We were on the top of a hill, so if a shot was misjudged, or slightly overcorrected, there was a very real possibility of a 105mm howitzer round hitting one of us in the face. Travelling at 472 metres per second and weighing a shade over nineteen kilograms, one of these would only need to land next to us to kill our entire detachment in an instant (which of course is precisely what they are designed to do).

After several long, stressful salvos, the fact that four little signallers were in the firing zone made its way to the gunline. The barrage stopped.

We glanced at the decimated hill across the valley. Huge, brown scars were rent across the grassy hillside and smoke trailed out of most of them. My ears rang, my butt was still clenched, and I managed a nervous giggle.

'Was that supposed to happen?' I ventured.

'Pretty much standard when the fucking gunners get loose,' said White.

'At least all the "tanks" are dead,' offered Knight.

Walker laughed. 'Yeah, hold on.'

He radioed in and cheerfully informed HQ that the enemy tank division had suffered huge casualties, but that the sigs on the hill, despite the gunner's best efforts, were still very much alive.

SERGEANT COLLINS HAS A PLAN

WITHIN THE ARMY, there are what we call Standard Operating Procedures that dictate how you do your specific role. If the infantry have to attack a hill with a machine gun post dug into it, they have a whole book on exactly how they ought to do it. The same is true of signallers, engineers and even the army PTs. However, there is always space for creativity, initiative and ingenuity. Within certain parameters, squadron and platoon commanders throughout the army are always looking for new and creative ways to get the mahi done.

In training exercises, and later deployments, with various national militaries, I came to learn that New Zealand soldiers have a reputation for this out-of-the-box, Number 8 wire-type thinking.

In the world of New Zealand Electronic Warfare, Sergeant Tim Collins was like MacGyver. He was a mad scientist, with hangars full of expensive equipment, and twenty-odd guinea pigs who would do any mad shit he asked of them. His vision for what NZ EW could be was mixed, to say the least.

Sometimes his ideas were great. They were modern, cutting edge and could be downright fun.

A good example was the mounted configuration we adopted for SK 2013. It was one of my first exercises with 3 Signal Squadron. I arrived there as one of six 'newbie fucks' and was hurriedly thrown into a detachment. We had these Pinzgauers on loan from QAMR (Queen Alexandra's Mounted Rifles) that had a hatch in the roof and a platform in them so a machine gun could be placed on a swivel mount and fired while the wagon was driving.

All those months of carrying the biggest, dirtiest weapon on corps training was finally paying off. We went through contact drills, in the event of the tyres being shot out or the engine block being damaged. My job was to leap up into the turret and start firing off rounds out of the roof while everyone else got the radios and sensitive equipment safely out of the wagon. Then, someone would drop a smoke grenade right by one of the doors, and I'd have to detach the gun from the swivel, leap through the interior of the pinny and jump through the smoke, landing on the ground holding my machine gun while everyone else covered my exit. That was definitely one of Tim's cooler ideas. We took the mounted operations to its tactical extreme. We covered the vehicles in camouflage netting, spray painted every single detachable piece of equipment, and placed black insulation tape over everything that could possibly create shine. We spent a serious amount of time debating over how to stop the windows from reflecting light too. After some truly terrible, potentially fatal ideas were tossed around, we settled for coating the inside of the windows with blackout curtain. We had no choice but to leave the front windscreen unobscured. The vehicle drivers were strangely insistent about needing to see where they were going.

A not-so-fun innovation was Sergeant Collin's obsession with digging in. Having spent my first major exercise with 3 Sigs as a 'mounted' troop based out of a large utility vehicle, I was less than thrilled to be going back to being dismounted. Even less so when Sarge explained his latest concept.

'These days, you have to assume you're being watched from above,' Sergeant Collins said one frigid Tuesday morning.

The usual rotation of the year was as follows: inventory our squadron's ungodly amount of gear and specialist equipment to assess what we actually own, get said gear ready for large brigade exercise, go on large brigade exercise and lose/destroy 10% of all of it, spend months cleaning/replacing/fixing it, and then squeeze in some training before the next inventory. We were in the training phase.

We stood huddled around in the bays, like camouflaged penguins bracing against the Antarctic chill.

'If you get into a good LP, set up your kit and just lie flat on the ground, you're going to get spotted by the first thing with a camera that flies over you,' he continued.

We exchanged glances. Nobody liked where this was going.

So, what we need to be doing is *digging in*. We need to get our infil sorted, find a good position, and then spend our first night digging an LP that the whole det can fit in that can be completely covered with a couple of hoochies.'

I stuck out my hand (soldiers don't raise their hands, but thrust them directly outward, like a socially-inept robot offering a handshake). 'Sarge, when you say "we" need to dig ...'

'I mean you dickheads.'

Everybody chuckled.

'OK, I get the obs from above thing, but why not just put two hoochies over the det? How does digging a hole help?' someone behind me asked.

Sergeant Collins was ready for this. 'Has it been that long since basic training that you've all forgotten about IDF? Our current area of operations is ...?'

'Afghanistan,' we chorused obediently.

'And the Taliban fucks who want to blow you to shit are very fond of mortars, RPGs and whatever else they can fling at you without having to actually get into a firefight with armoured opponents.'

This was a good point. NATO forces, being trained in squad fighting tactics, preferred shoot-outs where their body armour, high rate of fire and numerical superiority could be used to their advantage. Guerrilla forces like the Taliban preferred hit-and-run tactics like mortar ambushes and IEDs (improvised explosive devices), where their manoeuvrability and lack of manpower were assets.

When you're at war, there's one thing you want to avoid at all costs: a fair fight.

'So, how big do these holes need to be?' asked Hughes.

'About two hoochies wide should fit four of you, plus the kit. Leave one side open about a foot for observation and peg the hoochie to the ground on the other three sides.

'That's a fucking big hole,' someone murmured.

'How long will this take to dig?' asked Griffon-Graham (GG).

Tim grinned. 'We've got all day to find out.'

As I've said before, a surprising amount of soldiering is spent holding a shovel, not a rifle.

The problem with digging is that bigger holes take exponentially longer to dig than small ones, even if you have more people involved. Two people can dig twice as fast as one, but that's where the gain in efficiency peaks. After that, it's impossible to work in a small space without getting in each other's way.

Tim had a very specific vision for how these 'pits' should be constructed. Three feet deep, minimum: just enough room to crawl around under the roof of the hoochie and occasionally prop yourself up on your elbows if you wanted to make a meal or take a drink of water. The front of the pit, with the small open observation slit, needed an extra deep part so that the two people on watch could sit and face out with their feet in a hole. Sort of like a below-ground couch made of dirt. It was fairly comfortable, compared with other night-watch positions I've endured. But that extra foot and a half of depth we needed added considerable time to the overall construction.

Once the hole was complete, there was still the matter of placing out radio antennas and threading their cables into the pit and then creating an overall level of concealment that would appease Sergeant Collins.

We took large chunks of turf and laid them on the edges of the hoochie to try and blend the hide's profile in with the scenery. At a distance of more than fifty metres, it actually worked fairly well. As with most military camouflage, there's no invisibility cloak. If someone is close enough, they will see you, regardless of what you're wearing. Camouflage is merely for concealment at a distance.

If you're fast and motivated, a single-man shell scrape can take as little as an hour, but we found that digging a hole large enough for four men, plus equipment and all of Tim's other specifications, took four people almost three hours.

Each detachment completed two 'dig ins' that day. Then, just as 1600 rolled around, we filled in the second hole and stomped back to camp, covered in dirt, exhausted and thoroughly unenthusiastic about our latest and greatest squadron tactic.

The very first time we implemented this on a large-scale exercise, it was a hilarious (although not at the time) disaster. It resulted in a situation that lives on in infamy in 3 Sig Squadron to this day. But I'm getting ahead of myself. Before those hard times, was exercise Hard Times.

HARDER TIMES

SERGEANT COLLINS, SERGEANT PHILIPS and a handful of the other senior NCOs from the squadron wanted us to head out on a squadron field exercise. They named it 'Exercise Hard Times'. At the very least, it was a suitable moniker.

We were arranged into detachments, with the notable exception being that the usual det commanders, all corporals, were not going to be in the dets with us. The senior sigs were instead going to have a crack at det commander position, while the corporals had a crack at the sergeants' jobs, and the sergeants … well, the sergeants did *something* for two weeks, I'm sure of it.

We were out at Mount Sunday, an unbelievably scenic piece of Canterbury that I utterly took for granted because, in all honesty, it's very difficult to appreciate the landscape when you're crawling all over it carrying a pack that would be described as 'painfully heavy' if you took half the stuff out.

If you're familiar with Mount Sunday, good for you. If you aren't, you may have seen it on a movie screen before. It's the location where the *Lord of the Rings* films placed Edoras, the capital city of Rohan.

We were at the top of a huge hill, overlooking the car park. We spent all night climbing up and managed to throw up a hoochie just in time for rain to come in sideways at us. We slept in a row under the single hoochie, like sardines in a tin. Each man spent ninety minutes manning the radio, passing it along to the next person as their shift began. The rain came harder, and harder, until tiny rivers began to form and the ground beneath us became spongy and riddled with waterlogged worms.

We spent the next week and a half listening, watching and doing our best to avoid the relentless efforts of the sergeants to find our various hidey holes.

PATROL PROCEDURES

IT WAS AN UNREMARKABLE weekday in Burnham Camp. It was sunny, but in mid-May a clear day only meant it was colder. It was about three degrees outside. PT had been the usual gruelling hour of crawling over frozen grass and trying to stop my hands from going blue. As usual, we had rushed from PT straight to the showers. I crammed my face full of cereal, shaved, changed into a clean uniform and sprinted to the bays, only to be told to 'Wait, wait out.'

So, here we were, forty minutes later. Jordy and I we were standing outside the bays, smoking our third consecutive cigarettes and talking absolute shite. Out of the HQ building, Staff-Sergeant Sallow (or 'Staff' as people of his rank were addressed) came stomping over. He was most paradoxically grumpy man I'd ever met. He was only pissed off when there was nothing around to be pissed off about. He was only in a good mood when there was something worth yelling at you for. As one of his underlings, it was tricky to navigate, but you got used to it.

We had been at 3 Sigs for nearly three months now, and in that short time our demeanour towards rank had turned from cautiously formal, to casual, to downright smug. Jordy turned and, with his inexhaustible supply of pep, let loose with a Bugs Bunny-esque, 'What's up, Staff?' right in his face, from a distance of under three feet. Sallow looked like Jordy had just offered him a blowjob. I took it a step further and gave him a frat-bro head-flick that would have earned me about a thousand push-ups had I tried it back up in Linton.

Sallow fired right back with a, 'Shut-up, Coolibar. Palmer broke his foot, so now we need one of you idiots to go on Recon Patrol Procedures in his place.'

He now had our attention.

Patrol Procedures was a highly coveted course. It was essentially a ground-up recon skills course for infantrymen who had made it into 2/1 Battalion Recon Platoon. A few years ago, someone in 3 Sigs had managed to convince Recon that we should send a detachment of signallers on each course to learn recon skills and improve our overall soldiering ability.

That in itself was a small miracle. Infantry thought of everyone outside their corps as a bunch of useless geeks. Allowing us to participate in specialist training must have taken some smooth talking indeed, or possibly even the aforementioned blowjob. What made this offer from Sallow even more tantalising was that 3 Sigs had been subsequently banned from going on patrol procedures since the ill-fated 'Banner incident' of approximately one year previous.

Banner, a Military Intelligence private recently promoted to lance-corporal, was on a TOD (tour of duty) to 3 Sigs. MI privates get sent to various units to learn how and where the information they receive is collected. Good in theory. Unfortunately, the kind of people who end up in MI don't do so well crawling around in mud, which was easily 50% of the job in 3 Sigs. So the short of it was, an MI soldier who was uncomfortable in a signals squadron had ended up very uncomfortable on a six-week field exercise for elite infantry. Needless to say, he didn't cope so well.

The climax of this particular fiasco resulted in his detachment slogging through snow, upwards of ten hours a day, with the usually office-bound Banner in charge. They had been out in this for nearly two weeks when Banner reached the end of his tether (I was not eyewitness to this, but by all accounts …). He stopped in the middle of the patrol to unleash a toddler in supermarket-style tantrum about how it was too cold and he was too tired and that he didn't want to be a corporal ANY MORE, the finale of which, I'm told, included him literally tearing the rank off his shirt and hurling it to the ground.

Spectacular performance, to say the least. I'm sure he was in the running for an Oscar.

Naturally, 3 Sigs didn't send any more detachments to patrol procedures after that. Yet, here was Sallow, glaring at us both, informing us that one of us could be representing signallers again on this trial.

We were both eager as hell. Staff loved that. I could see in his eyes that he wanted to make us grovel for it, or maybe have us fight each other over a vat of acid. Something else must have taken priority however, because he simply left his withering stare on Jordy for another moment before flicking his head at me and saying, 'Davidson, you're up. Go fill out the forms.' Then he wheeled around like a bear after a quite unsatisfying mauling, and stalked off in search of another victim. I tried not to rub Jordy's face in it too hard. His ego was like an ornate chandelier: enormous, obvious and very fragile.

He nearly did an actual guffaw. 'Why'd he pick you?'

I shrugged. 'It is winter in Dip Flat. Maybe he thinks I'll die.'

This response seemed to soothe him a little.

'Yeah!' Jordy responded cheerfully 'Maybe you will.'

Later that day, I was told to report to the Recon hangar with the other 3 Sigs personnel who would be comprising the detachment for Patrol Procedures. In charge was Lance-Corporal Sam Platt, AKA Alleycat Platt. I never got solid confirmation out of him, but apparently the nickname came from a steamy late-night rendezvous with a local girl, in a literal alleyway. He never denied it and seemed to have no issue being called Alleycat, so I can only assume that the story was either true, or the actual events that transpired were even more shameful. His dad was from Bedford and his mum was from El Salvador. So, he looked like a South American footballer (complete with 90s-era spiked haircut) and spoke like a Led Zeppelin roadie. He had excellent taste in music, terrible taste in women and looked about ten years younger than his current thirty-two. I liked him a lot.

With me from corps training was Aaron Taylor. The golden boy, the unit Superman. He was always the front of the pack on every run, pack march, CrossFit session and beep test we did. He sneered at everyone eating pies and would hover around people who smoked cigarettes, berating them while he chewed handfuls of almonds. Not surprisingly, he was built like a Greek statue. He aced every theory course they had ever put in front of us. He even had some aspects of corps training changed by suggesting more efficient ways to teach. He was the kind of person who you wanted to dislike for being so goddam amazing

Above: In my first set of DPMs, 2011. Note the name tag made of tape and the red rank slide, the unmistakable marks of a recruit.

Left: Standing (centre) at 'present arms' position on my final parade as a recruit, Waiouru, 2011.

Jordy, me and Andrew taking the application of cam paint extremely seriously.

After a run in the hills above Palmerston North during Signal Corps training. From left to right: Andrew, me, Jordy Coolibar, Aaron Taylor, Reid. The hand gestures are meant to spell 'EW' (Electronic Warfare).

Above: One of many weekend pilgrimages from Palmerston North to Wellington, 2012.

Left: After a year in Linton, four other EWOPs and I are ready to move to the South Island to learn the art of hiding in the bushes, 2012. Our fellow corps trainees are bidding us farewell.

Me and Ziggy Stardust in my Burnham barrack room, circa 2013/14.

Four grubby signallers ready to go bush for a week or two, Canterbury somewhere, 2014.

Left: Anzac Day 2014. After several hours of parades and ceremony, we would eventually find ourselves in a local RSA, swapping stories with veterans who would insist on buying us beer. This one was in Templeton, Christchurch.

Below: Command tents set up on a unit exercise. Our officers and sergeants would devise our orders from here and send us scurrying into the hills to fight invisible foes. Whenever we radioed 'Zero-Alpha' for orders, it was this location that we were contacting.

Almost all of 3 Signals Squadron in one photo while on exercise in Canterbury. The multitude of uniforms reflects the NZDF's transition from DPM to MCU camouflage at the time.

The rolling hills and jagged mountains of Canterbury offer steep climbs, and treacherous footing even on a sunny day. The lack of cover meant you had to move quickly to avoid detection, and there was never any respite from the wind, rain or snow, which would descend without warning.

Buzz (left) and me sitting on the roof of our building in Taji base, Iraq, 2016.
Just after sundown was the magic time of the day when the heat dropped from
unbearable to merely unpleasant.

Our ANZAC team of Kiwis and Aussies at Taji base. Here we are posing with our
armoured 4WD (courtesy of the US Army) in front of an unfinished building around
the back of our compound. I'm the one kneeling on the left.

Above: A typical soldier's room at Taji base on a typical day. There is a second, equally crowded bed about two feet to the right, and that's about it. Not pictured: the smell of four consistently moist armpits.

Left: Four soldiers (that's me on the right) on leave in Dubai , UAE. Deployment moustaches are virtually mandatory.

at everything, but you just couldn't. He had these huge teeth and laughed like a Disney Viking.

His one weakness, if any, was that he was a pathological troll. If there was ever an opportunity to wind someone up, or trick someone in some way, he had to do it. It didn't matter if it was his best friend, a superior officer, or even a complete stranger. Because of his natural charisma, it rarely got him into trouble. But when it did, he always considered it a fair trade.

Also in our det was Steve Ainsworth. If Aaron was our unit superhero, then Ainsworth was something along the lines of our Dwight Schrute. He was a recluse and frequently put people on edge with his combination of weird, inappropriate jokes and occasional temper tantrums. I wasn't exactly thrilled to be spending five weeks in a high-stress environment with him. But even the prospect of being potentially killed and eaten by the unit loon wasn't enough to curb my enthusiasm for the course ahead.

We spent almost every day for the next two weeks at Recon Platoon's hangar on the other side of camp. It was tucked away behind 2/1st Battalion's regular lines, so for four signalmen, we were very much in enemy territory. Despite the animosity between the two corps at times, we found from day one that the Recon staff were very amicable. They seemed happy to have us along and spent a lot of time with us in those two weeks going over the sorts of skills we would need to brush up on to excel on the course. Luckily for us, the main skills being emphasised were things that we as a squadron practised regularly already, in particular honing the art of Break Contact Drills (BCDs).

Despite what Hollywood and *Modern Warfare* would have you believe, Recon forces are not attacking troops. Their role is primarily scouting, gathering information and sitting in the rain. A successful recon mission ends in the detachment silently leaving their location and vanishing without a trace. In short, if you're a recon soldier and you have to fire your weapon, something has gone terribly wrong.

One of the main reasons for this is that recon detachments are small. Four to five men in enemy territory are going to be outnumbered in any enemy encounter, unless they happen to surprise someone who's just wandered off for a shit. Because recon forces move quietly, deliberately and slowly, they rely on enemy forces announcing themselves and giving the detachment time to duck away or hide while they go past. The films you see where two guys with a machine gun and a Claymore mine ambush thirty enemy soldiers and emerge with only a sexy cut to the cheek to show for it are just nonsense.

But despite all the sneaking around and hypervigilance and generally acting like a family of deer during open season, sometimes recon soldiers do come face to face with enemy forces. It could be that the enemy platoon is resting and not making much noise. The bush can be so dense that you can't see someone until you're pretty much standing on them (soldiers wear camouflage for a reason). It could be that noise interference like rivers, airfields or really terrible weather has masked the footsteps of thirty men moving nearby. Most jarringly, there could be five other idiots just like you trying to sneak through the bush without making a sound. Sometimes recon soldiers come within spitting distance of a hostile soldier holding a loaded weapon; nine times out of ten, there is only one course of action that makes sense.

It is done without question and conducted with maximum SAS: speed, aggression and surprise. This tactic is only possible after weeks of rigorous training and a high level of individual fitness.

We run away.

It's a very structured running away, not quite like King Arthur and his knights fleeing in *Monty Python: The Holy Grail*, but that's exactly what it is.

The general reasoning is as follows.

As a recon element, almost any enemy force we come across will be better manned and better armed than we are. Even if they aren't better armed than we are, they're bound to have more friends nearby than we do.

The goal is to break contact as quickly as possible. This means disrupting any sort of attack that the enemy force might be trying to organise. Assuming that we've encountered the enemy head on, the scout will be the first person to spot them. If kneeling down quietly and hoping they won't notice us isn't an option, the scout will (after identifying beyond doubt that these are, in fact, enemy troops) scream 'CONTACT FRONT!', and spray his entire magazine in the enemy's general direction on full automatic. This will take about two seconds and will be all the time the rest of the detachment has to get into position. Everyone behind the scout takes a few big steps to the side, alternating left or right (so if the person immediately behind the scout goes left, the next person goes right, and so on).

The idea is to make a sort of 'corridor' of people. Now that the scout has emptied his magazine, he'll turn and sprint down the middle of the detachment, all the way to the back. As soon as he's passed the first person, that person will start firing. They should get through ten to fifteen rounds, not aiming for specific zones but rather trying to cover as much of the det's frontage as possible. Once they've done so, they'll turn and run down the corridor.

This can continue for as much as a hundred metres. The idea behind firing so many bullets so quickly is to keep the enemy from organising an attack and to project the illusion that they are dealing with a larger force than just five men. Whoever is carrying the machine gun is going to be firing like bullets are going out of style. In training, I always fired like a maniac because, by my logic, every round I fired into the bush was one less round I had to carry.

In all seriousness, there is an art form to being an effective machine gunner. It involves finding a good firing position, keeping tabs on the leftmost and rightmost enemies (it's up to the gunner to make sure the squad is not flanked) and mentally counting your bullets as you use them. Once you have to reload the gun, the rest of your squad can quickly become sitting ducks, so you have to maintain a balance between firing enough rounds to be effective, but not burning through ammo too fast. Covering fire is an extremely effective way to not get shot. If your enemy is avoiding your bullets, they aren't shooting at you.

Once the det commander feels like there is enough distance between the detachment and the enemy, and they aren't pursuing too closely, he will likely scream 'Bomburst!'

This is the signal to all run away from the point of contact, in different directions. It can often mean that a few people take off at right angles from each other. The general rule of thumb is to run two hundred metres back and regroup, directly behind where the bomburst originated, but to have everyone approach from a variety of angles. This means that any individual being pursued will hopefully not compromise the rest of the det.

Most of the first week at Recon Platoon's hangar passed the same way. We'd get up at 0600, eat a meaty, oily breakfast provided by Ben, the chef, load up our packs, belts and webbing with full, first-line ammunition (for rifles, this was 300 rounds; for the machine gun, it was 1,000) and head off into the bush. Then we'd patrol as silently as possible, trying to move like a big cat stalks.

The best way to move quietly through bush is to gently place the outside of your foot down and wiggle it slightly. This moves small pieces of debris aside and prevents those ghastly 'crack' noises that small sticks make. Once the outside of your foot is down, you roll the rest of your foot down slowly until your big toe takes the weight. Repeating this for each and every footstep is not only mentally and physically exhausting, it's also slow as fuck. It's not uncommon to move less than one kilometre per hour when patrolling like this.

We practised for more than six hours a day those first few days, patrolling back and forth, up and down the same hill. You couldn't relax, or even get complacent for a moment. Every so often, without warning, an instructor might fire off a few rounds or throw a Thunderflash at us and yell 'CONTACT!' and we'd have to go through our BCDs. If we didn't run fast enough, or communicate our movements effectively, we'd do them again, and again, and again, until we were slumped over, sweating and swearing.

Spending my days alternating between creeping around in absolute stealth or crashing through the bush firing our weapons and screaming at one another began to take a toll. I collapsed into my skinny bunk each night and slept like a rock for as long as humanly possible.

Towards the end of the first week, we began receiving longer assignments. We were given a stretch of road or a particular stream to monitor. We'd patrol there, in complete silence, communicating only with hand signals. Then we'd establish an OP (observation post) and watch the target in pairs. We'd have to record every person we saw coming and going: vehicles, registrations and so on. The people we saw would be instructing staff wearing disguises, or carrying random assortments of objects. Sometimes we'd observe for an hour or less before receiving the radio call to return to Dip Flat. On one of the days we lay there for seven hours, well past sundown. When we got back to base, our detachment would be questioned by one of the Military Intelligence Operators to ascertain if we had gathered accurate and important information.

It was on one of these assignments that the final test was sprung on us.

We got up, nodded politely at Ben while he shovelled more fried grease onto our plates and huddled around Corporal Spinney to receive our morning briefing. It was freezing cold, despite the morning being completely cloudless.

The Dip Flat training area is in the middle of an enormous valley. A sheer mountain range rises steeply in the east, and the wide river to the west quickly gives way to more thick, steep bush. This means that in winter you don't actually feel the first rays of sunlight until it's nearly noon. Then it becomes unbearably hot as the sandflies, mosquitos and wasps emerge to harass any and all mammals they can find (especially tall, furless ones moving quietly and cautiously). After spending the middle of the day creeping and crashing through the bush at sporadic intervals, we'd be drenched in sweat and dirt and cobwebs and that weary feeling you get when you know the end is nowhere in sight. By 1600, the sun would be nestled on top of the horizon. About thirty minutes later the temperature would plummet once again.

We had a morning of theory, which involved relearning the ERV (emergency rendezvous) drills and practising more hand signals. This was one of my favourite parts of the course, as we were now at a level where we could nearly have entire conversations with only one hand, and very little speech.

We were standing around Everly. Alleycat and I passed a cigarette back and forth. Even with my webbing and a beanie on, it was crisp and cold. Everly pointed out the building that we were to survey and the route we were to take. I was so familiar with the valley at this point that I only needed a glance to realise that the 'enemy building' was just another part of the camp. It was about 300 metres away, as the tūī flies. We would be taking a slightly longer route, out the back of camp and hooking around to approach it from the bush, instead of cutting through camp. It would take us less than an hour by my estimation. Good. I was sick of creeping around, flinching every time someone stepped on a leaf.

We began shouldering our packs and I nudged Taylor. 'Staff are getting a bit lazy, aren't they? That building is legit a part of camp. It's just over there.' I gestured with the barrel of my gun.

Aaron nodded and stood on his tiptoes. At over six foot, he could see further than me.

'Lazy as, bro. I can fucking see it from here.'

I laughed as he shrugged his pack on. 'Whatever, maybe we'll get to eat lunch in camp today.'

'Yeah, wouldn't want our grease levels to get too low.'

'Hey! Doctors recommend that you drink eight glasses of grease a day. You gotta stay on top of that.'

We kept joking as we strolled through camp. When you walk with a heavy pack on and your arms are cradling a weapon, you can't help but adopt this ambling gait that is reminiscent of someone in one of those old-fashioned diving suits. It also compels you to crack terrible jokes and replace the word 'yes' with the phrase 'fuckin' oath' at several octaves below your speaking voice.

We quietened down once we reached the edge of the bush. It was go time.

One of the first things you do before going into any patch of deep bush is to acclimatise. This means entering the tree line, making sure you're out of sight and just kneeling for five to ten minutes. You close your mind off to thinking about the mission, or whether you brought enough extra rations or not, and you open up your senses. Look at the colour of the bush, the layout of the forest floor. Listen for the consistent noises: birds, bugs, running water, whatever it is that you need to categorise as background noise. The same goes for smells. Each bushland has its own unique, earthy smell. All of these sights, sounds and smells need to be sitting in your mind, so that you can instantly notice when something is amiss.

Long before you see an enemy soldier, if you're alert to it, you'll hear them. Not crashing footsteps or the sound of them sliding a magazine into their rifle. You'd only hear that if they are a pack of absolute fucking muppets. You'll hear the silence they create. Birds are smart enough to stop singing when large, predatory animals go walking beneath them. Many of them will in fact have a secondary call, which I'm sure translates roughly to, 'Holy fucking shit, what are *those*?!'

Once you've been a decent amount of time staring at fallen leaves, you start to notice sign pretty quickly. Nothing in nature even remotely resembles a boot print.

The acclimatisation also gives you time to get ready for the long stints of absolute silence. It sounds strange, but for most people (especially chatterboxes like myself) you don't realise how much unnecessary verbalising we do. Once you're in the bush, two or three days can go by with only a few whispered sentences being exchanged between the five people in your det.

Everly gave us the 'knife hand' gesture and we 'shook out'; in other words, he made his left hand into a karate chop shape and pointed directly into the bush, and we arranged ourselves in marching order. He swept his arm in a straight line, indicating we were patrolling in file, and then extended his fingers and clenched his fist twice. Two fives, meaning ten-metre spacing between each man in the file. For relatively open bush such as this, this was fine. In dense bush or jungle you need to be closer to avoid losing sight of each other. You need to observe how the man in front of you navigates each obstacle, such as a fallen tree or patch of bush. This minimises the sign you leave behind and reduces the chance of you stepping on a huge, dry branch and making a crack that 'can be heard in Canada' as the instructors would warn us.

We patrolled slowly, silently. Aaron was in front, taking long, cautious strides and scanning constantly. There was almost certainly a group of instructors out there waiting to jump us. We needed to spot them and hit them with the old 'defensive attack' before they had too much of a chance to start causing large casualties in our group. As tough as BCDs in the bush were, crashing through the bush with a pack and a weapon is even more tiring when you have to drag one of your 'wounded' comrades.

Behind Aaron was Platts, wielder of the map, constantly communicating with Aaron through hand signals to keep us on course. I came next, then Ainsworth with the radio, and finally Everly in the 2IC position so that he could watch and assess. We moved with the utmost caution and managed a kilometre in slightly over an hour. The hot part of the day was approaching and I was dripping with sweat. The bush began to fill with the sounds of swarming insects. They buzzed around my neck and exposed forearms. Military-issue mosquito repellent is so chemically toxic it's practically a war crime. If you left it top-down on a counter-top overnight, by morning it would have melted a decent hole in the surface.

I had hastily run repellent over myself that morning. Despite this, sandflies began landing on my arms in the tiny gaps I had missed. They swarmed to these spots, covering my arms in stripes of buzzing, flapping, feeding parasites.

I managed to use my left hand to sweep a few off my arm, but I didn't dare remove my right hand from the grip. Taking your master hand off your weapon on patrol was a cardinal sin, and Everly, the literal sniper, would 100% see if I committed said sin to do something as trivial as trying to keep some blood inside my body.

Another hour and 600 metres later (we hit some thick bush) we stopped for 'a ten'. Slowly moving into a large circle, we took our packs off one at time in painstaking slowness. Dropping to one knee, you have to leave your weapon hanging from its sling (extra fun with the ten-kilogram machine gun), unclip one of your shoulder straps and slide your pack around to rest on your extended thigh. Then you pick up all thirty kilos, which your arms don't even encircle properly, and lower the pack to the ground as silently as possible. The last six inches are a biceps workout all on their own. For five people to do this takes ten minutes; a ten-minute rest often ends up being over half an hour.

We sat on our packs, weapons at the ready, facing out. One at a time, we were allowed to reach into our outer pockets and retrieve a snack and a water bottle. We all carried a small amount of food and two litres of water in our webbing, but you did your best to save this until absolutely necessary. If you ever get separated from your pack, you need to have as many rations on you as possible.

Ainsworth did our radio check and informed HQ in a hushed whisper that we were on track and less than a kilometre from our designated OP.

I was one of the first to have my pack on, but I had to remain kneeling until everyone had theirs on too. It was right then, at this critical moment when I was precariously balanced and my hands were full of machine gun, that the wasp appeared.

I was wearing ballistic sunglasses, mostly because I thought they looked cool as hell with my face paint and the skull-emblazoned buff I wore around my head.

It landed right on my left lens and buzzed a challenge at me. I flinched. The wasp did not. It stood there, less than an inch from my open eyeball, buzzing and yellow and huge. I gently blew some air upwards at it, trying to emulate a gentle breeze. The wasp went in the opposite direction I wanted it to. Instead of flying away, it crawled downwards to the bottom of my glasses and proceeded to climb up *inside of the lens*. I felt its wings graze my eyelashes.

I was sweating 'like a vegan at a barbecue' as Corporal Arapeta used to say. Of course, nobody else in the detachment had any idea I was going through my own version of the *Saw* franchise. They were facing out, looking for lurking NCOs in the bushes. I was so distracted by the threat of being blinded, I doubt I would've noticed if a platoon of clowns had come bursting out of the foliage playing trumpets. Every single atom of my focus was directed at the wasp. I *willed* it to leave. It crawled around on the lens in lazy circles.

I was shaking now, straining from the stress and the heat and the balancing act of staying on one knee with my huge pack on my back. I noticed out of the corner of my eye that everyone was beginning to stand up. I didn't dare move. I didn't want to speak or signal either. I decided that imitating a tree was the best strategy for keeping my eyeball un-stung. As far as I knew, wasps didn't attack trees with the same reckless hate that they attacked everything else with.

Everly obviously noticed that his det gunner was still on one knee, staring straight ahead, evidently not breathing, because he approached me. I heard the faintest murmur next to my ear.

'You alright, bro?'

As soon as his hand touched my shoulder, the wasp simply dropped off my glasses and flew away.

Just like that. Fucking magical. I resisted the urge to start kissing Everly's boots and instead just nodded. He didn't need any more explanation; he just patted my shoulder again and we shook out and carried on walking.

We patrolled on, checking our arcs in wide sweeps and settling into the balance of quiet but (relatively) quick travel. Just as we were approaching the last stretch before the proposed OP, Aaron held up his hand for a halt. Strangely, Everly didn't seem to notice. He was staring at the same treeline as Aaron, but didn't approach him. Platts did though. I saw Aaron raise his rifle to look through his scope. Everly was staring intensely into the trees. I saw movement. A bird? Or was that a hand in a black glove? I craned my neck for a better angle.

Aaron let loose with a spray of automatic fire into the treeline, at about his ten o'clock. The sound of gunshots disintegrated the silence of the bush.

'CONTACT FRONT!' he screamed.

Legend: he'd spotted the enemy party before they pulled the trigger on their ambush. That made us look good already. I was already moving before Aaron had finished saying 'front'. I saw a fallen tree, sprinted towards it and landed so I was practically riding it like Harry Potter nose-diving for the golden snitch.

There was loads of movement in the trees now. Shots began to ring out from several spots in the treeline. I saw glimpses of faces and heard barked orders as the Recon NCOs began to organise themselves into a firing line. I heard the hiss of a Thunderflash being sparked, aimed my gun towards the sound and flicked off my safety catch, then squeezed the trigger. My immaculately oiled machine-gun began spewing blank rounds. The belt disappeared into the maw of the hungry gun as I went through the first forty rounds in one long burst. Being the machine gun in a firefight means making your presence known; a machine gun can fire more rounds in five seconds than *three* rifles. A long burst says to the enemy, 'Here I am. Get your fucking head down, or I'll take it off.'

My ears were ringing already. Brass and link glimmered on the ground amongst the deadfall. I kept firing, shorter bursts this time. Three to five rounds with each tiny squeeze, aiming at any and all movement I saw ahead of me. It felt like we were doing well. To my right, the boys were shooting and moving through their BCDs. There were definitely less rounds coming at us than we were firing back. It seemed like we could actually win this contact. All that Everly had to do was to direct us to attack and—

'BOMBURST, GO GO GO!' Everly's usually quiet voice punched through the firefight like a foghorn.

Bomburst? Shit.

It was time to get out of there. The det started firing and moving away from the contact. I kept firing until I was sure everyone was behind me. I was rewarded with a hissing sound as a silver canister arced over my head and landed on the ground ten feet in front of me. Thick, acrid vapour poured out of the smoke grenade. It was an oily green colour and it stank. It stained the ground where it landed and began to obscure the bushes I'd been firing into. Hopefully it obscured me too. 'MOVING!' I yelled to my det for some cover, then hoisted the gun up, turned and ran.

I was crashing through the undergrowth, occasionally stumbling as my foot punched through a mass of twigs and cobwebs that looked like solid ground. I saw Platts briefly, but he was running at almost a right angle to me, as he should be. We were supposed to be running to where we had last halted. It shouldn't take long at full speed. I risked a glance backwards and saw Ainsworth leaning against a tree and firing back towards the enemy. His medal would arrive in the post, I was sure. I kept running. Suddenly, I heard more shots ring out, away and up the hill from our original contact. Whatever it was, I wanted to be far away from it. I altered my course so I was running directly away from the new sounds of gunfire and people hoarsely barking commands.

I later found out that Alleycat-Platt had decided that the OpFor was less likely to chase him uphill. He had sprinted up the small bank, thinking he was in the clear, only to walk directly between the rest of the OpFor and the other recon section they were just about to attack, or 'bump' in recon slang. Getting bumped meant going through BCDs. OpFor kicked off their assault early, and the recon detachment thought that Platt was there flanking them, so they began firing at him with extreme prejudice. What ensued was an extremely confusing clusterfuck of a BCD, with OpFor firing at the det, the det hollering commands at each other and firing at Platts, and an exhausted Platts firing at everyone and screaming at the top of his lungs, still running as fast as he could.

I kept crashing though the bush, heading slightly downhill. As a general rule, when trying to escape a contact you run as hard as you can and as fast as you can, for as long as you can. For me, with my pack, webbing, machine gun and everything else, that meant running for about three straight minutes. Once I was gasping and my run had become a limp-footed shuffle, I sagged against a tree and tried to quieten my heaving breath while taking stock. I had no idea where anybody else was. I was still a couple of hundred metres away from the rest spot with the wasp, so I decided I would try and approach it as quietly as possible. The time for madly crashing through the bush was (hopefully) over. Time to go stealth.

I gulped down some water and heaved myself to my feet. Once I could see the ERV, I sat back a distance and tried to conceal myself in a thick bush. I couldn't see any of the guys from my det, so I assumed I was the first to make it back. Fine, I'd wait for the others here. SOPs said that I should wait five minutes for them and then move through the rest of the OTR (on the run) drills. I knew that there was an OTR component to Patrol Procedures, so I was hardly surprised when nobody showed up. That was that, then: I was now going to be hunted through the forest for however long it took for the Recon NCOs to find me. I chewed on a fruit bar while I made up my mind how to move forward.

The rendezvous point that we had been using for all our tasks so far was about 6 kilometres away, up and over some roads, back towards the turn off from the main highway leading into the Dip Flat training area. I hadn't actually been there yet, and because RVs were so often notional in training exercises, I hadn't given much thought to where it was, exactly.

I was determined not to get caught. Or at least, not get caught before anybody else. I was a signaller on a grunt course. There was some serious corps pride on the line here. Not only that, but the last time sigs had gone on this course it had been a disaster. I thought of Banner, hurling his rank slide onto the snow and stomping his feet.

No fucking way. If these guys wanted to catch me, they'd have to drag me out of the top of a tree or from deep inside a hole in the ground.

A stick cracked less than ten feet away from me.

I swung around immediately, my machine gun ready. I couldn't see anyone. I started squirming my feet around, ready to jump up and start legging it. Then I heard a noise, similar to the sound people make when trying to convince a cat to approach them. I knew that noise really well, because Aaron always made it when trying to get someone's attention without speaking. Whistling was an amateur mistake, because a human whistle carries really far (hence why farmers use it to talk to their dogs) and whispering was nearly as bad. A small 'ch-ch' could be just about anything. Except this time, it was definitely big Taylor.

His head poked out from around a large tree. We made eye contact. I sagged with relief and Aaron grinned. His giant, tombstone teeth stood out amongst his roughly slapped-on cam paint.

Aaron and I quickly jammed ourselves into a nearby bush and exchanged anecdotes from the 'bump' in hushed whispers. Once we agreed that this was definitely the OTR drill, we decided to whip out the map and decide on a route to the ERV.

Aaron was the one who decided on the route in the end. He was already a scout, and better with maps than I was. I also happened to be holding the much bigger gun, so I scanned all around us, with my head on a swivel, while Aaron was concentrating on working out where we would go. Once he seemed satisfied, we slipped our packs on and set off down the hill. We made it about ten steps before another obstacle presented itself.

Aaron stepped off a large rock and dropped about two feet. I went to do the same, and the moment my boot hit the ground, the clip of my left pack strap exploded in a shower of overworked plastic and my pack swung off my back, smashing into the ground and dragging me with it. I lay there, in a heap of confused DPM, and managed to wriggle upright.

Aaron was there in a flash. He looked concerned for me, but not nearly as concerned as he was about the absolute racket I had just made. We agreed, in hurried whispers, that my clip was pretty well fucked, and I settled for tying it back together with an ugly, but reliable, reef knot. I had used this pack since basic training. It had spent more time in the bush than some trees at this point. I could replace the clip, but not here. For now, I would have to undo my pack only on one side and leave the left side tied up tightly. Fine, whatever. One more inconvenience to add to the list.

While I made a ramshackle repair of my pack, Aaron and I had a pep talk. We needed to get into a winning mentality.

The next twenty-four hours or so were likely to be extremely unpleasant, but Aaron and I both agreed that we would not go quietly. Not only were we both competitive individuals by nature, we wanted to give our squadron a good name. It wouldn't look good if the first signallers allowed back on this course were the first to get nabbed.

We spent the next hour or so walking silently along the side of a slope, keeping the river on our left and freezing every time we heard any sort of movement. There was still the occasional sounds of gunfire and vehicles careening down the dirt roads that snaked through the bush. But the gunfire was further from us each time and only once did a vehicle drive along the road that was directly up the hill from us.

When all your focus is on the here and now, it's amazing how quickly time can get away from you. Although we were making terrible time in a patrolling sense of the word, before I knew it we were three-quarters of the way there. Aaron asked if we should do dinner, and I realised it was pretty much dark. We scanned around and found a thicket wrapped around a tree stump. We dropped down onto our stomachs and crawled into the middle of it, dragging our packs in after us. We decided to sleep until an hour or so before dawn, then we'd set off again.

Not daring to take our boots off or do anything else that might slow us down if we were found, we each wrapped our sleeping bags around ourselves and dozed fitfully, one at a time, while the other kept watch. I don't know how the winter Patrol Procedures managed this part. It was thoroughly cold and miserable.

About half an hour before I was due to wake Taylor up, I heard movement. It was someone walking along, doing their best not to make a noise. I tried to turn my head without disturbing any of the foliage I was resting in. With the sliver of moonlight and my eyes filled with visual purple, I saw a head, and the outline of a rifle. The figure was ten feet away from me. Then, they stifled a cough. A familiar, honking sort of cough I had heard many, many times before.

I clicked my tongue twice.

The figure went down on one knee, trying to figure out where the clicking had come from. We remained in this stand off for several long, uncomfortable moments. Then, finally, Aaron broke the silence.

'Ainsworth, hurry the fuck up and get over here.'

Ainsworth's shoulders sagged with relief. He shuffled over and squeezed into our rough hide. He explained in a hurried whisper that he'd almost been encircled by the staff and had ended up hiding under an overhang for the better part of the day, listening to vehicles rumble back and forth over his head. He'd only started moving again once the sun had gone down.

It was before dawn, meaning that visibility was almost nil. Usually, this means you avoid moving because of the risk of making a racket, but since Ainsworth was there, and we were already awake, we thought, fuck it, let's try and make the ERV before the staff wake up and start hunting again.

We made it in less than an hour. At one point we did have to leap down a muddy bank to avoid being spotted by a ute that came bursting around a corner at high speed, but otherwise it went without incident. We confirmed the coordinates on the map and found a small ranger's hut at the ERV. We nervously knocked on the door, rifles raised in case it was some sort of trap. It wasn't. A bleary-eyed Recon sergeant opened the door and frowned at us.

'What.' It was an accusation, not a question.

None of knew what to say. We had just survived the escape and evasion phase, hadn't we? Were we supposed to have done something else? There was a long silence. My shoulder ached where my ramshackle packstrap had been digging into it. Eventually, the ever-chipper Aaron spoke up.

'We've gone through our rendezvous procedures, Sarge.'

The sergeant wasn't impressed. 'So what? You want a fucking cookie?'

Aaron, a man born impervious to sarcasm, looked as though he was about to ask if the sergeant had any cookies of the chocolate chip variety.

The sergeant shot him down with a glare, and then sighed heavily.

'Let me get my fucking boots on and I'll drive you back to camp.'

That's the thing about the military. If you're given a task, even if it's impossibly difficult, or dangerous, nobody gives you a pat on the back or special treatment for getting it done. They simply acknowledge that the task is complete and then start looking at what else they can get you to do.

It's your *job*, after all.

We were driven back to Dip Flat, cold, exhausted and a bit battered, but stoked that at least three members of our det had made it without being captured. We found out later that five people were caught by the roaming staff, not including one poor unfortunate soul who had dropped his pack and recklessly crossed the river to escape capture, only to spend the night shivering, wet and alone. After that whole ordeal, he was reprimanded for endangering himself so thoroughly that it was as though he'd failed anyway. To be fair, being on the run without any of your gear, and possibly hypothermic, is not exactly a 'clean getaway'.

That was the last major event of Recon Patrol Procedures, one of the hardest but most rewarding courses I ever attended.

PART 3

FUN AND GAMES

NO WAY DOWN

IT WAS LATE 2014 and I had been in 3 Signal Squadron for almost two years. We were hosting a medium-sized exercise that included four Canadian EWOPs who had been sent to our squadron for six months on exchange. They were all brilliant, but I got on particularly well with a tall, gangly, bespectacled dad named Bobby. He had been a solider for a good long while, but despite this was a very positive and optimistic sort of guy.

Our squadron was out in full force. We had taken over yet another random field, generously lent to us by some patriotic farmer, and were about to start sending detachments up into the mountains to establish LPs. This was a strange exercise for me because, for the very first time, I wasn't in a det. I had been assigned to Headquarters. That meant sitting back in the FOB, manning the radio, doing sentry and all the other shit jobs that officers and sergeants don't want to do.

I was hilariously out of practice at being around the command team. Although it's true that working in the dets is cold, exhausting and sometimes downright punishing work, at least you don't have to shave your face each morning or relocate an entire antenna array every six hours because the replacement duty sergeant has 'just had a great idea'.

Being with the HQ team was like being back at camp, but with all the downsides of being out in the field. I quickly decided that it was the detachment life for me, so I was actually relieved when they told me that Hugo (one of the Canadians) had ruined his ankle and would need me to take his spot in his detachment.

I was tossed into 66-Bravo with Bobby, Granger, Aaron and good ol' Corporal Walker, and off we went. Our first infil was difficult, to say the least. We were dropped off in the dead of night on the side of a gravel road. When we looked at the map, our route in looked as though we would have to work our way straight down a gulley to a streambed, and then cross the stream in order to climb up the other side. It looked bloody steep, but was only a three-kilometre walk before we could set up our LP and start collecting. I was cheerful. It was almost 2200. With luck, it wouldn't be long after midnight before I was in my sleeping bag.

You would have thought by now I would have learned a thing or two about optimism.

The slope was impossible. We started working our way down the gulley, only to watch it turn from a steep hill to a gravel mudslide, and then further down it became a vertical drop into a deep and wide river. Telling us to remain where we were, Walker and Aaron took off their packs and scurried down to take a closer look. They were gone for almost twenty minutes, but even before I heard their boots on the rocks, I knew what they were going to say.

'There's no way down,' whispered Taylor as he wriggled his pack back onto his shoulders.

Walker shook his head in agreement. 'Only way we'd make it down there is with some abseiling gear and a fucking raft. This map is either outdated, or just written by some lazy prick who didn't actually take a look down there.'

I had to agree with him. The four of us knew what a steep slope ought to read on a map, and this vertical descent had not been represented at all.

After lighting a cigarette and frowning at the map for a while, Walker finally worked out the only route that was an option to us. 'You're not going to like this, lads,' he whispered as we huddled around him. He used a tiny red light to show us where we would be walking (soldiers use red lights because it doesn't travel as far as light in other wavelengths) and moved the edge of his compass to show our proposed route (you never use your finger to point things out on a map, because they're round and therefore cover hundreds of square metres when you place them on a map, making them horrendously imprecise pointing tools. I always opted for a blade of grass, or a pen).

Grass or not, the route was easy enough to spot. We had to carry on down the rough road we were on, downstream to the east for a considerable distance, until the cliffs gave way to riverbanks that would allow a crossing. Then we simply had to walk back *up* the hill westward, until we arrived at our originally proposed destination.

All of us were frantically doing the same mental calculation, knowing the map's scale instinctively (almost all military maps use a 50,000:1 scale) and trying to work out how far this new route was going to be.

Aaron, of course, got there first. 'Almost nineteen kilometres,' he sighed. 'That'll be fun.'

Granger and Jackson were less cheerful.

'What the fucking fuck is this shit,' huffed Granger.

'Gotta say I agree with Granger here, fellas. This sure is fucky, eh?' chimed in Bobby.

We had no choice. We threw on our packs and tried to walk at a quick, yet sustainable pace. We didn't practise much in the way of tactical patrolling. We were miles away from any supposed enemy activity, at considerable elevation. It was a long night. We stopped every two to three kilometres, for water and a bite of something sweet. Except Granger, that is: at our first stop, I was amazed to see him reach into the top of his pack and produce a perfectly wrapped McDonald's cheeseburger. Nobody else commented and he ate it without saying a word.

Even walking as fast as we were, the grey light of dawn was just beginning to settle on the tops of rocks and tree branches when we arrived at our originally proposed LP. I was exhausted. It had been twenty-four hours since I last slept and the thought of being in my sleeping bag with my iPod going made me especially sleepy.

Aaron was the first on radio shift. He was still fiddling around with the settings and making minor adjustments to the antenna while I was laying out my sleeping mat and bag beside him. He got a hold of someone on the other end and started receiving a message. I was close enough to hear the exchange.

'This is 66-Bravo, we are halted, in LP, initiating collect, over,' whispered Aaron.

'66-Bravo this is Zero-Alpha. Understood. Message incoming, prepare to copy.'

Aaron, like any good radio operator, already had a pencil and paper sitting on his lap.

'Roger, send over,' he replied.

'You are to collapse LP and relocate to figures 667898, setup no later than 1500 hours over.'

I was getting into my sleeping bag, but at this I paused, one of my boots halfway off. Walker had also paused, midway through rolling a cigarette.

Neither of us said anything, but our thoughts were identical. 'Surely not.'

Aaron rolled his eyes as he responded.

'Roger Zero-Alpha, confirm that we are to collapse current LP and move to figures 667898 ASAP?'

'Roger, pack down and move. Zero-Alpha out.'

As one, we gave a collective groan. Knowing our current coordinates on the map, hearing the new grid reference meant we didn't even need to check the map to know that where we were going was at least several kilometres away. And not one of us had managed even a moment of sleep. Walker sighed and lit his cigarette. Granger reached into his pack and pulled out another perfect cheeseburger. He said nothing, merely chewed thoughtfully while I looked on in exhausted astonishment.

THE HILL HAVE EYES (AND PROBABLY SHOTGUNS)

DURING MY TIME IN 3 Signals Squadron, I was involved in dozens of exercises. Several of these were 'brigade level', which meant that a significant portion of the entire NZ Army (and the Air Force and Navy) were all involved at once. They were huge operations, often lasting up to a month. When you're a member of a small detachment, from a small unit, it's easy to be overlooked (as the incident with the artillery battery had taught me). One such exercise was Kiwi Koru, all the way back in 2014.

Our RRT was sent up to join a recon det for a task that would take one or two days. The usual business: helicopter onto the side of a mountain somewhere in the remote South Island, clamber to the summit and do the sneaky-sneaky until the all-powerful voice on the radio told us to pack down.

The det consisted of good old Alleycat Platt, Oscar Hughes and the long-suffering GG. We met up with the guys from Recon Platoon and got on the helo that was meant to take us to our DOP (drop-off point). From there we would walk the rest of the way to the pre-determined hide.

The helo took off and we spent about thirty minutes in the air, beelining to the DOP. I remember feeling grateful it wasn't a long trip, because I was desperate to take a piss; of course, as fate would have it, the helo had to abort due to cloud. This meant we not only had to back track, we had to fly all the way to a nearby air force base to refuel. It took nearly an hour. Flying through fog and low cloud in the dead of night might have been a magical experience, but all I could think about was how badly I didn't want to piss my pants. It was agony.

Finally, the helo touched down and I managed to hobble away into some bushes. If you've ever been bursting to the point of desperation, you'll understand how finally relieving yourself is practically a religious experience. I emerged from the bushes and was informed that we'd be driven to our location instead. It was well and truly nightfall at this point and the air was chill with moisture.

Two detachments, packs, machine guns and all, crammed into the back of a single Pinzgauer and started making our way to the deployment zone, with a brief stop at a local McDonalds along the way. It is fun to see the reaction you get wandering into an eatery in the middle of nowhere and asking for a quarter-pounder to go amidst ten camouflaged, armed soldiers.

Things started going wrong as soon as we hit the DOP. It was one of those gravel roads that loosely connect neighbouring farms. There was a distant house, a vast pine forest to the east, and acres of dairy farm all around. It must have been past midnight by this time, and not even one second after getting out of the wagon, gruff shouting erupted from a nearby house. It wasn't a friendly shout either (if there is such a thing). Mostly comments along the lines of, 'You bloody bastards, get the fuck off my land,' in a voice that resonated with generations of casual alcoholism and inbreeding. The farmer's house was semi-concealed behind a tall hedge that followed the curve of the road, so all we could see was his silhouette superimposed by the bright house lights he had on his front porch, maybe fifty metres away. We got all our stuff off the wagon and the driver gave us a 'good luck' before fucking off back the way they came as quickly as possible.

The recon det wasted no time and began barrelling up the road before us poor EWOPs had gotten our forty-kilogram packs on, loading each other up one at a time. By the time we stood up, they were a good 100 metres away from us. The farmer was still there, going berserk.

Platts made a gesture and we made a quick exit the opposite way, towards some dark sheds and away from the house. We walked fifty metres away and halted behind a shed before doing a nav check and realising that, of course, we had set off in the wrong direction. We needed to go back up the road and pass by the house again. We couldn't move further east of the house, as there was eight-foot deer fencing and it immediately opened into a deep quarry of sorts. We elected to wait until the farmer got bored of peering into the darkness.

It ended up being almost twenty minutes before the lights finally clicked off and we felt like we could move without being accosted by a shotgun-wielding insomniac. We walked as slowly and as quietly as we could, the dirt road crunching beneath our feet like cornflakes. As soon as we were coming up next to the hedge that enclosed the farmhouse, the lights turned back on, the front door crashed open and the farmer burst out onto his porch. We were now only about fifteen metres away from him, standing in dead silence.

We froze, praying that there was enough darkness to shroud us. His black silhouette loomed there on the porch. I swear I felt his eyes burning through the hedge, which now felt very sparse indeed. This went for an unbearable amount of time (probably not even five minutes in reality). My back ached under the strain of my pack. I craned my neck to look back at Oscar, who was nervously licking his lips, his eyes fixed on the shadowy figure. Finally, the farmer went inside and turned off the lights. We stayed there for another five minutes, then backed off slowly and regrouped in a ditch a few metres down from the house.

Looking at the map, we decided to go around the back of his property and get back onto the road further north. Once the insane farmer's house was at our back, we trekked hard and fast for a good 500 metres before ungracefully clambering over a small fence and into a large open paddock. The moon had crept out from behind the clouds and we had a clear view of the paddock and our route up to the treeline that was to become our LP.

The paddock was undulating, with sporadic clusters of gorse throughout. We moved in single file, making our way past some dozy-looking, but very much awake, cows, who by now were becoming curious at our intrusion. As we weaved our way through the herd, it occurred to me that they didn't seem at all worried by four strange mammals wandering through their midst. Instead of clustering together as cows usually do, they stood stock still and forced us to move around them.

We had been walking, halting and kneeling for quite some time, and my back was starting to ache. Evidently, so was everyone else's, because the next time we paused to give Oscar a chance to consult the map, GG leaned forward and shuffled his pack around on his back, a familiar jiggle that gives the wearer's shoulders a few precious moments of respite. As he jerked his pack forward to make it more comfortable, something happened. The sudden movement sent a ripple of wariness through the cowherd. It wasn't panic, yet, but they had most certainly changed their collective setting from curious to alarmed. The vibe was beginning to change.

I stared at the nearest cow, which was no more than five metres away. It was staring at an oblivious GG as he wiggled and squirmed his enormous pack around. The cow's tongue flicked out and it rolled its eyes. The moonlight glinted off its horns.

Horns? I thought to myself absently.

There were other cows drawing closer now. One of them turned away from me and GG and started strutting towards

Oscar and Platts, two gigantic testicles swinging between its legs like a pair of fuzzy kettlebells.

The penny dropped. Not a cow. In fact, there was not one set of udders to be seen.

Shit. We had wandered into a paddock of full-grown bulls, and the novelty of our presence was beginning to wear off. Without taking my eyes off the nearest bull, I stepped up to GG and gripped his arm. He stopped moving. I whispered to him, pleading: 'Stop.'

Oscar turned and waved us towards him. We slowly congregated at the base of the hill, where we figured the gorse would hide us and the bulls could carry on like normal.

We figured wrong. Unfortunately, once the bulls could hear and smell us but no longer see us, they stressed out even more. They became almost instantly agitated. As we grunted and strained to walk up the increasingly steep hillside, we heard them snorting and poking their heads through the scrub. Then, a thundering off hoofbeats grew terrifyingly loud as a particularly bold (or stupid) bull crashed through a bush right next to us.

'Jesus Christ,' Platts gasped as the bull careened past him, missing his pack by less than a foot.

We broke all pretence of tactical patrolling and scrambled our way through the labyrinth as fast as we could, bulls smashing around us wildly. As we neared the top, we could see the fence line. Each man broke for the safety of the other side and threw his pack over into the next paddock before diving over himself. We lay there on the pine needles. My hands shook with fatigue and fear.

Having made it safely to the other side of the fence, we checked the map. We were now about 200 metres north of the farmer's house, where we had started around two hours ago. We were also some five kilometres from our proposed position, and the sun was meant to come up in the next hour. Rather than risk our chances on the roads with the deranged farmer, we moved to the nearest high feature and called it in. We set up a hasty position and spent the next day there, feverishly watching from the bushes as the farmer chopped wood and did other mundane daily activities.

HOSKEN

OUR DETACHMENT WAS STILL lingering in the FOB, caught in the limbo that betides soldiers between missions. Our gear was drying out, we had restocked our food and ammunition, and we were wandering around camp like vagrants, tactfully begging for cigarettes. As usual, without ceremony or pomp, the exercise was suddenly over. 'Aunty Huia' was simply called over the radio one day, and that was that.

Aunty Huia is a piece of NZ Army folklore: a fictional kindly old woman who will take pity on suffering field soldiers, emerging from the bushes with baked goods and to do their laundry. She's nearly always referred to sarcastically. Corporals will look down on a cold, hungry recruit feeling sorry for themselves and chide them: 'What are you waiting for? Aunty Huia to come along with some muffins? Maybe she'll wash your clothes and knit you a scarf too?'

But it's also officially unofficial that when an exercise is over, the role-playing is done with and everyone can start getting ready to 'EndEx', whoever is in charge will get on the main radio net and simply say: 'All callsigns, this is Zero-Alpha. Aunty Huia. I say again, Aunty Huia.'

As soon as you hear that on the radio, everyone starts to relax a bit. You don't have to be silent, or post sentries. You can smoke freely, and so on.

As you can see, real or imaginary, everybody loves Aunty Huia.

However, the EndEx of Kiwi Koru was different for 3 Signal Squadron. We were heading to our HQ tent to retrieve our cell phones out of the lockbox and start responding to wives, girlfriends or (in my case) the local Tinder situation, only to see Sergeant Collins looking uncharacteristically grim. He told us to sit on the bench beside the mass of cables and blinking boxes that made up the EW Command Tent. Eventually, everyone in our squadron was gathered, unsure why we were there.

We were informed that Sig Hosken, who lived in barracks with us, had just died as a result of suicide.

We were stunned. I knew Hosk pretty well. We worked together, drank together, and he would tell me about his son. He always took the kid on these great adventures. But he was struggling, and nobody knew. That enforced stoicism, that 'I can handle it alone' attitude that society places on young men, had claimed another victim.

The entire squadron was at his funeral. The haka we gave him shook the walls and rattled the windows. We screamed ourselves hoarse.

Rest in peace, Hosk. The only other thing I can say to anyone reading this is, check on your friends. I wish I had.

THE CHILDREN OF THE CLAY

IT WAS ON EXERCISE Kiwi Koru that we first put Sergeant Collins's digging-in tactic to the test. The results were mixed, to say the least.

There were four of us in the detachment. Oscar Hughes (Hughey), a longtime 3 Sig solider, Griffon-Graham (GG), a guy even newer to the squadron than I was, and good old Alleycat Platt, our det commander.

We were dropped off on the side of a large terrain feature, late at night. It was so dark that we had to patrol wearing NVGs (night vision goggles).

This is nowhere near as fun as it sounds. In action movies, when the elite commandos burst in and start shooting up all the bad guys and the camera switches to night vision, it's always a crystal-clear representation of the world. This is not what you see when you look through NVGs. For starters, NVGs only show you things in two dimensions, there is no sense of depth, and everything can only be represented in one colour, that sickly, florescent green. In practice, a small rise in the grassy field you're walking along looks *exactly* the same as a small depression does. Patrolling with the crushing weight of a det pack and continuously stepping down when you should have stepped up, and vice-versa, makes for a very nerve-wracking, exhausting way to move around.

We walked along the side of the huge hill (more of a grassy mountain) and eventually wound our way up to a pine forest. We used the cover of the pine forest to reach our LP, which was to be set up near the top, facing down into the plains below us so we could survey a large area. It had started to rain. Platts and Hughes went ahead to find a suitable place to start digging while GG and I set up the radio for a quick chat back to base.

Platts returned and walked us to the spot they'd chosen. It was nothing special: a flat piece of ground about twenty metres below the large, flat top of the mountain.

It hadn't been a long walk up there, but it was steep, so most of us were covered in sweat. 'Why couldn't the fucking helo have dropped us off *here*?' I whined.

'Because then they wouldn't have made it back to base in time to watch the rugby, probably.' I grabbed my thermal mat and walked a short distance away to conduct overwatch. I needed a position that was relatively concealed and that allowed me to keep an eye on everyone in the det while also observing the main avenues of approach to our position. The rain was falling a little harder now, so I quickly jogged back to my pack and whipped out my rain jacket. I used it to cover the top of the gun – the last thing I wanted to do was spend the next three days scrubbing rust out of the working parts. Skin is waterproof, weapons are not.

The three guys had pulled out their E-tools and were now attacking the soft ground with the enthusiasm of men who had just one last job to do before a rest.

Platt looked up at me as I passed. 'One hour, yeah?'

I nodded. After an hour, someone would relieve me on the gun and I'd take their place digging.

By the time I had an E-tool in my hand, I was pleased to see the guys had made some serious progress. I dug the blade into the ground and found it was like going through a cold chocolate brownie. Grey and faintly yellow dirt was stuck to the E-tool.

'It's clay,' whispered Hughey, reading my mind. 'Super easy to dig into. We'll be done in no time.'

This was a pleasant surprise. Even in the rain, we were rapidly creating a deep hole that would be our home for the foreseeable future. Back in Burnham we had practised digging on the 189, a large field just outside of camp with earth made mostly of ancient, dried-up riverbeds, so you could never dig for more than a foot at a time without hitting some huge, solid stone that would have to be dug around and excavated at great effort. There were no rocks in this soft, yielding clay.

Even so, it took us almost four hours to get the hole deep enough. It was pretty good time by our standards, but it meant that it was virtually dawn by the time we were all lying in the hole with the antennas set up and the radios humming and blinking the way they were supposed to be.

The rain had been falling steadily the entire time and our clothes were soaked, but once we got into the hole I had to admit it was cosy and comfortable. Hughes drew up a shift roster and we quickly fell into the LP routine of listening, smoking, sleeping and talking about absolutely nothing of substance. We even had an *FHM* magazine that was read cover to cover over a dozen times on the first day alone.

I slept most of that first day, lulled into unconsciousness by the bone-aching fatigue of the infil and the dig-in, and the soft patter of rain on top of the hoochies. I wasn't cold so I simply lay down on top of my bivvie bag and went to sleep.

When I was roused for shift, I noticed that my leg was wet. I quickly assessed the source to be water that, using the clay bank as a sort of drainpipe, had run down the hoochie and then flowed back into the hole.

I made myself a tea, using my gas cooker with extreme caution in the cramped space. Once I sat up front in the 'sofa' I noticed more water. Some had collected in the footwell we had dug. Oscar noticed my frown.

'It's not a big deal, you just need to scoop it out every hour or so.' To demonstrate, he grabbed his cups canteen and scooped up the puddle. It didn't even fill the cup to halfway. He leaned forward and tipped out the water. 'See? Easy.'

'Great,' I murmured. 'Like being on a ship that's slowly sinking.'

'That's the spirit.'

My shift was largely uneventful, until we intercepted some local police radio. In much of rural New Zealand emergency services still don't use encrypted radio channels, so if you're on the right frequency and have a sensitive enough antenna, you can often hear police, fire and ambulance officers talking to one another and their dispatchers. Usually it's quite inane, run-of-the-mill vehicle accidents and such, but this evening we were treated to something a bit more engaging.

As well as everything else that reconnaissance work can be – tiring, stressful, dangerous, cold, miserable and so on – it is also head-bangingly boring most of the time. Nobody ever carries a smart phone or anything more diverting than a deck of cards most of the time, so if anything interesting ever pops up on the radio, everyone in the detachment usually clusters around, like wartime children gathering around the radio for story time. That particular evening, we were treated to the unfolding saga of a local man who had gotten too drunk at the local pub. Officers had been called to take him home (it sounded like a common occurrence: they referred to him by his first name). Once they arrived, however, he bolted, and was now the target of a miniature manhunt in rural Canterbury. He had fled through a paddock, so officers were chasing him on foot, breathing heavily into their radios as they pursued the drunken man up a very steep hill, if their laboured gasps were anything to go by.

With this entertainment to pass the time, my shift passed quickly. I slithered around Platts as he crawled up to replace me. The rain maintained its steady but gentle tempo on our little hide. I wiped away a puddle that was forming on my bivvie bag and crawled into bed. I had a good four hours until my next shift, and I intended to spend three hours, fifty-nine minutes and fifty-nine seconds of that fast asleep, if possible. Once I was in my bag, I put my headphones in and put on a Raconteurs album (*Broken Boy Soldiers*, definitely my favourite of 2014). I pulled my beanie down over my eyes and quickly drifted off to a warm, fuzzy doze that wasn't quite sleep.

Less than two hours later I was shaken awake to absolute chaos. I tried to work out what was going on, because there was a lot of movement but nobody saying anything. I sat up and immediately placed my hand into thick, cloying muck. Confused, I wriggled around, only to find that the muck was everywhere. The ground beneath our sleeping bags and ground mats had turned into a sludge the consistency of warm butter. Had water leaked in somehow?

I turned to Platts, who was frantically adjusting the roof of one of the hoochies, trying to divert the steady stream of water.

Oscar answered my question before I asked it.

'It's coming up from the clay. We must have dug below the water table.'

The penny finally dropped. We weren't being flooded, we were sinking. The water was coming *up* from the ground, not down from the roof. There wasn't a single inch of clay that wasn't utterly waterlogged. And there was nothing we could do about it.

I sat up further, trying to surreptitiously wipe my hand on my bivvie bag. I saw GG hunched over the footwell, scooping water out with his cups canteen. Except it was no longer a teacup's worth of water. He was filling and emptying his canteen over and over and over again. The footwell was half full. I wriggled around and started scraping the surface puddles I could see, getting covered in sloppy clay up to my elbows for my trouble.

Two hours of battling the tide later, we had reached a sort of equilibrium. I jumped on shift and divided my time between listening to the scanners and keeping the water in the footwell from spilling over my bootlaces.

This went on for another two days.

Why not abandon the hole? you may be thinking. This was an active military exercise, and if we moved we would have to tell HQ. They'd want to know why we were giving up an established LP, and risking discovery. In the army, if your answer to a query is, 'Well, I don't want to get dirty, sir,' you may as well put your credibility in a bag and toss it into a river.

By the end of the second day we were covered in a mixture of fresh and dried clay. We didn't bother changing shirts anymore. The rain had blissfully stopped for half a day, but that only meant a delay of the inevitable. At 0300 on the third day, we were practically swimming. We couldn't cook hot meals anymore, because the ground was so unsteady that our cookers wouldn't stand up straight. We abandoned the hole just before dawn, filling it in by heaping clumps of mud and clay with our bare hands as much as our E-tools. The end result looked like a shamefully dug mass grave, which, if we had stayed any longer, it might well have been.

We took shelter back in the pine forest, exhausted and filthy. Platts and I shared a cigarette and began to laugh at the sheer ridiculousness of it all.

The helicopter came to collect us a few hours later. The payload sergeant took one look at us and shook his head. 'You can't come in here like that!'

I must admit, panic took me. It was a long walk back to base and I was down to literal peanuts for rations. Before I could respond, Platts beat me to it.

'Take it up with my CO if you've got a problem. This guy's going into hypothermia.' He jerked his head towards GG.

The sergeant reluctantly helped us throw our sodden, filth-encrusted packs into the chopper and we clambered aboard. My boots were so caked in clay that I actually slid on the deck as I stepped inside.

We were dropped off at the 3 Sig encampment, a collection of tents, trucks and barbed wire that came with us on every major exercise. With support troops, our squadron numbered close to forty people (assuming nobody was in Afghanistan or Iraq on deployment). Nearly all of them saw us slide out of the helicopter, covered head to toe in dried clay. We hadn't even started taking the packs out before the laughter started.

'What the fuck happened to you?!' someone asked. I simply shook my head and started hauling my stuff towards the communal sleeping tent.

Walker stopped me. 'No fucking way are you coming in here. Not like that.'

Fair enough.

In the end, we managed to douse everything in enough water to get most of the clay off. The entire time we were scrubbing, hanging or drying our gear, people began referring to us as 'the children of the clay'. The name stuck. That became our unofficial callsign for the rest of the exercise. The part that really stung, even more than having to squeeze clay out of my socks, was what our CO had to say to us.

Our commanding officer, Major Thomson, emerged from the command tent. He marched right up to Platts, our det commander, and reprimanded him for 'endangering the detachment'. True, it had been a thoroughly miserable few days, but it wasn't like any of us was actually in danger. Even GG had managed to crack a grin once we were sitting in the chopper on the way out.

Platts was given a formal warning and treated with a general air of lofty disapproval by the officers for the rest of the exercise. That, apparently, is the prize you get for following orders.

PINNYS ON PARADE

WE WERE ESCORTING RADIOS and rifles from Burnham in the South Island to Whenuapai air base in Auckland, providing support for 2/1st Battalion's Recon Patrol Commanders course. We often worked closely with Recon, even to the point of being placed in the same det. So while the senior members of Recon Platoon were assessed on their ability to lead a detachment through mission scenarios, our job was to simply be bodies in their dets. No thinking involved, our favourite kind of exercise.

With a guaranteed two nights in Wellington, with more to be confirmed in Auckland, this was already being talked about as a 'piss trip'. Everyone was packing their bags full of town shirts and condoms, with barely a second glance towards our FSMO. Enthusiasm was off the charts.

Our Pinzgauers (or Pinnys) had to be moved too, so we went for a two-day road trip in a convoy of five vehicles, with fifteen or so young soldiers. We were led by our Command Team of Sergeant Tim Collins AKA The Silver Fox, and Lieutenant Lucy Williams.

Lieutenant Williams was twenty-two, fresh off OCS (Officer Cadet School) and had just been given command of a troop of all-male, socially impenetrable signalmen. She had been my commander at Depot Troop. Since then, she had trained in Australia for a year, learning how to be a signals officer. She had spent a lot of time out in the field learning about troop movements and radio theory. I had spent that year humping packs up and down hills and firing tens of thousands of blanks into the shrubbery. Obviously, we all thought of her as a desk jockey.

The first day was a stupidly early start, and also our first week wearing the new MCU (multi-camouflage uniform). I had grown up seeing New Zealand soldiers wearing DPM, disruptive pattern material. I liked it. I had been beyond excited when I first got my DPM on basic training and I wore it with pride. I liked ironing my collar flat and folding my sleeves until they sat snug against my biceps. Most of all, I liked wearing polished black boots.

The new boots were tan and began to fall apart about three steps out of the Q-store where they were unboxed. The MCU was a sad grey-brown of small, ugly squares. It was supposed to 'perform in all environments' as a neutral colour. But in reality we found that it just made you slightly stand out everywhere. As well as squares of grey and brown and light green, it inexplicably had purple in it, which I found I could see even in very dim light. We all suspected that instead of being a high-performing material, it had somehow cheaply found its way to the NZDF bean-counters. These suspicions were confirmed during our next joint exercise with British forces. As soon as they saw our beige-checkerboard shirts they exclaimed, 'Holy shit, lads! That's the uniform we nearly got issued!' Then they strolled off in their highly coveted multi-cam.

The most painful thing about the MCU was the hat. It is a difficult thing to explain to a civilian why a hat should be so important, but I will try. From your first moment off the bus for basic training, you see hats. You see huge, tattooed corporals in berets that droop over their red faces. You see platoon sergeants in wide-brimmed, mounted rifle hats. You see new recruits running in formation wearing stupid little black baseball caps. Berets are very synonymous with the military, but they are only worn on base or in the public eye. In the field on basic training, you see overburdened infantrymen in field-dress wearing J-hats (jungle hats).

In an environment where everyone wears the same uniform, personal flair starts to become a matter of fine details. J-hats are simple enough, merely a brimmed sunhat in DPM with a string chinstrap. Nothing much to it. But once you've been around a camp or two, or seen a large-scale, joint exercise, you begin to notice that not everyone wears their J-hat in the same way.

Here is a handy guide to help you deduce which kind of solider has just walked past you.

2/1 Battalion: obtain the smallest J-hats, even to the degree of making the brim smaller with scissors and re-hemming it. Some of their brims are no more than an inch wide. They then pull it mostly towards the front of their head, bunch up the excess hat that has now gathered at the top of their forehead and tuck it in. They pull the miniscule brim down until it has completely covered their upper eyelids. They now have to walk around looking down the length of their nose. This would seem impractical to say the least, but since the average 2/1st infantryman is about the height and shape of an expensive refrigerator, this is barely an inconvenience. You could point out that they look like a complete fucking idiot walking around half-blindfolded, but to my knowledge, nobody has thought this is a good enough idea to actually attempt it.

1st Battalion: North Islanders, so a little more formal in their wear of the hat. They don't go so far as making alterations, but they instead create the illusion of barely wearing a hat. The best I can describe it is that it looks as though they have pinched the hat in the very centre and dropped it onto their head from a metre up. There it sits, precariously balanced, complete with a little point. You can always spot a 1st Battalion soldier in a crowd from this tiny peak.

Engineers: are so busy being close to the ground, sniffing around for mines and tripwires, that they ram their hats down onto their heads, presumably to block out light and sound from having to listen to anybody from another corps speak to them.

Logistics: are also easily spotted. Having access to stores, and therefore all the new uniforms, a loggie's hat will always be the cleanest, nicest and newest hat in sight.

Medics: hardly ever wear a hat, because they've usually thrown it into the air out of sheer exasperation trying to figure out how the injured soldier in front of them could possibly be this stupid.

We drove up to Picton in a convoy of three Pinnys, scooted across the Cook Strait on the Interislander and made into Wellington without any significant hiccups. Or rather, there may have been hiccups, but I didn't notice. My usual MO for long journeys was to sit next to someone larger than myself (which happened to be pretty much everyone), put a Raconteurs album on, pull my beanie down over my eyes, use the large person as a pillow and sleep. This technique worked in Pinnys, Unimogs, aeroplanes, Land Rovers and more. For most of my six years enlisted, my iPod Nano lived in the left biceps pocket of my smock. On exercise, it came out nearly every day.

The second day of driving was long. We stopped off in Waiouru (prodigal sons returning) while our command team took care of ... something command teams take care of. Whatever it was, it gave the rest of us just enough time to stretch our legs, smoke cigarettes and sneer at the freshly shaved recruits scurrying around us.

We *finally* made it into Whenuapai air base later that night. The duty sergeant didn't look super excited to see us. He grunted a bit when he buzzed our convoy through the gate, and grunted some more when he gave us all our respective room keys. My room seemed tiny compared to other barrack rooms. But I felt better when I saw Jordy's. The foot of his bed actually touched the sink at the end of his room, and he was two inches taller than me. We all stood clustered in his doorway, sniggering while he unpacked and pretended to ignore us.

It was still only about 2000 at this point, and we were excited by the prospect of air force women around. It was a Friday night, so we changed out of our military uniforms into our civilian uniforms. Soldiers are the worst at wearing regular clothes. You can spot them immediately. Standard dress for a soldier in 'tidy civies' is as follows.

Collared shirt, usually with the sleeves rolled up enough to expose tattoos and forearm muscles.

Levis jeans with a dark belt.

Pointed leather shoes known as winklepickers (AKA 'brothel creepers').

An enormous G-Shock watch or similar that shows signs of extreme use. (Worn with the watch-face on the inside of the wrist, so that you can check the time while holding a rifle).

Enough cologne to make one highly flammable.

OPTIONAL: Two or three packets of cigarettes on your person.

Soldiers will then move around from bar to bar, in groups of four to forty, singing, shouting and periodically embracing one another with increasing degrees of affection, all the while trying to ensnare members of the local populace.

We got to the bar, which was conveniently downstairs from the guest barracks (commonly known as transit barracks), only to find it barren. It wasn't empty, but it was filled with dudes. Not a single woman in sight.

It turns out that prior to our arrival, the air force had put out a *warning* about the army coming to stay on base. We were regarded as something akin to a troop of wild pigs that was passing through: dangerous, dirty and clearly beyond being reasoned with.

The short of it was, we had the bar to ourselves for pretty much the entire time that we were at Whenuapai.

BREAKING INTO AUCKLAND ZOO

THREE OF US FROM EW were embedded into a recon detachment. The brief stated that we needed to find an overwatch position to observe a handoff that was going to happen somewhere around the outer fields of Western Springs. The plan was to move through the public park in the dead of night, set up our observation post somewhere in the bushes, spend the day peering through binoculars and be gone 'like a fart in the wind' the following night. Any civilians around should be none the wiser.

Of course, the maps we were given were older than I was. They showed the park being much larger. I knew we were in for a tough time when we all jumped out of the truck – in the dead of night, on a quiet suburban street – and instead of the bush that we were all expecting to see, we were instead treated to a three-metre-high fence topped with barbed wire.

'That's not supposed to be here,' murmured the detachment commander.

Brilliant, I thought to myself. That's what you want to hear when you're standing in the middle of suburbia covered in camouflage paint and holding an assault rifle.

The fence didn't slow us down too badly. One of the recon guys actually had a collapsible ladder strapped to the side of his pack for such an eventuality, so the eight of us were up and over the fence in minutes.

We 'shook out' into a loose formation and started patrolling through the bush. I was right behind one of the other EW operators that had embedded into the section with me. The recon guys were expert scouts, so there wasn't much for me to do besides walking quietly and trying to ignore the all-too-familiar ache that my cumbersome pack always brought with it. I had no idea where we were relative to Western Springs any more. Despite the moon being out, the bush was dense and dark. After a few hundred metres of this, we had to navigate our way down a steep, muddy bank. Difficult at the best of times, when you're carrying half your weight on your back and your hands are full of gun, it becomes an absolute ball-ache.

Nevertheless, we found our way down and were rewarded with the sight of a huge net, that started at the ground and disappeared above the treetops. I heard some confused whispering from the front of the detachment.

While they sorted that out, I took a moment to look around. I suddenly realised where we were. We were *inside* the Auckland zoo. That first fence had been the boundary. The net we were facing was the open-air aviary. This was confirmed when one of the recon guys prodded the net and about five kea were shaken loose and took off, swearing at us for disturbing their sleep.

We continued around it until we were rewarded with another fence, taller than the first, but not topped with razor wire. I smiled. I had been to the zoo many times, as an Auckland-raised schoolchild. Being in here at night with nobody around was even more fun. Unbeknownst to me, this information would have greatly benefitted the detachment commander and his scout, who were both South Islanders. They knew we were in the zoo, but that was about it. Their conversation (I found out later) went something like this.

'OK, next fence. Over you go.'

'Fuck that. It's an enclosure.'

'Don't be stupid. We're going around them. I checked the map.'

'That map's *ancient*.'

'This is the way to our OP. Don't be a pussy and get over the fucking fence.'

'And get eaten by a lion? Why don't you jump over, and I'll watch from here.'

'If there is something in there, just shoot at it to scare it off.'

'These are *blanks*, remember?'

This went on until a particularly bold and impatient recon member scrambled up and over the fence. There were a few breathless moments while the det commander waited for a large growl, but nothing happened.

Eventually, it was determined that there were no large carnivorous mammals occupying the area over the fence, and we clambered over without too much difficulty. We were surrounded by debris, mostly. Big pieces of wood and metal, used in enclosures, and a massive pile of woodchips were all we could see in the moonlight. We moved along until we found a narrow gap between two maintenance sheds, and were rewarded with a small, dense patch of bush that had a view of where we were supposed to be watching. We arranged ourselves in a defensive position and went to sleep.

I will never forget the sound of being woken up by a combination of African savanna creatures, the hooting of several unidentified apes, and a chorus of every birdsong I'd ever imagined. It started at daybreak and lasted well over fifteen minutes. We couldn't even whisper to each other: it was deafening.

At 0900, the gates opened. By 1000 the schoolkids had arrived, and they added their screeching to the background noise provided by the nearby aviary.

We lay there all day, occasionally hearing zookeepers bustling around the sheds that were only metres away. We had no idea if they'd been told we might be around. We were supposed to be unseen and undetected. So we lay still, didn't talk, and ate cold food all day and night. The Recon guy took turns on the binoculars and the EW guys took turns scanning the airwaves for short-range radio chats of interest.

Sometime that evening, while I lay in my bag, the handoff must've occurred, because I was being shaken awake and told to be ready to move.

Our journey out was only slightly less eventful. We had two more fences to climb over, and were told to meet the Pinzgauer at the end of the street. Of course, as I was literally on top of the final fence, with one boot on either side and ten feet above the ground, a security car came cruising down the road.

The guys below me silently went to ground, melting like shadows as they tried to flatten their bodies. The ability of a 6 foot 4 recon soldier to swiftly and silently hide behind a tiny shrub is uncanny. You have to see it to believe it. The car's headlights illuminated them for a moment, and then kept driving. My legs were shaking from the strain of keeping still. The fence rocked slightly. I was sweating. After what felt like an age, the sound of the car died away.

The recon commander's voice hissed unseen out of the bushes somewhere. 'Hurry the fuck up, sigs.'

I half climbed, half fell to the ground and gratefully crawled along to join the others in the bushes. We radioed the Pinzgauer and were told it was only a few minutes away. We moved as close to the edge of the road as possible, awaiting our pickup.

I saw the guard before I heard him. He was walking down the footpath, the same way the car had come. He looked like he came out of the same factory that all late-night security guards come from: a dumpy guy in his mid-thirties, moving sluggishly along, bored out of his mind.

We froze. I lay on my side, my legs wedged against a trunk and my vision mostly obscured by the bush that was giving me scant cover. I could see the guard's shoulder, and several of his chins. He stopped and looked into the bushes.

We collectively held our breath.

About a thousand years passed. Then he turned and walked back the way he had come. In our debrief, the commander told the officers that we had been 'almost spotted, but no civilians were aware of our presence'.

In hindsight, I'd be much more confident in saying: 'A civilian did hear us, and came to investigate. He saw eight large, camouflaged individuals holding automatic weapons and staring straight into his soul. He decided that the flashlight in his belt and the thirteen dollars an hour he received weren't enough to give him a sudden case of heroism. So he went back the way he came.'

LUCYS IN THE ARMOURY

WE PULLED UP AT Trentham Military Camp sometime in the afternoon. We had a ferry to catch the next morning, but all that anybody really wanted to do now was get some beers down them. Tim Collins AKA The Silver Fox and Lieutenant Lucy Williams made the questionable decision to let us head into town for the night.

We stood clustered around our superior officers in the small hallway, having dumped all our personal gear in our tiny rooms. Lucy spoke first.

'Alright, I need two pers to take the weapons to the armoury and then I'll release you so you can all head out and fail to impress the local girls.'

Tim delivered the crucial information we were waiting for.

'So, we're giving you a bit of rope here fellas, don't hang yourselves with it. We need to be at the ferry building at 0630 tomorrow morning, which means you will be back on base, ready to move by 0500 at the *very* latest. Drivers, you will not drink any alcohol tonight, got it?'

Hayden, the man perpetually entrusted to drive one of our Pinnys, looked dejected, but everyone else was rapt.

Once the weapons had been driven across camp and stashed in the camp armoury, and the specialist equipment was securely in Sergeant Collins's room (he was confident that he wasn't going anywhere for the night), it was straight into showers and town clothes. Lucy offered to drive us, using the camp van to make two trips. She and Tim had their own stuff to do back at base. (Most likely each other, but we had long since stopped caring about that situation. They were good leaders and, even more importantly, let us largely do as we liked outside of working hours.)

The night went much like any other night out with the squadron. Eighteen of us left camp together. Twelve of us went to the first bar we saw; ten of us stayed in there without getting kicked out, seven of us went to a nightclub next door three hours later, four of us talked to some girls until they got bored of us, three of us consoled ourselves with shots while telling ourselves 'they weren't even that hot', and by 0300 I found myself alone, wandering down Courtney Place trying to light my last cigarette.

It was windy in Wellington that night (obviously), so I was having some trouble getting my dart lit. I stopped at the traffic lights. A very cute girl with dark hair and glasses said she liked my shirt and I had the drunken confidence to offer to reward the lady's compliment with a drink at the nearest bar. She agreed, provided she could bring her friend with her. I regarded the bored-looking blonde at her side. A drink in a bar with *two* girls? Sure, why not. I had two hours left, who knew where the night could take me?

It seems that Lucy (that was the brunette's name) had an even more pressing curfew than myself, because after two drinks she started touching my leg and asking if I lived nearby. I wish I remembered what I'd been talking about that night, because clearly it was the right sort of stuff.

I tried to answer as nonchalantly as possible.

'Fuck yeah, let's go.' I was half out of my seat already, barely a sip gone out of my beer. If ever there as a time to abandon a perfectly good drink, it was now.

Lucy grabbed my hand. 'Mmm yeah but you have to find someone for my friend Lucy. OK?'

I considered explaining that there was plenty of me to go around, but the tale of Icarus cautioned me against it. Best to enjoy flying a little bit before aiming directly for the sun.

'But I thought *your* name was Lucy?'

She sighed. Clearly, this had already come up. 'It is, so is hers. Do you have any friends out tonight?'

My phone was in my hand instantly. I messaged the group chat and texted everyone from the squadron who wasn't married or better-looking than myself.

After ten long minutes, during which both Lucys regaled me with a carefully rehearsed speech about which of them deserved to be 'Lucy One' and why the other should be 'Lucy Two', I still had no messages. I made a deceitful, sneaky decision. I checked my phone and feigned delight.

'Oh, great news! My very good friend Jordy is home already. He'll meet us there.'

Of course, I had no idea where he was, but he was probably on his way back to barracks, right?

I was very much a 'cross that bridge when we get to it' kind of problem solver when I was 21.

The three of us left the bar, with Lucy One's hand firmly shoved into my back pocket. So far so good. I made a beeline for the taxi rank ... and nearly collided with Ainsworth.

Never in my life had I been so pleased to see that awkward grimace of his.

'Oh, hi Dario,' he droned, almost exactly like Eeyore.

'Ainsworth, uh, Steve! MY GUY!' my response was entirely too enthusiastic.

Ainsworth looked suspicious. 'What do you want?' he asked cautiously.

'You, my bro. This is Lucy Two.' I pushed him towards the blonde. 'And the four of us are getting into a taxi, right now. Cool?'

Even Ainsworth could recognise when an opportunity had fallen into his lap. If we had been fishermen, this was like a gigantic, blue-fin tuna squeezing itself into the can and paying its own postage.

It was after 0400 by the time we got back to base. We flashed our IDs and the girls walked in with us. They didn't seem phased that 'home' for us was a large military installation and not the 'flat' we had alluded to, but not explicitly mentioned. It was chilly that night, and a morning fog had rolled in. About 500 metres up the main road, I realised I didn't really know the way to our barracks. Ainsworth didn't either.

'The transit barracks?' I murmured to Steve as we walked, holding hands with our respective Lucys.

'This way, I think,' said Steve.

We started to go left, but Lucy One stopped us.

'Um, barracks are that way, right?'

Steve and I were too stunned to respond. The Lucys marched on, undeterred. After 100 tense metres in the cold, dawn air, we were rewarded with the ugly brown roof of the transit barracks dead ahead of us.

I caught up to her. 'How did you know?'

'I've been here before,' she smirked.

It occurred to me that I had not, in fact, gone out to town and pulled a good-looking girl solely on my charms and wit. Going by my earlier metaphor, I was most definitely the tuna in this scenario, *not* the fisherman.

I grinned around the metaphorical hook stuck in my lip. Fish or fisherman, the result was the same.

I checked my watch as the four of us made our way into the dimly lit transit barracks. It was 0440. I was cutting it fine to make it before 0500, but I was definitely not late.

Excellent. I assumed everyone else was asleep, so I tried to be quiet as I fished in my pocket for my room key. Of course, as anyone who has ever been flatting will tell you, it is physically impossible for four drunk people to return quietly past the hour of 0200.

Sergeant Collins's door opened and he emerged, looking surprisingly awake. He glanced at the Lucys with an amused grin.

'Morning, Dario. You got the others?'

I was still a bit drunk and very, very tired. 'Others? Nope, just one girl for me.' I gestured towards Sergeant Collins with my head. 'Lucy One, Tim. Tim, Lucy One.'

Tim shook his head and chuckled. 'The *others*. Sambo, Jordy, you know?'

I finally caught on. 'Shit, no. They're not back yet?'

'You're the first.'

My finely developed sense for a fast-approaching beasting was still sharp from my time in Linton. I unlocked my door without breaking eye contact and ushered Lucy One inside.

'Nope, no sign of them, I'm afraid. I should really try and get some sleep though. Meeting at 0530 still, yes? OK then. Night, Sarge.' I shut the door and locked it before he could respond.

Lucy One and I had just enough time to recite our favourite Bible passages to one another before it was time to get up, strip the bed and hurriedly stuff all my things into my duffel bag. I was moving at top speed, Lucy One was trying on my beret and taking selfies in the mirror. Good for her.

I emerged to see Sergeant Collins engaged in conversation with Emele, the unit Mormon. He definitely wasn't drunk.

Sarge said something I couldn't hear, and Emele nodded and hurried away out of the barracks.

Lieutenant Lucy came out of her room, fully dressed. 'Any sign of them?' she asked Tim curtly.

Tim nodded towards me. 'Just this smooth operator and Ainsworth.'

Lieutenant Lucy was pissed. The scowl on her face could've turned sunshine into drizzle, robins into pigeons, and rainbows into greyscale Instagram filters. Ainsworth chose this moment to emerge from his room, grinning from ear to ear. Lucy Two lurked in his doorway looking uncertain.

Like all good leaders, Lieutenant Lucy made a quick decision.

'Right. You two,' she said to me and Ainsworth, 'start stripping down everyone's beds and pack up their rooms as best you can. You two,' she directed at the women, 'are you alright? Do you need a lift home?'

The Lucys looked surprised. 'Um, yeah. Actually,' said Lucy One.

'Not a problem, we can do that. But first I need your help with something. We need to get some stuff from the armoury and I need an extra set of hands. Come with me.'

And so my lieutenant, in her full military uniform, led two girls in small dresses down the hallway, chatting amicably. I overheard Lieutenant Williams as she opened the door for them.

'I'm Lucy, by the way.'

Ainsworth and I exchanged glances. I addressed the most pressing issue.

'How are we supposed to get into everyone's rooms?'

Sergeant Collins materialised and threw a key at me. 'Master key for the barracks, do *not* lose it.' He went back to grabbing all the radios and other equipment out of his room.

Ainsworth and I proceeded to unlock each room and whipped the sheets off each bed while roughly shoving everyone's sprawled gear into the corners. It took us nearly twenty minutes, after which the three Lucys returned from the armoury. Lucy One looked like she'd just been on a rollercoaster, Lucy Two looked slightly more bored than usual and Lieutenant Lucy looked mildly amused.

'Alright?' I asked Lucy One.

'That was *awesome*. I got to touch all the guns.'

I was glad someone was still having a good time. It was now 0545 and there was no sign of most of our squadron.

Tim recruited Ainsworth and me to move some of the stores into the Pinnys, while Amy called Tupou, her arms folded in the universal stance of 'I can't believe these fucking idiots.'

Just as we had finished doing everything we possibly could, and the Lucys were sat in the Pinny, wearing our camouflage smocks over their dresses for warmth, I heard a vehicle in the distance. It wasn't coming from the road Ainsworth and I had walked in on. It was approaching from the other side of camp. I strained my eyes and squinted. Emerging through the fog, like a Valkyrie bursting through the clouds, was the van.

Emele was driving, a look of deep worry etched into his usually placid features. The sliding door of the van was open, and out of the side of the van came a blaring chorus of rock music, barely audible above the bad singing that accompanied it. Occasionally an empty can of beer would fall out of the open door and echo atrociously as it struck the ground on the otherwise silent parade ground.

The van pulled up and no less than eleven very drunk soldiers piled out of it. Sergeant Collins gave them the shortest, most brutal set of orders I'd ever seen and they scurried into the barracks, cackling like hags and trying to push each other into the hedge that adorned the front door.

Fifteen minutes later, we were driving through suburban Wellington, Ainsworth and I with a Lucy on each of our laps, while they directed the Pinzgauer full of rifles, radios and uniformed soldiers to their front door.

They clambered out when we had pulled into the correct driveway, I got a final kiss goodbye, and that was that. We made it to the dock just in time to join the back of the queue for vehicles boarding the Interislander ferry and collapsed in a grateful heap in the lounge.

Jordy and Sambo were shattered. I was just about to tell them the story about how I singlehandedly charmed two gorgeous ladies when Sergeant Collins loomed over us.

'Don't get too comfortable, assholes. There are two Pinnys below decks that need to be constantly guarded to make sure that no nosey passengers go snooping through them or nick the guns and radios. You two can go down first, someone will be down to relieve you shortly.'

I groaned and started to get up.

'Oh, not you Dario. You were back on time. You get some rest, mate. Same goes for Ainsworth.'

Hayden and Jordy looked aghast.

'But they brought *girls*, into barracks!'

'Those girls signed out everyone's weapons, so they were a hell of a lot more useful than you morons.'

I resisted the urge to chime in. Instead I pulled my beanie down over my eyes, rolled over on the bench seat and went to sleep.

BEING THE BAD GUYS

EW REQUIRES A HIGH security clearance. We use sensitive equipment and work with and around all the sneaky people that they make Matt Damon movies about. Getting a government security clearance is a pain in the ass. It takes literally years, and includes getting multiple referees, background checks and filling out lengthy forms on secure computers for hours at a time.

But there are perks. One of which is that it makes even a junior soldier qualified to be enemy party for an SAS exercise.

Four of us were up north anyway, and myself, Aaron and Jordy were tagged to go play bad guys for a few days. Something I realised early on in my career filled with military exercises is that it's a lot more fun to be the bad guys. You can wear whatever you like, you don't have to stick to such rigorous disciplines as you would being in a conventional unit and, best of all, you eventually get 'killed' and get to mince around camp waiting for the exercise to end while the good guys sweat and scramble around in the mud for a few extra days.

The scenario was that three of us had taken a hostage. There was a larger narrative that had been playing out for a couple of weeks, but we were only subbed in at the last minute. All I knew was that we were the bad guys, and the long-suffering

GG was our hostage. We were stuck in a woolshed out in the middle of nowhere, and we knew that at some point in the next few days an undisclosed number of Alpha Squadron were going to come and rescue him. We were given 'simunition' for the exercise. Simunition is similar to paintball, except that it can be fired through a regular rifle, with some minor adjustments. The rounds aren't as large as a paintball, although they fly faster and further, so they sting about the same. They also don't splatter like a paintball; it's more of a waxy residue. When you shoot someone, you can tell if they've been hit because they'll either be marked in bright purple spots or they'll be swearing at you.

The first day passed without incident. We sat in the shed, made pancakes and bacon in a tiny frying pan over a gas burner and took turns 'guarding' GG. We even had him tied to a pillar in the middle of the room, although we agreed we'd only tie his hands up if we knew 'they' were coming.

It turned out that it wouldn't be much of a surprise, because late in the afternoon of the second day the commander of Alpha Squadron waltzed into the shed. He was huge but friendly, in an 'I could kill you without breaking a sweat' kind of way.

He was accompanied by an equally large man who appeared to be wrapped in a mattress.

'It's a dog suit,' the guy explained in a muffled tone. 'We're training some new attack dogs, and I got the short straw.'

'Rather you than me,' said Jordy.

I had to agree. 'Yeah, have fun with that.'

The major smirked. 'Don't worry, the lads will get to you too. Just try not to flinch, or they'll go for you harder.'

That was ominous.

An hour later, Jordy and I were standing out the back peering into the woods. The dog suit guy, who had introduced himself as Alex, was out the front. Aaron was inside with a securely tied GG as his 'meat shield'. Aaron being Aaron, he was determined to 'kill' an SAS soldier before he went down.

Another hour passed. We were bored. There are only so many cigarettes you can smoke and 'would you rathers' that you can get through before a tired silence descends. It was dark. We were facing away from each other, to cover a wide angle of approach.

The SAS are depicted in films as ruthless, efficient special forces soldiers. But I wasn't some random, untrained insurgent. At this time, I'd been in the army for about three years. I had spent plenty of time with a rifle or a machine gun in my hands. But nowhere near enough for what was about to occur.

The first we knew anything was happening, I heard a thud right next to my boot. I assumed something had fallen out of my pocket, so I turned to see what it was. I was just starting to bend down when it exploded in my face.

A flashbang is a small, non-lethal grenade that makes a single, extremely loud concussive explosion of light and sound. It's designed for things like hostage situations, when you don't want to turn everyone in the room into bolognaise.

This wasn't a flashbang. It was what is known as a 9banger. It's well named. Instead of one loud concussive bang, it delivers nine of them, in slightly less than two seconds. After the first bang, your ears start ringing and your vision is streaked with the spots you get from looking into the sun. After the third bang, your head starts feeling like it's full of loose ball bearings.

If you're close to a 9banger that goes off, it's almost impossible to still be on your feet after the fifth bang, because the parts of your inner ear responsible for maintaining a sense of balance are literally vibrating with concussive force. Before the fifth bang even had a chance to pummel me into the ground, I was already being shot.

White jolts of pain hit my neck and ears, and one really nasty bastard struck my fingertip. Even more rounds peppered the body armour on my chest. I fell over, barely able to see anything, let alone fire back. Jordy was shooting, but I couldn't see how he was doing. My eyes *throbbed*. It was like someone was slowly, steadily pressing their thumbs into my eyeballs. I felt rather than saw heavy boots swarming all around me.

Somewhere in the distance, I heard a shout and a bunch more shots were fired. It was like they were happening underwater. I literally went into the foetal position and tried to will the ringing in my ears to stop.

All I remember after that was being flipped onto my back and searched. Once I deployed, I learned that this was standard practice for a kill team, making sure that every corpse is accounted for or anything of intelligence value (like a cell phone with a bunch of baddies in the contacts list) is found. They were thorough, pulling *every* item out of my webbing and tossing it aside.

It took almost ten minutes for my vision to fully return. The ringing didn't stop until the next day. Aaron was even less fortunate. He had tried to use GG as a human shield and the SAS trooper coming in through the door ended up shooting at the only part of Aaron he could see: the direct centre of his forehead. He had a red scab there for over a week.

It was my very own, up-close demonstration of what it meant to have the NZSAS come for you.

I can promise you this: it'll be over quickly.

Back at the unit, myself and the rest of the boys were presented with a one-off certificate that proudly said *I got shot, by the SAS.*

HURRY UP AND WAIT

'A SOLDIER? THAT'S INTENSE.'

'Must be full on.'

'All go, go, go.'

When I told people I was a soldier, they would often comment on the perceived intensity of the job. And it's true, it can be intense, except when it isn't. As a small cog in a very, very big machine, your responsibility as an individual solider is to simply be *ready.*

Being a good soldier isn't hard. Well, actually, it is fucking hard, but it's *simple.* I had a good career and six years of decent opportunities passed my way because of this simple formula I learned on basic training. For anybody reading this who is considering joining the military (or a similar profession) I can honestly say this is the most crucial ethos you can stick to.

All you have to do to be a successful solider, is *be where you're supposed to be, five minutes before you're supposed to be there*, with exactly the gear you're supposed to have on you to do the task at hand.

That's it. That's soldiering.

Because the commanders, the generals and colonels and so on, they are the ones with a job to do. All the corporals and grunts under their command are just tools in their gigantic Swiss Army knife. As one of those tools, being ready to do your specific role on command and then neatly slide away until you're needed again is the best thing you can do.

This analogy is especially true because most of the time, most of the tools in a Swiss Army knife are doing sweet fuck all.

Take our deployment for Exercise Hamel, for example. This was a large-scale Five Eyes exercise in Australia. US Marines, Canadians, British soldiers, all flying in from the corners of Western civilisation to sweat together and shriek at the Australian wildlife. Should have been a simple hop across the ditch for those of us coming from New Zealand, right?

Our unit was prepared. There were fourteen of us and two Pinzgauers being freighted by the air force. We made the drive to Ohakea air base and had a rough night's sleep on camp stretchers in a vast hangar. The skills needed to sleep when someone in your room snores, skills that I thought I had honed on basic training, were woefully insufficient in a cavernous space filled with almost 200 other people. We had been told to be on the runway, with our packs, ready to fly at 0800 hours. Naturally, this meant getting up at 0600 after what probably amounted to an hour of sleep. We packed the stretchers down, guzzled a sloppy breakfast of beans and eggs, and were all assembled on the runway at 0745, with the morning light beaming into our eyes.

But 0800 came and went.

So did 0900.

By 1000 hours, we finally had someone pass some information along. Apparently, the planes were delayed. But nobody knew by how long, or if there was another plan, so the orders were to remain in place.

Fortunately, someone had a deck of cards.

We sat on that tar all day, playing cards, smoking and generally complaining about our lot in life. Dinner came served in hotboxes, and still no aircraft were to be seen.

At 2130 I was dozing, with my beanie over my eyes on a bed made of two packs. An aeroplane landed less than 100 metres away from where I was sleeping.

Immediately, the sergeants and junior officers roared into action.

'Everybody up, let's fucking GO!'

'Hurry up, hurry up.'

Thirteen hours of doing absolutely nothing, and suddenly, it was back to moving as quickly as humanly possible. It was business as usual.

GRIEVOUS

WE HAD A HUGE, unexplored base to find trouble in. When there are fifteen of you sharing a room, you find any and all excuses to be elsewhere. On the days where we were done with exercise admin and had finished driving through town conducting 'training' (which largely consisted of tuning into Triple J radio station and cruising around Townsville looking at girls), we would go off for 'PT'. This was a great throwaway term that you could use to go off and do what you wanted. If we were off doing PT, our officers didn't have to find things for us to do, and we could saunter about in running shoes and shorts without anybody stopping us to ask what we were up to. On one such stroll through camp, we found a very quiet, out of the way gymnasium.

Army bases are like small towns and the base in Townsville has multiple gyms. We found ourselves near the boundary of camp, having followed a path that meandered around a large pond. After geeking out at the turtles and being divebombed by a colony of bats, we saw a huge, empty gym. Pleasantly surprised, we went inside. There were only five people in the entire building. Two old NCOs on treadmills, a janitor and two very bored-looking civilians manning the desk.

Just before we had left New Zealand, the squadron had been seized by a fever of a new game, grievous, where you take turns at hitting a ball against a wall. It was vaguely based off squash, with a few notable differences. You can play with as many as fifteen people at once; you use tennis rackets and a tennis ball; instead of one designated wall, you can use any vertical surface in the entire gymnasium; and if you miss your turn, or otherwise make a foul, you are out of the game and usually have to do a series of physical punishments on the sidelines. The earlier you go out, the more severe the punishment. So if you were the first out, you might have to do 150 squats, second out will do 140, and so on, until the winner only has to do ten or so.

We wanted to play a round of this, so we cautiously asked the civilian at the desk for tennis racquets and a few balls. No issues there.

'Can we use the gymnasium?'

He shrugged. That was all we needed.

We played most afternoons, running around the gymnasium, smashing the ball into walls, windows and doors and generally getting out of breath. At some stage, somehow, we started doing it wearing our body armour. It was great for cardio fitness and leg strength but was probably another significant factor in the degradation of my knees.

Once Exercise Hamel was actually about to start, things got a bit more serious. Our room was suddenly filled with ration packs, smoke grenades and boxes upon boxes of blank ammunition. The vehicles underwent various checks to make sure they could handle anything the Australian outback might throw at them (spoiler alert, they couldn't).

I had been sorted into the experimental 'leftovers' detachment. There were five of us. Sig Dalton, a small, soft-spoken type who was originally from South Africa, was technically in charge. Although he was a nice enough guy, he was about as suited to a leadership role as a fish is to playing the drums.

There were two Australians, Walsh and 'Mickey'. Mickey had a real name, but nobody ever used it. In another example of military nicknames, this guy was called Mickey and nobody ever got around to telling me why. He was the spitting image of Biff from *Back to the Future*. I mean like, identical. When I pointed this out, he assured me that people said that a lot. Unlike Biff, Mickey was actually pretty easy to be around, which is more than I can say for Walsh. He was very much the 7 Sig's equivalent of Ainsworth. He loathed soldiering, hated going on exercise and detested being in the field. So, as you can imagine, he was an absolute joy to spend five weeks in the outback playing soldier with.

Fortunately, the detachment was saved by the addition of a US marine called Brad. He was from Louisiana. I learned this is where Tabasco sauce comes from (of which he had a seemingly inexhaustible supply). He was having too much fun being in a foreign country to let the overall drudge of an exercise get him down. I spent most of my time in the detachment talking shit with him.

A common observation made by members of other branches of the military is that signallers do sweet fuck all. We are the roadworkers of the military. This is not entirely incorrect.

Let me explain.

The workload of an average infantryman over the course of a five-week exercise will not vary much from day to day. They wake up, care for their weapons and their kit, run out into the training area, point their rifles at foes (invisible or otherwise) yelling 'BANG BANG, you're dead' whilst being barked at by their sergeants, and return back to the FOB. Upon their mud-splattered return, in the midst of exchanging slaps on the back (and presumably, each other's asses) they will spy three signallers sitting on the roof of a vehicle, smoking cigarettes, suspiciously mud-free.

This leads them to the reasonable conclusion that signallers are a pack of lazy POG (pronounced 'pogue', as in 'vogue') fucks that wouldn't know real soldiering if it kicked them in the tits.

What the grunts *haven't* seen is the seven hours preceding this rooftop cigarette.

On a graph, the signaller's workload would look like the letter U. As soon as an exercise starts, there are lists upon lists of unique radio frequencies that each and every section of ten men, in a brigade with 2,000 people, will need to be assigned, without causing any sort of interference in a bandwidth narrower than a drinking straw, because the NZDF wanted to save eighty cents on purchasing frequencies (radio frequencies are like website domain names; you have to pay for them and the free ones are all garbage). On top of this, certain branches of the military use different radios, which perform with varying efficiency, at various distances, at a variety of frequencies. Confused yet?

Good.

After the headache of assigning these very specific freqs (pronounced 'freaks') you need to set up antennas around the entire FOB, to ensure that each HQ can talk to their respective units out in the field. If you think that the ability to communicate with their units would be a priority for officers when choosing where to place their command tent, you would be tragically mistaken. Some hapless signaller will arrive to place antennas, only to find the masterminds from engineering top brass (high-ranking officers) have decided to put their command tent at the base of a hill, behind a screen of large, wet pine trees, in a pond. Essentially, any spot that we are taught is terrible for receiving radio frequencies somehow looks like Fort Knox to officers in the field. So you spend your time trying to make it work, attempting to glean one single megahertz of communication from the airwaves, often for hours, on the roof of a vehicle, all the while having some gung-ho captain asking you every four minutes, 'Why don't we have comms yet?'

Of course, eventually, you do succeed. And you hand the radio handset over to the officer with a look of exhausted triumph on your face, happy in the knowledge that you're about to treat yourself to a shit you've been holding in all day, now that the latrines have been dug. This, of course, is when another gung-ho captain comes up (holding his rifle ready, as though Charlie is about to come bursting out of the trees at any moment) and explains that you actually need to move the entire command tent 200 metres *into* the forest, to make room for a truck that absolutely cannot be parked anywhere else. The life of a radio monkey will continue thusly for the first fifty or so hours of an exercise, and it will definitely happen at 0200, 0400 and 0500.

To hark back to the roadworker analogy: nobody gives a shit about what we are doing, until they need to use the road.

INTO THE OUTBACK

AS MENTIONED, I WAS in the leftovers detachment. Exercise Hamel was well and truly underway, the grunts had been taken to the exercise area and camp in general was pretty damn quiet. The rest of EW had been 'deployed' to overwatch or support various other assets, and 'the leftovers', as we were affectionately known, were still sitting around, doing not much. That was fine by me. In a job where you can be asked to work for thirty hours in a row, I was always more than happy to hide away somewhere with my beanie pulled down over my eyes and my headphones in, waiting for the mess to open for my next meal. This exercise it was all about Jack White and the Raconteurs.

When I wasn't playing air guitar in a dark corner, we kept tabs on the other detachments by lurking around the command tent and chatting to some of the EW higher command. We even got talking one afternoon to an Australian grunt who made and sold homemade beef and kangaroo jerky, specifically for large exercises. 'Jack rats' are snacks and treats carried to supplement the army-issued rat – ration – packs that are so disgusting that you can safely leave one opened in front of an unsupervised dog. They are always highly sought after before any lengthy stint in the field. We bought multiple bags of his soy sauce and chilli-flavoured jerky, for $15 a bag. He had a truckload of the stuff. The guy probably made a killing every time his company went out on exercise.

Literally two days passed like this. Some people may have found it boring; not me. Since I received my first iPod shuffle in 2006 and began cramming it full of my stepdad's Nine Inch Nails CDs, I have always found listening to music to be an ideal way to while away the hours. But, eventually, my little rag-tag team of rejects was given a mission. Well, sort of.

A recon section of grunts was heading out to a remote location, searching for an enemy flanking force. The infantry commander had asked for EW to be embedded into his section, but in order to keep the group size down, he only asked for two of us. This was something of a problem. As I've mentioned multiple times, EW equipment is heavier than a box of rocks. Usually, that gear is divided amongst four or five suffering men. Split between two was guaranteed to be absolute misery. As the detachment commander, Dalton elected to go, a decision I respected. 'Don't ask of your men anything you wouldn't do yourself' is a key tenet of military leadership, but it is commonly ignored by lazy, inept NCOs.

And, either because of my apparent competence or, more likely, because I was standing closest to Dalton when the tasking came up, I was the second man chosen.

To solve the issue of equipment, Dalton and I hatched a plan. We were only going for one night, which meant we didn't need much food or water. We elected to take the smallest radio possible and rely on satellite communications, which are reliable but you need to be out in the open for them to work. We placed every piece of equipment in a specially designed pack on my back, which was heavier than a patrol pack by far. Dalton carried a single sleeping bag (which we decided to take turns in), food, water and spare batteries on his back. All in all, it was a pretty sparse list of equipment, but we didn't have much choice.

The plan was to go out with the recon section, stay in position with them for a day and then move off to get picked up by the rest of our detachment once we had confirmation on where the enemy was (or wasn't).

Before we left I made sure to get all my belongings squared away, stashed neatly in my pack and left on my stretcher-bed, which was next to everyone else's in the large hangar we were sleeping in.

We decided on a pickup spot, Dalton and I said goodbye and our det told us they would see us the next day, with our vehicle and the rest of our gear.

Dalton and I jumped in a Boeing CH-47 Chinook, which was definitely a highlight of the exercise for me. It was one of those enormous, twin-rotor deals that made an immense amount of noise. It screamed along the ground and I watched the red dust swirl up, thirty feet in the air all around the landing zone. It was like a scene out of *Dune*. The Australian recon soldier barely gave us a nod as we all jogged towards the helicopter. The rotors were still going, so formal introductions weren't exactly an option.

We soared over the Australian outback. I kept my eyes peeled for kangaroos, but all I saw was sad-looking trees slowly suffocating on red dust.

We disembarked on the edge of some wetlands and Dalton and I filed into the recon platoon's marching order. Dalton had the mobile scanner going and gave the recon commander regular updates that nothing was, in fact, happening across the airwaves.

While Dalton played golden-boy force-protector extraordinaire, I lagged along behind, under the crushing weight of all our belongings, plus the spare batteries, not to mention the added weight of a very heavy chip on my shoulder. I was like Igor carrying his master's tools while the mad scientist bounded ahead.

Eventually, sometime around dawn, the recon platoon went to ground and told us in a hushed whisper that this was where our paths would diverge. Fine by me. The pack was digging into my shoulders and my heels were aching. I had already finished an entire canteen and was well into my second one.

New Zealanders always suffered in the Australian heat, and the sun wasn't even up yet. Dalton and I found an ugly thicket to climb into and did our best to make a bit of concealment. We threw up our antennas from his pack and started firing anything and everything we collected back to 7 Sig HQ. Technically, we were just waiting for Mickey and the rest of our det to come and pick us up so we could rejoin the main advance. But in reality, we needed recon to sweep the area and give it the OK, and then an infantry platoon had to come through and establish a defensive position before they'd even think about letting a lone vehicle full of specialist equipment roll through.

Considering that the recon guys were already moving out in formations and conducting their sweep, and the infantry platoon was on standby, all in all we guessed the whole thing should take no more than about three hours, four at a push.

It took nine.

We heard the whole thing unfold on the open radio channel. Recon had cleared the area, and was waiting for infantry to come and secure the position. But infantry couldn't decide which platoon it was going to send. There was a mix up. They almost sent two platoons at once. An hour went by, then someone realised they hadn't sent anybody. And then they almost sent an entire regiment.

And so it went. It was almost 1500 by the time we finally heard Mickey on the radio telling us he was about fifteen minutes away. There wasn't much of a road, so in their defence, the boys had to navigate the terrain entirely on their own. As anybody into off-roading will tell you, you can't just pick a direction and gun it. Not unless you want to get stuck and destroy your tyres and suspension after 100 metres. Even in a 4x4 with huge tyres, you have to take it slowly and keep an eye out for rocks, holes and venomous wildlife.

Even through the branches and foliage above us, the sun was beating down mercilessly. I was sweating buckets. The scanner's CPU was hot enough to burn you if you rested your arm in the wrong place. Dalton didn't seem to be fazed at all. He wasn't Australian, but he was a native South African, so it amounted to the same result under the oppressive heat of the midday sun. He was actually humming to himself as he checked through the frequencies, the bastard.

I had removed as many layers as I could without actually going shirtless. Because we had started the mission in the middle of the night, I had worn my warm socks. Deserts are surprisingly cold at 0200. I was itching to get into the rest of my gear and air out these sweaty socks for a bit. With water being a scarcity in the field, you don't get a chance to actually wash your clothes, but with lots of airing out and regular changing between uniforms, you can maintain an acceptable level of stench for quite a while.

Finally, I heard the grunt of the G-Wagon. I resisted the urge to whoop and instead flung down the antenna and got on one knee in the universal patrol soldier's pose for 'I'm ready to roll'.

They pulled up on the outskirts of the wetland. Dalton and I scurried out to meet them and clambered in.

I was so relieved to have that huge, unyielding slab of metal off my back that for the first ten minutes I didn't even move. I just sat there, flopped into the passenger seat like a comatose house cat. Then I remembered that I had beef jerky in my pack. I sat up and started rummaging around the sea of gear stuffed behind the seat.

My pack wasn't there.

'Did you guys strap my pack to the roof for some reason?' I asked.

Brad continued sleeping. Mickey and Walsh had one of those non-verbal conversations where all information is passed through a series of eyebrow waggling and head nodding.

Mickey broke the news to me. 'Yeah mate. About your pack ...'

This wasn't going to be good. Had they gotten it wet somehow? God, that would be annoying.

'It's back at base,' Walsh finished lamely.

'Sorry dude.' Mickey's condolences fell on deaf ears.

I took a moment to process this. There only seemed to be one course of action.

'FuuuuuuuuuuUUUUUUUUUUUUUUUUCK!' I hollered at nobody in particular.

I immediately started thinking of everything that was in my pack. Snacks, warm clothes, water, my sleeping bag, oh my god, fresh underwear and socks ...

And it was day two of a brigade-wide exercise that was supposed to last a month.

Fan-tas-tic.

I shan't spend too long, dear reader, on trying to describe the stench that followed your humble narrator around by the end of Exercise Hamel. There are only so many adjectives that can be sprinkled through a sentence before it loses its sting.

Rest assured, my stink did not lose its sting.

I managed to muddle through the next few weeks on borrowed kit: sharing a plate with Mickey, using Walsh's tea mug, and so on. The thing I missed the most was my toothbrush.

Rinsing my mouth out twice a day with a smear of toothpaste and a gulp of water didn't really do the job.

When the exercise finally did end, I took the rancid socks and the indescribably foul pair of underwear I had been wearing (and had feebly tried to wash with what drinking water we could spare) and tossed them straight into the first bin I saw. There was no saving them.

FOXY VC

IF YOU LOOK UP EWOP on the NZDF website, you'll see that 'force protection' is labelled as one of the job descriptions. Force protection is a generic term that encompasses a lot of different roles in the military, including activities such as security patrols, threat assessments, perimeter defence, intelligence gathering, access control, surveillance and the implementation of countermeasures to potential threats.

Electronic Warfare is one of those countermeasures. When armies, militia or insurgent groups go to war, they use electronic communications. They're going to be on radios and whatever else they have on hand to talk to one another. That means, in any sort of remotely modern warfare setting, there are going to be hundreds of *thousands* of signals flying around the battle space every day. If you have the right equipment, a few trained operators and a little bit of luck, you can turn these random squeaks and squawks of noise into pretty powerful intelligence.

It just so happens that what happened next happened while I was in the outback, sweating into the same pair of manky socks for my eleventh straight day. So, forewarning: this is a 'second-hand dit' (see page xx for translation).

Corporal Fox and Sig Harata were in the back of one of our Pinzgauers, listening to the open-wave radio to try and identify anything of interest. In places where enemies aren't conventional armies (such as the Middle East) it wasn't uncommon for hostile forces to use simple, unencrypted radios, much like you'd see a security guard using. These can be picked up relatively easily, and the best part is you can hear what's actually being said (it's especially easy if the people speaking are from Sydney, and not speaking some random dialect of Arabic that only eleven people speak).

Fox and Tarpara heard an Australian accent, definitely describing what sounded like a potential ambush of friendly forces. Roughly transcribed, it went something like:

> **VOICE ONE:** … and that'll be that. Can you see anyone up there?
>
> **VOICE TWO:** Not now. There was a guy in it, but he's moved.
>
> **VOICE ONE:** Do you have a clear shot?
>
> **VOICE TWO:** Roger. I can see straight into the tower from here.
>
> **VOICE ONE:** Confirmed. Remain in place until a guard is in the tower and stands still enough to be targeted.

It was at this point that Fox and Tarpara started wondering which tower was being discussed. They peaked out the corner of the wagon and realised that it could be any of the numerous guard towers that had been hastily erected for the exercise. They were all two-storey, temporary structures set up so that a cycling roster of infantrymen could sit up there and stare into the outback, looking for signs of the enemy party.

The radio net squawked into life again.

VOICE TWO: Standby, standby, we have movement.

VOICE ONE: Roger, is it a combatant?

VOICE TWO: Confirmed, uniformed soldier wearing a J-hat and a camelback with a blue carabiner is making his way up the tower.

VOICE ONE: Roger. Wait until he's in place and then take the shot.

VOICE TWO: Acknowledged.

At this point, Fox looked out the back of the wagon and saw an Australian infantryman walking up the stairs of the nearest tower. The guy had a jungle hat on, and his camelback had a blue carabiner.

Fox didn't think twice. He unlocked the back of the Pinzgauer and launched himself out of it. He sprinted across the compound and started taking the stairs three at a time. Just as the Aussie private was finishing his assent to the top of the tower, he was tackled around the legs from behind and thrown roughly to the deck of the tower.

'What the FUCK!' hollered the Australian.

Fox said nothing, he was too busy gasping for air. The Australian tried to get up, but Fox wouldn't let him. For a long moment, nothing happened. Then, a single shot rang out.

Tarpara came out of the back of the Pinzgauer and started whooping. Enemy thwarted, job done. Pats on the back all round.

Or so they thought.

You see, any large military exercise is a bit like being on a big-budget film set, everybody in different departments trying to get their own tasks done in order to make the whole vision come to fruition. Also like a film, exercises have scripts. Certain events that occur will trigger other events, and therefore lead the gathered mass of soldiers to a desired conclusion at a desired place. Exercise ends, everybody happy.

This was still quite early in the exercise, about two days in. The 'enemy' had not been engaged in combat, or even seen directly at this stage.

What was *supposed* to happen, was that the enemy was supposed to be heard, and then they would take a lucky shot at a friendly soldier, who was *supposed* to get 'killed' to justify the friendly forces sending out a large retaliation force into the outback, thereby kicking off the actual combat section of the exercise, which would go on for several weeks.

However, the soldier that was meant to be shot very much hadn't been. Fox had just 'saved' him. He was referred to thereafter as 'Fox VC', as though his actions had earned him a Victoria Cross medal.

The exercise organisers, who had spent months and months planning every hour of Exercise Hamel, now had to come up with a whole new chain of events to justify the deployment of several thousand soldiers into 'foreign' territory.

What that meant for everyone on the exercise was, 'Wait, wait out.'

The exercise stalled for two days. Everyone stayed where they were. No enemies moved, no troops manoeuvred, nothing.

Out in the middle of the outback, our G-Wagon was the only man-made object for literally miles around. Our little detachment knew nothing of Fox's heroics. We just knew that we had nothing to do. The order came through the radio to 'Remain in place. Conduct no scanning to conserve battery power.'

'What the fuck?!' I hollered at no one in particular. We rushed to get out here and now there's nothing to do? Can we at least go back to base and grab my pack?

Dalton, feeling sorry for me and being a very decent human being, actually asked HQ if we could do just that.

A resounding 'no' came back almost immediately.

I started cursing and swearing and kicking the back tyre of the G-Wagon.

'Yep, that's the ol' green weenie for ya,' drawled a voice from the roof.

I climbed the side of the truck to see Brad, the marine, lying starfished on top of the G-Wagon wearing nothing but his underwear and a pair of sunglasses. The Australian sun beat down on his skinny frame as he gleamed with what smelled like tanning oil.

'The green what?' I asked.

'The green weenie, you know. Every time you want or need something to get done, the green weenie comes along and fucks you. It's the army's special way of saying, "I hear you, and I don't give a shit."'

'Like when you have leave booked and approved and the

day before your flight, the army sends you on course,' chimed in Mickey from somewhere.

Brad nodded sagely. 'Indeed, my friend. That is a textbook example.'

I understood. The 'green weenie' had robbed me of concerts I had bought tickets to, dates with cute girls I had planned, and all manner of things over the years. Now, it had stolen my pack.

'Sooner or later, the green weenie fucks us all,' Brad went on.

'Exercise Hamel is a shitshow so far,' I huffed.

'Seems like it,' agreed Brad. 'That's why I'm not on Exercise Hamel.'

Mickey laughed.

I was interested. 'Oh yeah? What ex are you on then?'

Brad gestured to his glistening torso. 'This is OPERATION BRONZE, my friend. A crucial mission in which I must become a shiny golden god before my time in Australia comes to an end and they ship my ass back to Florida.' And with that, he rubbed more tanning oil into his chest.

I looked around. Mickey was still chuckling. Dalton shrugged. Walsh was … somewhere. I made up my mind. If I was going to be stuck out here, I might as well get a tan out of the deal. I stripped off and jumped onto the roof next to Brad.

'Op Bronze!' I shouted.

'Op Bronze,' agreed Brad.

FIELD EXPEDIENT ANTENNAS

ONE OF THE LAST entries in the appallingly long list of 'shit that we forgot' on Exercise Hamel was none other than our most high-gain antenna. It was nearing the end of this extremely long, dusty (and for myself especially pungent) experience. We had been moving further and further from the nominal 'front line' and were at the top of a large hill. The bag of monkeys that was infantry HQ and their multiple Zero-Alphas had officially closed down the radio, and so we were back to being directly under the command of 7 Sigs again. *Great, brilliant!* I thought. Dalton pulled out the freq-sheet and found the frequency we ought to tune the long-range radio to.

He set it up and looked over at Walsh. 'Mate, grab the antenna.'

Even if it hadn't been Walsh, even if he hadn't suddenly adopted the look of a man who's realised halfway through his descent that his parachute is in fact a knapsack, I feel like my instincts knew before he even replied that there was no long-range antenna in our truck. It was probably back at camp, next to my pack and my fresh, clean socks. We did have a ten-foot whip, but it was for a completely different radio, so it was about as useful to us as a tank full of diesel was to someone who was stranded with a Suzuki Swift.

Walsh started mumbling, Dalton groaned, Mickey swore, I swore, Brad laughed, Dalton swore, I laughed. It went round like this for some time. All of us knew that this wasn't a minor inconvenience. We didn't know where to rendezvous with 7 Sigs to head back to base and we were too far from any other unit to jump on a shortwave radio and ask them to pass along a message now that the infantry net had shut down and couldn't be used as a relay.

The only real option, it seemed, was to pack up and go driving around, blasting the shortwave until we either made contact with someone or literally bumped into them. The Townsville Field Training Area, our home for the last several weeks, was spread over more than 200,000 hectares of land.

We were in a real pickle here. We knew that if we went driving through the training area, in this heat, with less than a full tank of gas remaining, there was a real possibility of us becoming a rescue situation. If we didn't die of thirst before we were rescued, we would definitely die of shame, or perish in the fires of military reprimand.

It occurred to me, in one of those very, *very* rare moments in life, that something I learned in a classroom could be useful here.

One of the lessons covered during my purgatory at Depot Troop was on FEAs, Field Expedient Antennas. Another TLA that, in this case, meant homemade antennas.

I asked Dalton to write down the frequency that we were supposed to be transmitting on, and got Mickey to start slicing up a long length of copper wire that was supposed to be used for the dummy Claymores we were supposed to put out, but never did. I vaguely remembered the calculations for cutting copper wire to length for a half-wavelength antenna because it was one of the questions in our test. Radio Wave propagation theory 101 – this is an abridged version, but it goes a little something like this ...

Radio waves travel through the air. With me so far? Depending on what is creating them, and how much power it is using to push them through the air, these radio waves come in a variety of sizes. Small, rapid waves move quickly over short distances, using a lot of power, and longer, slower ones travel over longer distances using less power.

'Frequency' is a term that refers to the number of cycles (when viewed on a graph, the distance between a peak and the next peak) that a wave completes in one second, i.e. the frequency of waves that it completes in a second. These are measured in hertz.

Since radio waves always and only travel at the speed of light (which is roughly 300,000,000 metres per second), you can work out the size of a wavelength by dividing the velocity (speed) of the wave by its frequency.

How does this help four stupid fucks on the side of a hill with a radio but no antenna, you may ask?

Essentially, we needed a piece of conductive material (metal) that was as close as possible in size to the wavelengths that we wanted to send and receive.

The wavelength (size) of a periodic wave (essentially, the size of the signal) can be calculated using this equation:

λ = wavelength

λ = 300/frequency (MHz) x VF

VF is Velocity Factor. Radio waves travel slightly slower in different materials by this amount. It's different for different sorts of wire. We had a good amount of copper wire, which I remembered has a VF of .95. Not massive, but significant enough that if you forgot about it, you'd only be hearing static and not knowing why.

I somehow dredged all that up from my memory while I sliced the bottom off a glowstick and drained it of gloopy, toxic fluid. I now had a hollow tube that was open at one end. While I worked out a rough and ready equation that was a combination of memory and confident improvisation, I asked Mickey to cut three more lengths of copper wire to the same length.

I cut the four lengths of wire as exactly as I could, and then pierced the still-sealed end of the glowstick in four places like a cross so the wires could be fed out and pulled tight.

Now I just needed a mast. The rather useless ten-foot whip was my new best friend. I stuck that into the hollow glowstick, braided the four wires inside the glowstick together and sliced off the rubber sheath, exposing the copper within. I jammed this into the antenna port on the radio and screwed it shut.

It rattled around loosely, but this wasn't important; the point of it was to get it off the ground. I had the guys stake my four wires out like the points of a cross. Once I'd raised my antenna up (only about six feet, to keep the wires facing mostly skyward) I was done.

When deciding what kind of antenna I was going to make, I went for the spray-and-pray approach. I wanted as much signal as possible coming out of our radio, with a large, wide angle of receive as well. The antenna that does this best, in my opinion, is the NVIS.

We had in front of us a homemade NVIS antenna. NVIS stands for Near Vertical Incident Skywave. I chose this specific antenna because I wanted as much coverage as possible. A NVIS antenna blasts signal up towards the sky and uses a low enough power and frequency combination that it bounces off the ionosphere and falls back down (hopefully) onto a friendly radio. Imagine a sort of umbrella of signal falling back down to Earth.

The downside of a NVIS antenna is that if any sneaky EW Operators are out and about looking for you, using one of these is akin to firing off a flare gun and screaming 'COME GET ME'.

But I wasn't worried about that right now. All I needed was a response. I'd happily suffer a bollocking later if it meant getting back in touch with command.

We fired up the radio and, with only one small electric shock, gave it a go.

We got a reply almost immediately. It sounded like an absolute ocean of static with the barest hint of a human voice, so garbled it was impossible to tell who it was or what was being said. I knew what was happening: it was called 'Donald Ducking', because that's what the voice signal that comes through sounds like. This happens when the signal is largely lost in the ionosphere and only a portion of it makes it back down to the ground. It wasn't exactly bad news, it meant we had gotten through on the correct frequency, but unless we could understand the other end, we were still just as stuck as before. My small consolation was that my antenna was working correctly and actually sending a signal all the way up into the sky, instead of simply blasting along the ground as a 'groundwave'.

We rotated the wires a bit and tried again.

This time, the response was faint and muddied, but comprehensible. Dalton recognised the other operator immediately and we all began a series of horrendous victory dances.

The 7 Sig guys all recognised their gruff sergeant and did a happy dance of joy. Dalton started relaying our location and all the other good stuff to the other end and I wandered off to enjoy a well-deserved cigarette. Partially for the nicotine, and largely because it was one of my few remaining ways to avoid smelling myself for a few minutes.

PART 4

AROUND THE WORLD

ZIGGY STARDUST: BARRACK MASCOT

IN 2015, I TURNED twenty-three. I was single, I lived in barracks. The only commitment I had in my life was a Dutch blue lovebird named Ziggy Stardust that lived illegally in my barrack room.

I say illegally because technically we weren't allowed pets. But everyone knew I had Ziggy. Shit, whenever our after-work drinks spilled over into the soldiers' barracks and our sergeants and officers came stumbling into our rooms to drink our rum and tell us what outstanding fucking lads we were, it would only be a matter of minutes before someone would start a chorus of, 'Bring out the BIRD!'

And so I would.

Ziggy was about the size of a fat mouse with wings. He was very soft and loved to sit (and subsequently shit) on people's shoulders. The officers loved him. They were amazed that he just lived in my barrack room with me, happy as a pig in shit.

As I said, we technically weren't allowed any sort of pet in barracks. On the rare occasion we actually had to endure an inspection, I would take Ziggy, in his huge cage that dominated the middle of my tiny room, and pop him in my car for the half hour it took for these things to transpire. A quick vacuum to suck up excess bird seed and feathers, and the inspecting officer was none the wiser.

When I was on basic training, and even Depot Troop to some extent, barrack inspections were serious business. You clean your room religiously. Not to actually clean it, it's already cleaner than an operating theatre. It's more like a game of cat and mouse, where you try and rack your brain for spots that the inspecting officer will try and find a speck of dust, or a strand of cobweb. And the officer spends his morning trying to think of spots in your room that you haven't already polished fifty times.

Down in Mexico, inspections were carried out so that our lieutenants could tell their captains to tell their major that he could put a little tick in the box marked 'barrack inspections' so that a huge pile of ticks could land on the camp commander's desk twice a year and he could promptly ignore them because the camp commander of Burnham Military Camp had to deal with things like brigade exercises and deploying people to Iraq and drunk grunts burning down barrack blocks.

When we did get inspections, it was more of an opportunity to start the day off at a leisurely pace and generally shoot the breeze with the officer and accompanying sergeant while they strode around gawking at the elaborate setups people had in their rooms.

Once, Lieutenant King, who knew perfectly well that I owned a tiny parrot, was the inspecting officer. He strode into the room and glanced around as though he hadn't been drunk in there playing *Madden* with me three weeks earlier. Although it was in an orderly fashion, every surface of my room had either a speaker or a picture of an *FHM* girl on it. Except for my chest of drawers, which was completely bare and spotlessly clean. Macca stared at the spot where he knew Ziggy's cage normally resided. He looked around, in his best impersonation of an officer conducting an inspection, and casually sauntered towards the drawers.

'Morning, Corporal,' he offered as he glided past me.

'Good morning, sir.' I remained outside my door, standing at ease.

'Got anything in here you shouldn't have?' he asked facetiously.

'Definitely not, sir.'

He made a show of glancing around the room at all my posters. Girls with tattoos and impossibly shaped bikinis smirked back at him.

'These your girlfriends?'

'That's right, sir. Reminds me what I'm fighting for.'

He laughed and, as he did, he opened the top drawer of Ziggy's cage-stand. Instead of balled-up socks, or more porn, he found a seed bell, packets of millet and enough birdseed to choke an ostrich.

'Interesting,' he murmured. He was really enjoying the charade. Clearly things were a little slow in the command cell that week.

He strode back out into the hall to face me. His expression was twisted into a comical parody of an officer's scowl, but his eyes were laughing.

'So, Corporal Davidson. Are you keeping a pet in barrack lines, against standing orders?'

I feigned outrage. 'Absolutely not, sir! I would never compromise the safety of my fellow soldiers by allowing a wild animal to live amongst them. Not including Sig Buzz.'

Buzz was standing about three feet from me when I said this and nearly had an aneurism trying not to chuckle. I didn't manage to break Macca, he was too driven trying to either get me to confess to Ziggy's existence or commit to an outrageous lie. Obviously I chose option B.

'No? No pet? Not a bird, or anything like that?'

Sergeant Enfield beside him began to grin wolfishly. He knew Ziggy well. After a few rums, he used to put Ziggy on his shoulder and start exclaiming that he was a pirate.

'No, sir. Just me and the floorboards,' I replied.

Macca savoured the moment before delivering his damming question.

'So, why do you have all that bird food then?'

I paused.

'Fibre.'

Nobody moved. To his credit, Macca kept a completely straight face.

'Very good. Carry on!'

He turned on his heel and, in a display of hilarious over-formality, strode out into the next corridor with a chuckling Sergeant Enfield close behind. Buzz, Jordy and myself leaned against the walls and did our best to contain our guffaws.

Sadly, wee Ziggy died while I was over in Australia for a few weeks of training. One of the boys was taking care of him and returned to my room one afternoon to find the little guy cold and stiff. The breeder I bought Ziggy from told me he likely died from separation anxiety, not uncommon among lovebirds. After three years sharing a room, I was quite upset to lose my feathered companion.

So, with Ziggy now gone, Lance-Corporal Davidson had nothing and no one tying him to Burnham Military Camp. I had just returned from Exercise Listening Redback in Australia. It had been a joint training between EWOPs from New Zealand, the UK, USA, Canada and Australia and it was fantastic. Two weeks of competing in sports, going out for beers. At some point, Electronic Warfare was briefly mentioned.

I had my annual leave booked for the day after we got back from Australia, so I jaunted over to Hawaii for ten days of, you guessed it, more beers. It was while I was in Hawaii that I received a military email to my civilian account. These always stand out alarmingly, because the military has a sort of internal network that they use for emailing each other all day. Emails have to be individually cleared to access the 'real' internet.

It was on my second day in Hawaii, sat on the beach waiting for a lovely American girl to return with two oversized alcoholic slushy concoctions. I checked my phone. The words -------UNCLASSIFIED------ *Lt King* were glaring on my screen. I skimmed the email briefly to find out that, a week after I was due to return, I would be heading off on some more training. Something called 'Long Look'.

For six months.

In England.

It was now July and I had spent less than two consecutive weeks of the year to date in my barrack room. Such is army life for an unmarried, unhoused individual.

I was absolutely chuffed to be heading to England. Not only was 2015 the year that England hosted the Rugby World Cup, not only had I never been to England before, but the unit I was going over to train with were none other than the Royal Marine Commandos, Y Squadron. I didn't know much about them beyond their military reputation for being a genuine, 'over the top, lads' fighting unit.

I was told to be at the front gate at 0430, where the airport shuttle would take me and Palmer to the airport. As was my tradition, I packed my single allotted bag the night before, after having spent all afternoon at the corporal's bar drinking beer, watching rugby, and shooting pool with Walker. Naturally, this meant I had about thirty T-shirts and nothing actually useful. The shuttle arrived and I heaved my comically overpacked army duffel bag into it and leapt into the van. We zoomed around the corner to the army housing area to pick up Corporal Palmer.

I was absolutely buzzing to spend the next six months in a foreign country. I could hardly sit still as we pulled into Palmer's driveway. Palmer shuffled out and flopped into the car, palpably less enthused. Not only was he quite a bit older than me, and therefore less hyperactive, he wasn't even an EWOP. He was a military intelligence soldier posted to our unit, for what was supposed to be a year or so to see how our squadron did business; so far he had been used as a stand-in operator in every field exercise and piece of foreign training. Due to the constant injuries plaguing our operators, 3 Sig command had learned to snatch any passerby with a security clearance and a working set of knees and throw them into the dets. Additionally, Palmer's wife had just had their first baby about a month ago.

I was stoked about travelling to foreign lands and drinking strange brews and liaising with exotic women. Poor old Palmer, on the other hand, saw it as being exiled to a completely different time zone away from his favourite two people in the world.

I must confess, once we had checked in and got onto the plane, my excitement got the better of me. Since we weren't in uniform and we had a full twenty-four hours of travelling ahead of us, I did the only thing any solider would do with a comfortable chair and no place of parade in my immediate future. I got extremely drunk. Not throwing up or loudly singing 'Bohemian Rhapsody' drunk, but enough that I was asked to 'please stop air drumming' by the passing flight attendant. Although I was understandably upset at being interrupted in the middle of a very technical drum solo, I managed to offset this tragedy by grabbing two handfuls of tiny liquor bottles directly from the trolley when the flight attendant served the person sitting across the aisle from me. Palmer watched me do it, his mouth agape. He barely managed to keep it together when I tapped the flight attendant and politely asked if I could trouble her for one more Bacardi before she left.

With my pockets full, Palmer and I played cards until I fell asleep somewhere over the ocean. I don't remember much of the stopover in Dubai, except for the immense struggle to remove my belt when going through a metal detector and giving Palmer a lot of hugs. Palmer told me later that his legs did most of the walking for the both of us, of which I have no doubt. I am eternally grateful for that man's ability to manoeuvre a highly intoxicated person through a liquor-free airport. Being detained on the way to a new military posting is a great way to suffer the wrath of two separate chains of command.

We landed in Heathrow, blinking like newborn sheep in the light and repeating the travellers' mantra of, 'What day is it?' As we stumbled out of the arrivals gate, it occurred to me that I had no idea who was picking us up. I'd met a few of the commandos on Listening Redback, but I didn't know any of them well. Anyway, Y Squadron had about forty people in it, how was I supposed to … Oh wait. There. The two huge guys wearing multi-cam and pointing at us. Well, that was easy.

The two guys asked us if we were from 3 Sigs. I laughed at the obviousness of the question before I realised that I was wearing jeans and a T-shirt in an airport filled with white guys in jeans and T-shirts. I was then mystified how they'd known to ask us specifically. One of the corporals, who introduced himself as 'Egg', said that we 'had the look', whatever that means. The other corporal was one of those annoyingly handsome, tall, tanned Brits. He flashed me a perfectly straight smile and shook my hand. 'I'm Cat.' He beamed.

These guys certainly looked like elite forces. The small one had eyes as hard as flint, and Cat was built like Captain America.

Cat and Egg. Did everyone in Y squadron have a random noun in place of a name? Was this some weird commando thing describing what they'd used to complete their first kill? If that was the case, I was immediately scared of Egg, and morbidly curious about Cat.

It felt as though Egg and Cat intentionally held back when they were in the car with us, and that passing through the threshold of Stonehouse barracks freed up their ability to revert to their mother tongue, because they started speaking a foreign language. I wasn't ready for the sheer volume of slang, jargon and utter gibberish that marines use each time they open their mouths. It was almost lunchtime, I was quite sleep deprived and more than a small bit hungover, and this is how my first interaction with the commandos' full screw went.

'Morning, Corporal.'

'Alright? What a hoofin' day, eh? Have ye scranned? There's pusser's in about an hour but it's pretty dog-shite so if you take a smally bimble up to the lads they'll sort ye out a janner pastie and a hot wet. Alright?'

I blinked like a stoned owl. Besides the fact that 'alright' was both a greeting and a question, there was a lot to unpack here. The above paragraph translates roughly as follows.

'How do you do? Lovely weather we're having, isn't it? Have you eaten yet? The mess hall will be open in approximately an hour, but its culinary reputation is lacking somewhat. If you take a small walk to the rest of the squadron, they'll show you where you can get a Cornish pastie and a cup of tea, sound good?'

Once you get the hang of it, bootneck slang was actually quite intuitive and straightforward. I must admit, my first week or so at Y squadron very much felt like I was learning a foreign language, so I treated it that way. The best way to learn a new language is to speak it, so I began inserting every commando word I could into my vernacular. I have compiled a small, but not exhaustive Bootneck-to-English dictionary.

-bats – Added to the end of words for emphasis. 'It's
  fucking rouge-bats in here.'
-pigs – Same as above.
Bimble – A walk.
Smally bimble – A short walk.

Dit – Short for ditty, a story.

Shit dit – An implausible, dull, or otherwise unlikeable story. 'He talked for twenty minutes about his lawn.' 'What a shit dit.'

Second-hand dit – 'I wasn't there but I heard from someone else.'

Drip – To complain. 'Having a drip.'

Elsan – The brand of field toilet that commandos use. Describes a useless or otherwise unliked person. 'That sergeant is an absolute elsan.'

Essence – So good, or very attractive. 'See that girl Smudge was with? Absolutely essence, mate.'

Fat one – Head.

Swede – Also head.

Grots – Barrack rooms.

Honkin' – Bad, foul tasting, ugly or otherwise unpleasant.

Hoofin' – Great, good.

Janner – A Plymouth/Cornwall local.

Matlow – Navy person.

Neggers – Short for negative, means no. (NOTE: Be careful how you pronounce this one.)

Pitchers – Dark (as in, 'pitch black').

Pongo – Army person.

Pussers – Official or issued equipment. 'Are those boots yours or pussers?'

Redders – Hot.

Rouge – Also hot.

Royal/Bootneck – A Royal Marine Commando.

Run Ashore, or Ashore – A night on the town.

Threaders – angry, annoyed or irate.

Waz – Really fucking good.

Wet – A drink, usually a beer.

A hot wet – A tea or coffee.

Yomp – A pack march. Can be used as the verb 'yomping'.

LOST LITTLE SOLDIERS

Y SQUADRON WAS TO be a part of a joint army/marines exercise held in the vast training area of Dartmoor. It was to be my first time actually out in the field with the Royal Marines and I was expecting a high degree of intensity, given their war-dog reputation. The night before we were due to leave, I'd been issued a pack, rifle and everything else I hadn't been able to take on the plane from New Zealand with me. I had the British ration pack laid out on my bed, which was, I'm pleased to report, superior to the NZDF's ration packs in every conceivable way. Better snacks, better meals, M&Ms, and these wonderful peanut butter/biscuit hybrids that I've never been able to find since.

I was determined to get through my packing, and then I was going to go to bed.

Of course, this was not to be. Charlie came bursting into my room shortly after dinner.

Charlie was the squadron rogue. He was about as disobedient as possible without actually breaking any rules (not obviously, at least) and was charming enough to get away with it. He was obsessed with baking. On more than one occasion I would wander into his barrack room and see him, oven mitts and an apron on, poking a skewer through a fresh loaf of banana bread he had made in his tiny oven. He watched *The Great British Bake Off* like it was an MMA fight, yelling and thumping the walls whenever his contestant 'absolutely nailed that brioche, mate'. He was undoubtedly a character, and quickly became my closest friend at Y Squadron. After partnering up for a particularly brutal PT session, and winning the fireman's carry relay race, we became inseparable.

However, like any good best friend, Charlie's real talent lay in getting the both of us into trouble.

He sauntered into my room under the pretence of helping me pack. He started tossing items from the rat pack out.

'Don't need these, these are fucking honking, these are wazpigs though, you'll want these.'

After about two minutes of this, he delivered his pitch.

'Looks like you're about done here. It's pound a pint night at Mousetrap. Shall we?'

Pound a pint was a weekly special where one might procure a pint of beer or cider for one pound sterling. Was it good beer? No. Was this an idiotic way to spend a Tuesday night before a field exercise? Without a doubt. Was I in Mousetrap fifteen minutes later, talking to two local girls about my far-off land, Middle-earth? Absolutely.

My recollections of the rest of the evening are foggy, having spent all ten pounds I brought with me, but I remember the following morning, vividly.

It was awful.

Smudge kicked my door open at 0830, wondering 'Why the fuck didn't you turn up to the armoury?' I was wrapped up in my blankets and my tongue was drier than an old sponge, so my response wouldn't have been comprehensible, even if it had been a wonderful excuse.

He sighed and told me he'd sign my weapon out for me if I could get my shit together in ten minutes or less. I groaned in a mixture of agreement and nausea.

I dozed the entire drive to the exercise. Before I knew it, I was in a four-man detachment, with a pack full of rations, batteries and equipment that was (figuratively and literally) worth more than my life.

It was a standard exercise: arrange EW soldiers into dets, send those dets into the woods for a week and tell them to look for baddies.

By this stage, this was mostly what my job back in New Zealand consisted of, so I was quite used to it. Highlights included an inquisitive fox that stopped by to check me out while I was on sentry, and being tasked to find a detachment of British soldiers that had gone missing.

Much like every military, the different branches of the British armed forces regard each other with thinly veiled contempt. A soon as the command came over the radio that an army detachment had missed several radio checks and that we were to go out looking for them, there was a chorus of woe from the marines I was with.

'Fucking useless pongo shites.'

'What a pack of absolute *elsans*.'

'I'm absolutely threaders with this lot.'

And so on.

We spent more than a few hours crashing through the undergrowth, hissing and shining torches, but in the end it was another detachment that found the lost little soldiers.

Shortly after my arrival at Y Squadron, it became evident to me that they weren't exactly prepared for a foreign soldier to be at their workplace for months on end. Being in an army unit is a bit like being enrolled in university, except everyone in your class has different degrees and different assignments that they want to complete on different days. Soldiers are always coming and going away for licensing, firearms qualifications, and a thousand other 'courses' that comprise a military career. Not only that, but because of the way security clearances work, I was only allowed to see and hear about half of what was being discussed in Y Squadron on a daily basis. On my third or fourth day, once I knew my way around, Y Squadron's enormous platoon sergeant pulled me aside.

'Look mate, this exchange, it's quite new to us. Also, this is a hectic time here at the squadron, with getting lads through their security clearances, and NCO courses and such ... Anyway, what I'm saying is, I'm not going to spend the next six months telling you what to do every day, alright? You do as much or as little as you like.'

And that was that. I hung around the squadron most mornings, attended PT with them, and partook in various training activities. But if something didn't appeal to me, most times I would just excuse myself and stroll away to the barracks. By the end of the first month, I had a pretty firm daily routine.

0730 – Wake up, breakfast and shower (or catch a taxi back to base from wherever I happened to be staying).
0800 – PT with the squadron. Commando PT was rough, especially hungover, but it was something I told myself I

would always attend, no matter what. I didn't care much about what the senior officers thought of my work ethic, but I didn't want the marines to think I was soft.

0900 – Walk to the squadron, drink tea and eat biscuits while listening to the day's agenda. Maybe run an antenna from the roof of the fort or something.

1100 – Sprint to lunch, eat in less than ten minutes and spend the rest of my lunch fast asleep in bed.

1300 – Cleaning. Y Squadron is a clean unit, even by military standards. Their fort is spotless, because thirty guys clean it for an hour every day.

1400 – Start planning with Charlie which bars we'll be out to that evening.

1500ish – Finish work for the day, back to bed.

1800 – Wake up, eat dinner, and start getting ready for a night out.

1900 – Watch TV with Charlie while drinking beers.

2000 – Out for a 'run ashore', spend the night drinking and looking for whichever local girl enjoys making fun of my accent the most.

Sometime around 0300 – Find a kebab and stumble home, back to barracks to fall asleep and do it all over again.

This wasn't *every* day. But it was a lot of them.

EXERCISE IRON LUNG

A WEEK 'YOMPING' AROUND the mountains of Wales, twenty to thirty kilometres a day, in sleet.

It was my final big excursion with Y Squadron, a bunch of lads I had come to like as much as anybody back home in New Zealand. Exercise Iron Lung was absolutely rough, but virtually all military friendships are based on mutual suffering. I made it through all five days without succumbing to injury or falling behind, a point of personal pride for a wee Kiwi signaller trying to match pace with the Royal Marine Commandos.

Finally, one cold and blustery day, it was time to fly home. There was a small, informal ceremony in which Y Squadron presented me with a plaque that the lads from the squadron had signed the back of for me. To my everlasting frustration, two days after I moved back to Auckland that plaque was stolen from my car, along with a backpack filled with unit patches I'd collected from all over the world, and the knife I'd carried with me every day. I never saw it again, but I think about it often. It was a bag of some of my most treasured memories, and whoever found it would have gained absolutely no monetary value from it. I hope they step on Lego.

It was December 2015. I had been in England for most of the year. I'd almost forgotten that I had a home unit; I'd become so used to being the foreign exchange student, it was strange to think I'd be heading back to New Zealand to actually do my job once again.

I was so desensitised to acts of depravity and sheer fucking cringe that I failed to rise to even the most obvious of pranks. I shuffled off the plane, exhausted, hot and at the precise midpoint between drunk and hungover. Instead of going to barracks, I rolled straight to Walker's new house, in all its domestic glory. I came inside to a chorus of cheers, and no sooner was a cold drink in my hand than the boys directed me to a squat Scottish corporal sitting on Walker's snot-green couch. (Despite being able to spot a single wilted leaf in a forest, virtually all military men are colourblind as far as interior decorating goes. Walker's couch and carpet resembled a used tissue.)

The Scot licked his lips, and asked me with as much nonchalance as a man in a doomed submarine, 'Yeralrite mate, ver seen a coak-queef?'

I barely blinked as I sat down next to him.

'Go on then.'

He then proceeded, against everything I thought I knew about human biology, to pull out his penis and squeeze it in a way that eventually coaxed a small but definitely audible 'fart' out of his urethra.

Everybody has a talent, as they say.

WELCOME TO THE WAR MACHINE

BEFORE THEY DEPLOY TO a warzone (we don't say 'war' anymore, we say 'global conflict') or ever set foot on foreign soil, every solider and officer must undergo pre-deployment training (PDT). For those of us in 3 Signal Squadron, this started the moment we got back to work in January from Christmas leave. For the first week back, all we did was fill out mountains of paperwork, frantically update our security clearances and work on our wills.

It feels a bit strange, writing a will at age twenty-three, but once it was done it wasn't like it was a recurring issue. I assume it was a bit more significant for those with wives and children. Mine was the formal version of 'give everything to my mum'.

The second thing they have you do is to take your death photo. This is in case you get killed on deployment. They want a nice, formal picture of you smiling that they can hang over your coffin, because in all likelihood, if you get killed in Iraq, there won't be much left of your face. So, you get into your dress uniform, look as good as possible, try not to think about the four-hour lecture you just had on the extreme effectiveness of IEDs, and smile for the camera.

Because we were being deployed with Australian soldiers, under an Aussie command, most New Zealand elements had to learn some new ways of doing business. EW operators were no exception. In fact, we had to spend over a month in Toowoomba, learning new pieces of equipment and a bunch of radio theory. Of course, we had all gone through such study on our respective Signaller Corps training, but that was years ago. In the realm of communications technology, specialist knowledge can legitimately become redundant within a year of learning it.

The month in Australia went by quickly. We spent a lot of time in classrooms and got to know the six Australians we would be deploying with, but also joined the rest of 7 Sig Squadron for morning PT sessions and drinks at their base bar. It was during one of these sessions that I saw a solider lose a bet, and subsequently drink beer using an orifice usually reserved for disposal. Until I watched the last 'gulps' of liquid disappear from the bottle into the grimacing soldier's body, I wasn't certain such a thing was biologically possible. There was another one of life's mysteries solved.

We got back to New Zealand, freshly trained and amicable with our Australian counterparts. The rest of PDT was a grind. We had to learn about the country we were going to, its history, the people, and the enemy we were going to face. The content was objectively interesting, but the delivery left a lot to be desired.

Imagine being at a university lecture, except everyone in the room has ADHD and the person teaching the content has only learned to read out loud that same morning. I did my best to stay tuned in to what was potentially lifesaving information, but the droning sergeant's voice sent my conscious brain scurrying for cover while my head filled with daydreams.

There were practical parts to PTD too: learning how to assemble and arrange body armour, for example. Humans have been wearing armour for thousands of years. It's good at keeping the red squishy bits in and the pointy bad bits out. Looking at old-fashioned knights in suits of armour that weighed over twenty kilograms, our issued RBAV (Releasable Body Armour Vest) at eight kilograms is arguably not that bad. Modern body armour is basically a vest that goes over your clothes and has inserts where you place thick ceramic plates.

Why ceramic? 'The specific composition and manufacturing process of ceramic armour allow it to dissipate the energy of incoming projectiles efficiently, reducing trauma to the wearer.' So goes the official statement. In simple terms, you want it to break. Bullets travel so fast (it's hard to comprehend just how fast) that if one hits you in the chest and you're wearing a large piece of metal that won't break, it's your ribs that do the shattering.

Ceramic is also lighter than metal, which is a bonus if you're trying to run around all Captain America-like. Just be careful not to drop them or breathe on them too hard. Dumping your armour on the ground after a full day on patrol can be a very expensive mistake (in the ballpark of $8,000 or so).

They're supposed to be able to stop one or two 7.62 rounds (which are what come out of an AK-47) and after that you had better hope the person shooting at you has been shot in return.

We also learned the basic structure of common IEDs. These probably started being used in guerrilla warfare approximately one week after gunpowder was invented, but they've grown more significant over time. The ones you see in movies, where people call a phone and a huge bomb goes off that levels a building? Totally real, unfortunately for anyone in the building.

There was also the matter of my hair. Soldiers are not allowed to have piercings, 'extreme' haircuts or what they describe as 'obviously dyed hair'. I feel as though this was to account for women in the military who habitually dye their hair subtly darker or lighter and have done for most of their adult lives. Nobody gives a shit if Wendy from logistics is actually a dark blonde and not a brunette. I don't believe the rule allows for a man with dark brown hair who suddenly turns up blonder than Madonna. And yet, that's exactly what I did.

During our training in Australia, I had made a wager with Bailey about the outcome of the Oscars. Unfortunately, DiCaprio won, which meant that I lost. I paid my usual hairdresser and (after asking if I was *really* sure) she diligently proceeded to dye my entire head white-blonde. It was awful. I looked atrocious. When my det got to PTD in New Zealand,

I had to act as though nothing was wrong, even though every senior NCO in the room was staring daggers at me every time I took off my beret. My eyebrows were as dark as ever, which only made me look more insane. Matters were not helped by the fact that, each time I pulled my beret off and the senior soldiers and officers stared at my head as though I had a swastika shaved into the side of it, Bailey, Stevens and the rest of the boys would start badly containing their sniggers.

I was only able to tolerate a week of this, and that weekend I made a decision to fix my hair. A box of supermarket dye only succeeded in turning my hair from an eye-watering blonde to a very conspicuous jet-black.

Fortunately, this strategy proved to be just enough to avoid being made to shave my head and start over, because the aggressive glares subsided to derisive sneers. Fine by me.

WELCOME TO TAJI

WHEN I TOLD PEOPLE I was going to Iraq, the heat was always one of the first things to come up. The curious thing was, almost everyone I spoke to about my destination had the same strange reassurance for me.

'Oh, well sure it's hot. But it's a dry heat, you know it's the *humidity* that gets ya.' 'It's not so bad if it's a dry heat, you know.' And so on.

Interestingly, nobody offering this sage advice had ever actually been to Iraq, or the Middle East at all, for that matter. But that didn't deter everyone from trying to console me with the knowledge that nine months of dry heat wouldn't be so bad.

I can assure you, dear reader, when the average days are forty-five degrees Celsius, with some special bonus extra hot ones, 'dry' or otherwise, it's absolutely so very, very bad.

Not only was Iraq hot, dusty and generally stifling, it was *relentlessly* so. What I mean is that the temperature ranged from uncomfortably hot to unbearably hot, and it strafed between the two. It never rained in Taji, not a single drop, for the entirety of 2016. I could count the number of clouds I saw during my deployment on one finger. One.

But nature is all about balance, and less than a fortnight after my rotation departed Taji, there was a rainfall of absolutely Biblical proportions. The entire camp flooded and then became a quagmire that sucked down vehicles and soldiers alike. We received photos of two American squaddies actually rowing an inflatable dingy across what had been a vehicle mustering point. The camp was thereafter referred to as 'Lake Taji'. (Where they got the dingy from, I have no idea, but given the American military's record of supply and logistics, I was surprised it wasn't a frigate.)

We had flown to Dubai and conducted some last-minute training at the American air base there. We were flown into Taji in a C-130, aka a Hercules. They are extremely loud, slow and uncomfortable aircraft. Most guys watched stuff on tablets or phones, or tried to sleep wearing earplugs. I always had the same solution; headphones in and turn up some loud, angry music.

Pendulum's *The Tempest* was playing when we could see the faint lights of Taji base in the distance out of the tiny, Titanic-style windows in the Herc. Anyone who hadn't noticed was suddenly alerted when the night sky lit up just outside the plane. Scores of flares were being deployed out of the Hercules. It wasn't uncommon for the local insurgents camped out on the hill to take pot-shots at the plane with their rifles. But the flares weren't for that. They were on the off-chance that one of them had a Stinger, or other similar shoulder-mounted rocket launcher that could possibly take down the plane. Deploying flares was an expensive, but comprehensive, safety measure.

When we landed it was already unpleasantly hot. I was doing my best to pretend I could hear everything the logistics sergeant was yelling at us over the collective roar of the active airfield we were standing on. He said something about indirect fire and, right then, the nearest helicopter got far enough away that I could hear him.

'So, the Iraqi Army retreated from the nearby base and ISIS seized some of their artillery, along with a few tanks and fuck knows what else. But the important part for you is, ISIS knows this base is full of "Americans" and have been taking pot-shots with their new toys at the base a few times a week. Luckily for us, they've got shit aim and haven't actually managed to hit the base yet. But they have hit the nearby town of Tarmiya. The short of it is, if you hear a big loud fucking siren that doesn't stop, get your helmet and body armour on, even if you're in the shower, and lie down. If you hear a series of sirens, grab your shit and run to one of the shelters scattered around base. Someone will point them out to you tomorrow. That's all for now. Welcome to Taji.'

('Americans' described any foreign soldier who spoke English as a first language, so that included us Australians and

Kiwis. I got used to being called American by the end of the first week.)

My detachment and I looked around and saw everyone was moving into the back of a large American truck. We clambered in. When you have body armour on and a rifle to look after, you take up far more room than usual, so the ride felt extra cramped. We passed through a security gate where serious-looking Fijian soldiers waved us through. The truck wove its way through the chicane, which was made from the shell of a burned-out car and barbed wire, and we rounded the corner. I got a quick glimpse of the base in full.

It was mostly grey, with areas of grey-brown. T-wall stretched on forever: huge, imposing slabs of cement that the US used to build FOBs. They were about four metres tall on average and they were arranged through camp to make streets and lanes as well as encircling the entire camp. Almost every single piece of T-wall was covered in graffiti. Not the good, colourful artsy kind that councils pay to make their skate parks look hip. It was the toilet-wall scrawlings that you can find in military installations all around the world. We got off the truck as we arrived at the Australian/NZ HQ and I was close enough to read one of the inscriptions. It was one of many, but the reference to Plato drew me in. In a neat, no-nonsense script, it read: *Only the dead have seen the end of T-Wall.*

That about summed it up.

A large military base is like a small town. Taji base is like a big town. It's about twenty-seven kilometres north of Baghdad and has been under American control since 2003. In true American style, before 2010, the food court also included

Taco Bell, Popeyes Chicken and Seattle's Best/Cinnabon. These days, it's more like a vast cafeteria you'd see in a school or a prison. It has a dining hall (the mess/galley/chow hall/whatever stupid name your parent military calls the place where the food is), several gyms, a few stores where heavily vetted locals are permitted to sling their overpriced wares to bored soldiers, and, of course, a church. We were told on our first night that the church was currently 'closed' because someone had broken in the night before and stolen every single bottle of communion wine. We found this especially amusing.

Unsurprisingly, being in such a dangerous area, Taji was a dry base. This meant that absolutely no alcohol was permitted to be sold, bought, consumed, made or otherwise imbibed on camp. The exception, of course, was the Catholic right to drink wine once a week, under the guise of pretending it was the blood of Christ.

We were shown to our 'rooms', which were actually converted shipping containers. There were hundreds of them, arranged in rows to make strange little neighbourhoods in this surreal place. They were sporadically interrupted by chunks of T-wall, designed to prevent artillery from wiping out an entire block of us at once. It made for a very ramshackle aesthetic. Especially when you added all the shanty-town clothes lines, regimental stickers and spray-painted graffiti that adorned every inch of 'the lines', as the living district was known.

There were two men to a room, and we each had slightly less space than was allotted to us on basic training. The container had a linoleum floor, with a pair of cheap metal tallboys, the obligatory rusted, springy metal beds, and a hilariously small 'air-conditioner' in the corner of the room. A tiny window in the back gave me a view of the next container, which was less than an arm's length away. This is where I would live for the rest of 2016.

We met up with the Australians we had trained with for PDT and also saw a familiar face. It was Mikey, one of the boys from 3 Sigs that we were there to take over from. There was a week of overlap between us arriving and them leaving, so that a handover could take place. We walked down one of the dusty main 'roads' of camp and arrived at our walled-off compound. Inside, we were introduced to our interpreters.

Obviously, one of the major barriers for any overseas operation is that of language. We had received exactly one classroom lesson in Arabic, the predominant language in Iraq, and between the six of us we probably knew about six words, which would undoubtedly be mispronounced. Fortunately, the US-of-A had an abundance of citizens with Arabic as a first language. Many of these were people who had been born in Iraq and left as children with their parents following the first Gulf War. This was the case with Margaret and Sam, except that Margaret was actually from Armenia. Regardless, the two of them now worked on Taji base as civilian contractors, interpreting for us, teaching us about Iraqi cultures and generally just making our jobs possible. Without them, we would have been more useless than a submarine window.

There was a third interpreter, a man named Abbas. He was at least sixty, with an immaculately shaved head and a goatee that he dyed black. He was an absolute unit, with that layer of fat that covers muscular guys who drink beer and eat meat their whole life. He had been living at Taji for two years by the time we showed up. The current rotation of guys warned us that he was a good interpreter, but otherwise a grumpy asshole. No problem, I just filed him under the category of prickly NCOs I had dealt with in the past and thought no more of it. It should be easy enough to just avoid him where possible, right?

Of course not.

Most of our work took place during the day, but not all. If war stopped when everyone went to bed, that would be great, but unfortunately it's not the case. We needed to have someone awake all night, working with an interpreter to go through any and all new information that came through our various sources, even if that info came through at 0300. It had been set up by the last crew to have two people on night shift every night. In my position in the detachment, it fell to me to write the shift roster. Nobody wanted to be on night shift. It was a two-week rotation, and meant living like a vampire, trying to sleep during the day when the temperature rose above thirty degrees before 0900. I doubted the longevity of any such schedule, and so placed myself on night shift before subjecting any of the lads to it.

It was awful. I tried to rest that afternoon but was still adjusting to the heat. Combined with the glaring sunlight that worked its way through the shades and the crack in the door, and the roar of heavy vehicles that seemed to be driving laps around my container, sleep was nearly impossible.

Nevertheless, eventually 1800 came around and I woke up and walked to the mess hall while everyone was getting dinner so I could get my 'breakfast'. I sat with a few of the guys from my detachment and, all too soon, they were returning to the lines to sleep while I walked along the road towards the compound where our work was conducted. Buzz was there, being the last worker of the day shift, and Abbas was outside smoking a cigarette.

Abbas and I sat down and began work. I think I managed about ten words out of him that whole first night. It was long, exhausting work, but eventually 0600 arrived. The compound door opened and one of the cheerful Australians poked his head in. Abbas didn't miss a beat. As soon as Sam, the day translator, showed up, Abbas was out of his chair and heading for the exit. I followed suit; I was shattered.

This was how my first two weeks in Iraq went. Working from dusk till dawn, spending my days caught between a doze and staring at the flimsy plywood ceiling of my container. It became clear to me beyond all doubt during this fortnight that humans are most certainly not nocturnal. My health deteriorated. I was irate, constantly tired. I lost track of time far too easily and I found that I couldn't concentrate on anything for more than a few minutes.

I also built a pretty good rapport with Abbas. I realised very quickly that he wasn't a grumpy bastard at heart. He was a bit gruff, sure, but growing up in a country run by Saddam Hussein was unlikely to forge anyone into a cuddly optimist. He was prickly because he'd been stuck on night shift for two months before we arrived. I had been at it less than two weeks and was about ready to burn the whole place down.

Abbas was actually a great guy. He had been a mortar-man in the Iraqi army in the 1980s, and had therefore fought in more conflicts than almost everyone else in the building combined.

After the third night, he started trying to teach me Arabic. I can say with utmost sincerity that he was a pretty decent teacher, and I was a terrible student. Arabic is a difficult language at the best of times. It wasn't just learning a new alphabet, or different concepts for sentence structure than I was used to in English or Italian. The most difficult part for me was training my mouth to make sounds it had never made before. Once you've grown up learning a language, your brain tends to think that all the vowels and consonants you know are all the sounds that there are. Any new words you learn in your native tongue are just different combinations of those sounds. Of course, there are many, many, *many* more sounds that the human mouth can make. And Arabic is made up of lots of them.

It was coming up to the end of my two-week stint on night shift, and Bailey was scheduled to take over. I couldn't stand the idea of anyone in my det suffering through what I had just done; I was even less enthused about it being my turn again in another six weeks. On day thirteen, I showed up for shift an hour early and went through our workload, tasks pending, and other such details. I devised a plan that would make sure we didn't fall behind, and nobody would have to sit on night shift any longer.

It was passed up the chain of command and a mere three days of bureaucratic buck-passing later, night shift had officially been abolished in our SCIF.

ATTACK

WE WERE ON THE RANGE with the Iraqi Security Forces when it happened. I say 'we' were on the range, but really it was the ISF that were doing the shooting. They were being coached by a few sergeants from 2/1st Battalion, while the corporals and privates stood around in a defensive perimeter. These guys did this almost every day. Drive outside the inner gate, set up a perimeter, stare at the desert. Rinse and repeat. I know my deployment wasn't pleasant, but I do console myself with the thought that at least I wasn't a security guard for eight months. It was definitely made worse by the fact that there were hostile combatants out there somewhere, so you can't switch off the way that you would if you were on exercise in Dip Flat, for example.

It was a boy, no older than sixteen, who had gotten into a car that had been converted into a bomb with wheels. He drove it towards camp, making it as far as the outer checkpoint before he was challenged. There were several Fijian security guards and a platoon of ISF forces by the gate.

And then he pressed detonate. It wasn't likely to be an actual button; probably just two pieces of wire held apart by a sliver of cardboard. Pull the cardboard tab away, the wires touch, circuit complete and bombs away.

We all heard it. I was talking to the commanding officer at the time. He was responsible for all Kiwi soldiers outside the perimeter. Because of the non-circular design of the base, we were going to have to go right past the attack site to make it back to the ANZAC lines.

My vehicle, with two EWOPs, an infantry gunner and a driver, was second in the convoy, so we got a good look at ground zero. I saw the plume of black smoke over the T-wall as we approached. Before we rounded the first corner, I saw an Iraqi truck speeding towards us, with a bloodied man sitting in the passenger seat. I didn't turn to watch where it went, but I could hear the voices of several men yelling in Arabic as it passed. One of them was screaming.

We came around the corner and I scanned for the gatehouse. I thought we must have been further away than I thought, because there was no sign of it. Then I realised it was gone. There was virtually nothing left besides a flat foundation of cement, mostly obscured by rubble and the black stain of burnt carbon.

There were more injured men here. There was one only metres away who had lost his leg above the knee. Two men desperately wound a tourniquet around his thigh while he lay there and shook violently.

Five Iraqi soldiers died.

Twenty-eight were injured.

And one ISIS recruit gave his life to kill his countrymen.

That's the part that hit me the hardest. This boy had been indoctrinated, radicalised and then driven to commit suicide in order to murder his own people. I'm sure that the goal of his attack was to kill 'Americans', but it didn't happen. He was yet another Iraqi casualty in a country that has been the centre of conflict, on and off for most of the 21st century.

Much of the indoctrination is done by local religious leaders, imams (basically priests). Obviously, not all imams are out there recruiting for extremist groups, but some are. They convince these young men with no direction that there's some great purpose in suicide.

It was especially heartbreaking one day to listen to a mother, pleading with an imam to let her boy come home, instead of going through with the task that he had 'volunteered' for.

It could be my cynicism, or maybe just my personal experience, but every imam we came to know over there gave me zero impression that they actually believed the doctrine they were spouting. I seriously doubted that they believed in the afterlife, or the 'seventy-two fruits' (which is a more accurate translation than the oft-quoted seventy-two virgins, or so I've been told). They enjoyed the prestige of being respected, they enjoyed the money that ISIS gave them, and that was where their loyalties truly lay.

One of the difficult parts for me to understand, as a foreigner, was the sheer number of factions contained within Iraq. In simple terms, we were over there to assist the ISF in their battle against ISIS. ISIS wanted to control Iraq and Syria by overthrowing their elected governments and replacing their constitutions with 'Sharia', the legal doctrine set out in the Islamic religious text, the Qur'an as they interpret it. Without delving into too much detail, one can see how this system is not ideal for anyone unfortunate enough to be born LGBTQIA+, or a woman.

Beyond this, we found that a lot of the issues we were dealing with were more deeply rooted than the relatively recent appearance of ISIS. Iraq is largely a Muslim country. In 2015, 98% were Muslim, 1% were Christian, and another 1% were 'other'.

But much like Christianity, there are sects of the Islamic faith. Iraq's Muslim population is two thirds Shi'ite, and one third Sunni. They both follow the Qur'an and the teachings of the prophet Mohammed. Do you think that they see eye to eye? Absolutely not. A lot of the daily conflicts, shootings and localised violence didn't even involve ISIS. It was Sunni vs Shi'ite. So locals have their religious allegiances to consider. But they also all belong to tribes based on what specific area they are from, much like New Zealand's localised iwis. Tribes in Iraq can trace their lineage back literally a thousand years or more, and disputes are often settled by AK-47 instead of the small claims court.

Because of marriages and movements, people can often be in the same tribe as one another, but be from different religions, and vice-versa. As if this isn't complicated enough, tribes and religions can be superseded by familial ties. So every Iraqi local has three (potentially conflicting) allegiances to consider when making big decisions about their futures.

Throw decades of Western invasion into the mix, and you have a nation of people who are not only tragically used to violence and warfare, but they're unbelievably hardened by it all. Which brings me to the final group of factions: the militia. Once ISIS started invading Iraq and Syria, groups of locals started banding together to defend their homeland from these aggressors. They weren't members of the military or any other officially sanctioned group. They would be several male members of the same family or tribe and they would give themselves a name and fly a flag of their own making from the back of a pickup truck. Some of these militias have been around for several decades, having fought *against* the Americans in the first Gulf War. They often made themselves uniforms and would gather in groups of up to 100 strong. Officially, they were on the same side as us and the ISF, so we were told to treat them basically how we would treat a small, allied country in the same battle area as us. Unfortunately, this didn't hold so well in reality. These guys were unpredictable, untrained and answered only to themselves. They would show up at the base at random, demanding ammunition or additional weapons, in exchange for 'intelligence'. They would claim to know the position of thousands of ISIS troops or places they had seen ISIS placing mines.

Most of the time it was utter horseshit. Sometimes, however, they would show up with a truck full of freshly dead bodies, again wanting ammunition or some other reward for 'killing ISIS'. We had no way of knowing if these corpses actually were ISIS or just some unfortunate rival militia they had come across.

As you can imagine, it also didn't take long for ISIS to clue onto the sort of access that these guys had to American and other Western forces, so they started embedding their agents into militia groups, which made things very fucking stressful for us.

If you want to know what a typical day on Taji base was like, it's difficult to give a simple schedule. Not only did things change constantly, but as the 2IC for the detachment and liaison between the Australian and Kiwi corporals running our SCIF, my days were anything but consistent. The only regular occurrence was waking up in a puddle of sweat and immediately downing a bottle of piss-warm water.

There was virtually no plumbing on Taji base, with the possible exception of the mess hall, I assumed. All our showers were transportable units hooked up to vast tanks of water, much like you'd see at a festival. The toilets were portaloos. If you ever want to regret owning a nose, try using a portaloo at 1400 when it's forty-eight degrees outside (making it approximately 400 degrees inside the festering cubicle) after a platoon of infantry on a high-protein diet has rolled through.

The lack of central plumbing throughout base meant that our drinking water came in plastic bottles, brought in by the thousand. Not thousands of bottles, thousands of shrink-wrapped *pallets*, delivered to base from the US via aircraft constantly. They were the cheap, thin plastic that crumpled instantly. Pallets were simply strewn around the base and people would tear into them without rhyme or reason. Half-finished pallets were often stacked on top of unopened ones. Each bottle held 600 millilitres of water. On a slow day, when I wasn't spending too much time outside, I'd go through five or six of them. On the days when I went out on patrol or was stood at the range watching the ISF narrowly miss each other with live rounds, I'd drink a dozen or more.

From the moment you wake up, you sweat constantly. It just becomes a layer that sits on your skin until you don't even notice it. Except you notice it on everyone else. Everybody has a unique sweat smell, and after a few months, I could tell who had been sitting in a chair before me based on the whiff that came off it.

I am one man. Drinking an average of eight bottles of water a day, multiplied by the 214 days I was in Iraq, means I drank about 1,712 plastic bottles of water. There were over 5,000 soldiers on that base. To my knowledge, not one of those bottles was recycled. We had bins that everything from food waste to bullet casings were dumped into without ceremony. The plastic water bottles are the tip of the iceberg when it comes to the waste, pollution and inefficiency that the military wreaks upon a country it's 'saving'. Is recycling a pressing issue when there are mortars and artillery being aimed at your base each day? Probably not. But it's definitely food for thought when you consider that Iraq, Afghanistan and dozens of other countries have been occupied by foreign troops for the better part of the past fifty years.

BLACK WATER

AS A RENTING OR ratepaying adult, you'll definitely know the term grey water. One day while walking across base, I saw huge tanker trucks with the words 'black water' spray-painted ineptly across the side of them. The mystery of what this ominous liquid could be was solved when I saw a huge pipe coming out of the truck attached to one of the portaloos.

The trucks were driven by locals. Apparently some local entrepreneur had assembled a ramshackle fleet of these vehicles and was being paid an exorbitant amount of cash to cart away our shit.

I was talking to an Australian logistics officer about an unrelated issue when one of the black water trucks rolled past one day.

'Where do they take the shit?' I asked.

He dragged on his cigarette and shrugged. 'Probably to a local sewage site that his brother owns or something. As long as it's not here, who fuckin' cares.'

And I assumed he was right, until I was out on patrol one day beyond the main perimeter of the base, where hundreds of buildings reduced to rubble were the only scenery for literally miles around. The only living things you regularly saw out here were skinny stray dogs picking through the debris for scraps of food or a partially decomposed arm to gnaw on.

Every time someone spotted a vehicle that wasn't a part of our convoy, we had to radio it in and keep an eye on it, lest it drive into another building and detonate. Someone spotted one of the black water trucks, and so we stopped the convoy and watched it. It was pulled over on the side of the road. Two guys were on the roof, pivoting the large pipe the shit was sucked up through. They carefully steered the open end of the pipe into a murky body of water that was too small to be a lake, but too wide to be a pond. One of them flipped a switch or something similar; and thousands of litres of piss, shit and, without doubt, a fair amount of sperm was vomited into the pond by the truck. We were a few hundred metres away and the smell rolled over us like a shockwave.

So that was Iraqi waste disposal, apparently.

ON THE MATTER OF RECYCLING

AS YOU ARE NO doubt aware by this point, I worked in a secure environment. This means that almost all information either coming in or out of our building was heavily policed. Literally every scrap of paper, or anything that had a hard drive in it, was scrutinised. Almost everything was stored digitally, of course, by there were certain things that ended up on paper that at some point had to be destroyed. We followed a simple mantra when destroying classified paper information.

Shred, Burn, Drown, Bury.

This meant that everything had to be put through a cross shredder (it reduced an A4 piece of paper into almost a thousand tiny squares instead of long strips of paper that could, in theory, be jigsawed back together). Then, it would be lugged outside in sacks to be thrown into the 'burn bin': an old oil drum that was completely blackened by soot. Once it had been reduced to ash, water was added to make it into a sort of slurry. Finally, we took it out to the far end of camp and 'buried' it by flinging shovelfuls of the grey muck onto a mound of dirt and garbage. Apparently all of that was *just* enough to ensure that the enemy didn't sneak past 100 armed guards, slither into camp and restore the puddle of sludge to a classified document. Did I mention that the intelligence community is a tad paranoid?

One day, I was in charge of the burn bin. It wasn't the worst job. You got to stand outside and smoke while setting fire to things. However, it's not as easy as it sounds. You see, paper burns exceedingly well. But shredded paper, essentially confetti, does not. I'm not an expert in thermodynamics, but my general understanding is that the pieces are too small and combust too quickly to generate enough heat to keep the usual flammable chain reaction going. Which means you need accelerants to get things humming along. So, yet another piece of the overall Mad Max aesthetic is me, wearing ballistic goggles and my headphones blasting Pantera, my shirt off to avoid getting it covered in smoke and soot, smoking a cigarette and pouring petrol onto a flaming barrel with a derelict building in the background. I wish someone had taken a picture of it, to be honest. My tinder profile goes wanting.

On this particular burn day we had received some batteries we had been waiting for. They came packed in cardboard and huge chunks of Styrofoam. It was my job to get rid of this trash, along with the contents of the burn bag. Being the efficient (lazy), forward-thinking (lazy) and environmentally responsible (lazy) lance-corporal that I was, I decided that I would simply burn the lot.

The cardboard went up fine. It helped the shredded paper along, so I was able to stir the flaming contents of the bin with a rusty pole we had lying around. Then, I flung in the long pieces of Styrofoam.

This was news to me, but apparently it's common knowledge that Styrofoam is made from oil. It certainly burned like it was. In a matter of seconds, the long pieces were engulfed in flame. They quicky started spewing black smoke (which I later found out is toxic enough to cause nerve damage directly to your brain). I had to take several steps back, but I wasn't worried. The stuff was about to be floating in the breeze, so things were very much according to plan.

If only I had looked up.

The vast majority of the smoke went straight upward. There was enough of it that the base fire department was called. Of course, in a hilarious example of military bureaucracy, they couldn't get into our compound because they lacked the security clearance to know our gate code. So I stood there, throwing more and more foam onto the pyre, while the despairing fire crew was 100 metres away from me, hollering into their radios trying to figure out who the fuck resided behind the gates on this end of camp. I heard their sirens distantly through the roar of speed metal in my ears, and completely disregarded it. A siren of some sort goes off on base every twenty minutes or so in Iraq. After the first two weeks, you barely notice them.

The pillar of jet-black smoke billowing into the sky could be seen by the grunts out on the firing range, apparently. It was about three kilometres away.

So, when you consider the undoubtable damage done to my brain and lungs from the Styrofoam smoke, the two packs of cigarettes I went through a day, the lack of sleep, and enough daily stress to develop a tick in my face (that I still have to this day), my time in Iraq was not the best for my overall health. However, there was one silver lining.

Being a dry base, while I was in Iraq, I didn't drink a single drop of alcohol, obviously. Not that I got much down time, but when I did get some, there wasn't heaps to do with it. There was also a large, American 'store' filled with just about every supplement known to man (and horse). The combination of all of these factors meant that during my time in Iraq I went to the gym virtually every day. The only exceptions were when I was out on patrol all day, or had actually been sent off-base.

The results were not bad. I weigh about seventy-five to seventy-seven kilograms on average. By the time I got back in December, I was eighty-four kilograms, and had less than 10% body fat. A friend of mine I was meeting in Wellington actually walked straight past me, because apparently my frame had changed so dramatically.

DISCHARGE

IN CASE YOU HADN'T gathered by now, I did not enjoy my time deployed to Iraq. It wasn't the heat, or the seven-day work weeks. It wasn't the long stints of boredom interspersed with very real danger.

It wasn't even the impenetrable bureaucracy that dogged your every move.

It was the gut feeling I had from day one, and what I came to know by day 215: our military presence was of very little (if any) help at all to the people of Iraq.

I had joined the army for various reasons, but it was always underpinned by the idea that, in a big picture sense, I'd be making the world a better place. I naïvely thought that it was as simple as, 'Join the good guys so we can beat the bad guys.'

Of course, real life doesn't work like a DC comic.

We (the coalition of US, UK, AUS, NZ and so on) spent millions and millions of dollars to send thousands and thousands of people to a country that has many deeply rooted problems (like all countries), thinking we could solve them by teaching a few citizens how to hit a target with a rifle.

There's a well-known mantra in the intelligence community, which has trickled down to most military forces that have spent time in and around the Middle East.

'Every time you kill an insurgent, you create two more insurgents.'

And if I learned nothing else from my time in Iraq, I can confirm that this is absolutely true. Every time we send the groupies to kick in a door and shoot a few ISIS members in the face (who, based on the kind of shit they get up to, really do need to be shot in the face for the good of the community and mankind in general) there is a knock-on effect that nearly always occurs.

ISIS member is followed, surveyed and confirmed to be involved in some terrible activities. Placing IEDs in highly populated areas, for example. We spend weeks or months figuring out where he sits in the big picture, and then kill him, either by drone or by gigantic SAS soldiers kicking his door down and emptying a rifle into him.

His family learns about his untimely death, most of them grieve, some of them shake their head and accept it as a consequence of his choices. But there is always a young cousin, or a little brother or a son, or even a close friend. This individual only knows the pain of their loss, and looks for somewhere to direct this pain. They know their country is filled with foreign invaders, who have killed their dear relative. If only there was a way to get back at these people.

And ISIS, or the Taliban, or a similar group, has just gained its newest member.

This happens time and time and time again.

I don't have all the answers. I was about as far from the top of the chain as one can get.

I don't know what the solution is. But I do know that the current method that we've been following for over fifty years isn't working. We might not be dealing with ISIS anymore, but the fundamental problem remains. *We*, the good guys, are creating our own enemies, in a cycle that chiefly results in the death of young soldiers on both sides, and innocent civilians, with little or nothing gained.

So, when I returned to New Zealand, exhausted, drained and disillusioned, and my sergeant-major started talking about my 'next deployment' as soon as six months from the day I returned, my 717 discharge papers were on her desk the very next morning.

I enrolled at Auckland University to study writing. And three months later, I handed in my room key and camp pass, and drove out of Burnham Military Camp for the last time.

LIST OF ACRONYMS

ALICE All-purpose Lightweight Individual Carrying Equipment

BCD Break Contact Drill

BFT Battle Fitness Test

DPM Disruptive Pattern Material (camouflage)

ERV Emergency Rendezvous

EW Electronic Warfare

EWOP Electronic Warfare Operator

FOB Forward Operating Bases

FSMO Field Service Marching Order

IDF Indirect Fire

IED Improvised Explosive Device

ISF Iraqi Security Forces

LP Listening Post

LSW Light Support Weapon

NCO Non-commissioned Officer

OpFor Opposing Forces

PDT Pre-deployment Training

PT Physical Training

SCIF Sensitive Compartmented Information Facility

TOETS Test of Elementary Training Skills